ᴵᴱ DUE

American Congregations

American Congregations

VOLUME 2

New Perspectives in the Study
of Congregations

EDITED BY

James P. Wind and James W. Lewis

The University of Chicago Press
Chicago and London

JAMES P. WIND is a Program Director in the Religion Division of the Lilly Endowment in Indianapolis, Indiana. JAMES W. LEWIS is Executive Director of the Louisville Institute for the Study of Protestantism and American Culture.

Published with the generous assistance of The Lilly Endowment, Inc.

The University of Chicago Press, Chicago 60637
The University of Chicago Press, Ltd., London
© 1994 by The University of Chicago
All rights reserved. Published 1994
Printed in the United States of America
03 02 01 00 99 98 97 96 95 94   1 2 3 4 5

ISBN: 0-226-90188-2 (cloth)

Library of Congress Cataloging-in-Publication Data

American congregations / edited by James P. Wind and James W. Lewis.
      p.   cm.
   Includes bibliographical references and indexes.
   Contents: v.   1. Portraits of twelve religious communities—v.
2. New perspectives in the study of congregations.
      1. United States—Religion.   2. Religious institutions—United
States.   3. Church work.   I. Wind, James P., 1948–   . II. Lewis,
James Welborn.
   BL2525.A525   1994
   291.6′5′0973—dc20   94-4136

CONTENTS

PREFACE

THANKS TO A GRANT FROM the Lilly Endowment, Inc., the University of Chicago Divinity School initiated the Congregational History Project in 1987. Based in the Divinity School's Institute for the Advanced Study of Religion, the project was codirected by James P. Wind and James W. Lewis. Convinced that American congregations are both extremely important and strangely ignored by historians, the Congregational History Project sought to focus fresh scholarly attention on American congregations by means of three major programs—a publication project, a dissertation competition, and a seminar on congregational history.

The publication project produced the two-volume *American Congregations.* The first volume, *Portraits of Twelve Religious Communities,* includes historical essays on twelve significant and diverse North American congregations. Building on these historical studies, the essays in the second volume, *New Perspectives in the Study of Congregations,* reflect on the various contexts of American congregations, the congregational tasks of faith formation and theological reflection, and the role of congregational leadership—all with the history of at least twelve particular congregations firmly in mind.

As an investment in the future of congregational studies, the Dissertation Fellowship program sought to identify and support promising new scholars studying the congregational dimension of American religious life. During the three years of the program, seventeen scholars, working in a variety of academic disciplines, were named Dissertation Fellows.[1]

The Congregational History Project seminar included each year's Dissertation Fellows as well as a variety of scholars with an interest in the congregation.[2] During its five meetings, the seminar explored the relationship between congregational history and congregational studies and reviewed the draft chapters of both volume 1, *Portraits of Twelve Religious Communities,* and volume 2, *New Perspectives in the Study of Congregations.* In addition, each Dissertation Fellow presented his or her dissertation project to the seminar.

The three-part Congregational History Project was unified by common attention to several core tasks. First, the project sought to transcend scholarly provincialism by assembling a group of scholars who work from various methodological perspectives. While seeking to identify the genius, or distinctive character, of the congregation as a religious institution, the project also attempted to broaden the descriptive horizon by studying a group of congregations that reflect significant religious and cultural diversity. As its name implies, the Congregational History Project sought to advance the historical understanding of the congregation, but it also encouraged participation by traditional theological disciplines which have contributed infrequently to the conversation about congregations. In addition, the project attempted to clarify the strategic position of the congregation on the borderline between the public and private spheres of American life. Finally, to a limited extent the project attempted to assess the significance of congregational studies for American religious history, theological education, and religious studies.

The codirectors of the Congregational History Project wish to acknowledge our deep indebtedness to a long list of people who have assisted at various stages. Perhaps our largest debt of gratitude is to Robert W. Lynn, of the Lilly Endowment, Inc., who first directed our attention to the important topic of congregational studies and worked with us in securing generous funding for the inquiry. Equally supportive has been Craig Dykstra, Robert Lynn's successor at the Endowment and our valued colleague.

We also enjoyed the consistent institutional support of colleagues at the Divinity School of the University of Chicago, including a former dean, Franklin I. Gamwell, and the current dean, W. Clark Gilpin. The deans' administrative assistants, Sandra Peppers and the late Delores Smith, were always helpful in many ways. Jennie Browne, a Ph.D. student at the Divinity School, was a valued and energetic research assistant, indexer, and good friend. In addition we owe special thanks to Chicago's distinguished historian Martin E. Marty for advice and counsel from the very beginning of the project.

We are grateful to the members of the seminar of the Congregational History Project for their sage advice throughout the project. For their hard work and patience with our never-ending editorial suggestions, we express our thanks to the authors of both volume 1 and volume 2. As the two volumes neared publication, we relied on the extraordinary editorial skills of Helen Creticos Theodoropoulos and, especially, Barbara

Hofmaier. We would also like to thank Alan G. Thomas, our editor at the University of Chicago Press, for his wisdom and good judgment.

Finally, to our spouses, Kathleen Wind and Marcia Lewis, we owe much more than gratitude for their patience and support in this and many other ventures.

NOTES

1. Timothy R. Allan, Kevin P. Demmitt, Dana Fenton, Karla Goldman, Shirah Weinberg Hecht, Timothy I. Kelly, Carol A. Kitchen, Fred Kniss, Doris O'Dell, Kristin Park, Mark A. Peterson, Joseph T. Reiff, Beth Barton Schweiger, Susan Myers Shirk, Clinton Stockwell, William Sutton, and Wayne L. Thompson.

2. In addition to the Dissertation Fellows, regular seminar participants included: Dorothy C. Bass, Eileen Brewer, Don S. Browning, Phil Devenish, Jay Dolan, Carl Dudley, Robert Franklin, Franklin I. Gamwell, Langdon Gilkey, E. Brooks Holifield, L. DeAne Lagerquist, James W. Lewis, Martin E. Marty, R. Stephen Warner, Jack Wertheimer, and James P. Wind.

INTRODUCTION

Introducing a Conversation

JAMES P. WIND AND JAMES W. LEWIS

FROM 1987 TO 1991 THE Congregational History Project focused fresh attention on the significance of congregations in American life. The project's centerpiece is a collection of congregational histories, which constitute *Portraits of Twelve Religious Communities*, the companion volume to this one. By placing these congregational histories alongside each other the first volume offers a rich sampler of American religious life in its complex, local particularity. By looking historically at mainline Protestant, new evangelical, immigrant urban Catholic, old-stock rural fundamentalist, Eastern Orthodox, African Methodist Episcopal, Mormon, Islamic, and Hindu congregations, it reminds us of the variety as well as the vitality of American religious life at the local level.

Moreover the project, which intended to produce more than historical case studies, was an inquiry done in a pronouncedly *Chicago* style. To be sure, the project "resided" in Swift Hall, home of the University of Chicago's Divinity School and its Institute for the Advanced Study of Religion. At least since the deanship of Shailer Mathews (1907–33), scholars have debated whether such a thing as the "Chicago School," a distinctive social-historical perspective on religion (especially in biblical studies and church history), ever existed. Some readers of *Portraits of Twelve Religious Communities* may see the Congregational History Project as the latest incarnation of this perspective, while others, aware of the variety of historical approaches in that volume, may see no continuity at all.

These days there is only occasional reference in Swift Hall to the Chicago School of church history. More frequent topics are pluralism, hermeneutics, the postmodern study of religion, and "conversation," a recurring metaphor for the Divinity School's increasingly interdisciplinary character. The Congregational History Project shared that ethos, seeking to constitute a conversation about American congregations.

1

Here the Divinity School's David Tracy, whose work has helped shape Chicago's current intellectual character, is instructive. Authentic conversation, he claims, "occurs only when the participants allow the question, the subject matter, to assume primacy. It occurs only when our usual fears about our own self-image die: whether that fear is expressed in either arrogance or scrupulosity matters little. That fear dies only because we are carried along, and sometimes away, by the subject matter itself into the rare event or happening named 'thinking' and 'understanding'."[1] We believe that the congregation as subject matter often "carried away" the Congregational History Project's participants, that individual fears about self-image frequently gave way, and that fresh thinking and new understanding emerged.

This particular conversation had several components. First, sixteen scholars participated in a core seminar that met twice a year for three years. While there were Chicagoans in the mix, they were joined by scholars from seminaries, religious studies departments, and divinity schools from across the country. Further, although the project centered on congregational history, the seminar included as many nonhistorians as historians. Sociologists, systematic and practical theologians, and ethicists were co-inquirers; senior scholars, mid-career professors, recently-minted Ph.D.'s, and advanced doctoral students sat at the same table. In terms of religious identities these scholars brought a variety of Protestant, Catholic, and Jewish perspectives as well. Although at any point this interdisciplinary and interreligious conversation could have led a scholar beyond the safe territory of familiar explanations, the combination of topic and conversation partners carried participants to new understandings and appreciations.

As the project proceeded, this core seminar refined the project's research agenda, immersed itself in the particularity of the twelve congregational histories, and finally developed a series of thematic essays on the congregation and the study of it. Those essays constitute this book. As the reader will quickly notice, our conversation focused on many dimensions of congregational life and acknowledged a variety of explanatory strategies. The project encouraged seminar members to engage in conversations with authors of the individual histories, making it possible for scholars who normally do not study particular congregations to encounter hitherto unnoticed dimensions of congregational life and raising new questions for the historians as they returned to their investigations. It also brought into the conversation seventeen dissertation fellows, thus expanding the horizon of fundamental questions and interpretive options available for consideration.

Throughout, the congregation shaped the project as questions like the following drove the conversation. What makes a congregation a congregation? What is new about the contemporary congregational situation? What do congregations really do for and to Americans? Given all the changes and challenges of American existence, why do congregations endure when so many other patterns of association seem to be withering? How important have they been in previous times and how important are they now? What can we really expect of congregations as we move into the twenty-first century? What can congregational studies teach us about the broader shape of religion in North America?

A History of Congregational Studies

The inquiry called "congregational studies" is not, strictly speaking, a discipline. In fact, its practitioners represent a variety of scholarly disciplines and are united more by their common subject than by their methods of inquiry. Although no comprehensive account has been written of the historical development of congregational studies, some of the contours of that history are now becoming clear.[2] Some of the earliest congregational studies, for example, were conducted by turn-of-the-century Protestant ministers seeking to respond more adequately to the new reality of urban America. Thus Walter Rauschenbusch, after a demoralizing but ultimately transforming eleven years as pastor of a German Reformed congregation in New York City, and Washington Gladden, after a similar seven-year pastorate at Springfield, Massachusetts, began to re-form their religious heritages into a "social gospel" which took seriously the challenge of the urban congregation.

This concern about new congregational problems led early in the twentieth century to the seminal effort of H. Paul Douglass and Edmund deS. Brunner to create a "sociology of the congregation," an effort which initiated formal research on American congregations. In its thirteen-year career (1921–34), their Institute of Social and Religious Research (largely funded by John D. Rockefeller, Jr.) pursued the most ambitious study to date of American congregations, producing at least forty-eight separate research projects and more than seventy-five volumes on these important religious institutions. These descriptive sociological inquiries into thousands of American congregations have been recognized for their

3

contributions to both congregational studies and the development of sociology itself.[3] Confident that objective research could help American churches overcome the problem of too many congregations, too few educated clergy, inadequate congregational resources, and American religious competition, these scholars developed an evolutionary model of congregational sociology and history.

In *The Protestant Church as a Social Institution* Douglass and Brunner summarized more than a decade of effort to regard the church "scientifically." They reported encountering resistance from pious folk who opposed tampering with their cherished institutions. They also identified "a considerable body of Protestant opinion which has reached a highly unfavorable estimate of the religious values of the present church." Discovery of a tendency by many to make congregations into a collective "whipping boy" revealed a perduring tendency in American religious circles to minimize the importance of these institutions. While Douglass and Brunner did not share this basically negative opinion of congregations, they identified it earlier than anyone else and found it among professionals and laity alike.[4]

Not even the largess of John D. Rockefeller, Jr., however, could assure a permanent future for Douglass and Brunner's institute and its scholars. What Robert T. Handy called "the American Religious Depression" took its toll on both congregational life and attempts to study it during the years between the stock market crash and the Second World War.[5] Consequently, the next moment of creativity in the study of the congregation occurred during the so-called revival of religion in the 1950s. During the Eisenhower era American congregations embarked on an unprecedented period of new church construction as congregations proliferated along the arteries to, and through, the suburbs. For their part, a significant cohort of denominational researchers issued studies that sought to understand and guide that proliferation.

In the midst of the economic and social reorganization of American neighborhoods came alternative congregational styles and ways of approaching congregational problems. Led by Gordon Cosby, the Church of the Savior, for example, aspired to break out of the typical congregational mold as it sought to minister in the city of Washington, D.C. Over the span of two decades Cosby and his followers initiated coffeehouse and retreat ministries as alternatives to conventional congregational ministries. Cosby was, however, only one prominent participant in this experimental episode in American congregational life which began in the late 1940s and continued through the 1960s. In addition to the

Church of the Savior (1947) and the East Harlem Parish Project (1948) were the Detroit Industrial Mission (1956) and Robert Raines's effort to provide a Koinonia (fellowship) structure for faltering congregations (1961). Historian Sydney Ahlstrom described this explosion of new institutional alternatives as a "tidal wave of questioning of all the traditional structures of Christendom, above all, of the so-called parish church." By the late 1960s the Department of Church Renewal of the National Council of Churches counted more than 350 experimental ministries, including storefront, apartment, racetrack, and coffeehouse ministries which had arisen during these decades of effervescence and protest.[6]

While the advocates of church renewal generated tremendous institutional innovation, others sought to apply to the congregation new insights from industrial psychology, management science, and social psychology. Congregations became systems to be improved, change a process to be encouraged and guided, and conflict something to be managed and channeled. Lyle Schaller, Loren Mead, Paul Dietterich, and Robert Worley, among others in a new cohort of congregational consultants, learned how to intervene in congregational situations, identify their problems, and suggest structural or managerial strategies which could alleviate congregational problems.[7]

Hovering near the center of much Protestant attention to congregations was the suspicion that congregations were finite structures which could never do justice to the infinite treasure they sought to offer to the world. The congregation remained a "whipping boy" but now began to receive serious theological criticism which surpassed the earlier judgements identified by Douglass and Brunner. H. Richard Niebuhr, for example, sounded the note of a nervous neo-orthodoxy when he warned against the dangers of a "church-centered" henotheism for much of modern religion.[8]

What Niebuhr discussed in a few paragraphs became the central concern of several scholars who developed a detailed analysis of congregations immobilized by a pervasive cultural captivity. Peter Berger in *The Noise of Solemn Assemblies* described America's congregations as culturally established institutions whose chief function was to keep religion irrelevant to the dominant challenges of the modern situation. Gibson Winter, after tracing an enervating process of religious suburbanization, argued for a restructuring of America's religious institutions. Bemoaning the "morphological fundamentalism" of American congregations, George Webber argued, as did the World Council of Churches, that congregations had to assume a new missionary structure if they were to make an impact upon their environment and remain faithful to their traditions. Theologian Langdon Gilkey found within the history of American congregations a process in which both sectarian and churchly types of religious institutions lost their distinctiveness. Instead they blurred into a common denominational type of institution which offered little sacrality, having lost access to both the authoritative traditions and powerful religious experiences which once compelled them.[9]

These critiques of American congregational life protested the assimilation of various types of American congregations into a vague "religion in general" which Will Herberg and others thought was engulfing American Protestantism, Catholicism, and Judaism.[10] To various degrees, these theological and sociological criticisms were part of a larger process of radical questioning which sought to embrace secularity and to free the major religious traditions from formalism while recovering the roots of their faiths through renewed biblical and theological scholarship.

While scholars like Berger saw little hope for congregations, others like Martin E. Marty and James Gustafson attempted to criticize them without abandoning them. In 1958 Marty, wary of the problem of congregational "multitudinism" (pluralism), urged renewed study of the local parish. Previously he had developed a series of articles in *The Christian Century* which profiled significant American congregations. James Gustafson employed the same metaphor for congregations used by H. Paul Douglass and Edmund deS. Brunner more than thirty years previously when he suggested studying the earthen vessels which bore the treasure of the biblical heritage. Gustafson outlined what could be called the first interdisciplinary model for congregational studies, arguing that congregations should be viewed as human, natural, and political entities, communities of language, memory, interpretation, understanding, belief, and action. The result of this type of approach would be a social and theological interpretation of the church.[11]

Throughout these middle decades of the twentieth century other scholars posed different questions concerning the congregation. C. Ellis Nelson inquired into the role of congregations in shaping the understandings, ethos, and values of members and emphasized the need to understand the culturally formative role played by congregations, rather than merely viewing them as reactive to the culture.[12]

Several scholars initiated inquiry into the public character of congregations. James Luther Adams called attention to the historical significance of American congregations in shaping American voluntarism. For him the Sunday offering plate became a key religious symbol for the "voluntary principle" which flowed from American congregations into their larger public life. In the 1970s Peter Berger and Richard John Neuhaus stressed the role of congregations as "mediating structures" between the private sphere of individuals and the larger public realm. More recently Parker Palmer and Martin Marty, rejecting the cultural captivity perspective, sought to make a case for the role of congregations in creating both public space and concern for the public in American life.[13] The Congregational History Project, in fact, can be seen as a collaborative, scholarly effort in the same corrective direction.

In the 1970s still other scholars employed an anthropological approach to describe the actual behavior of individual congregations. Michael Ducey, Samuel Heilman, and Melvin Williams pioneered in this type of research, spending years observing and interpreting the lives of particular congregations.[14] Their ethnographic accounts and the groundbreaking work of the late James Hopewell on congregational worldviews and value systems inaugurated a new approach to the study of the congregation that seemed to offer a way beyond either statistical analysis or theological opining.

To mention James Hopewell, of course, is to mention one of the persons most responsible for the current lively interest in congregational studies. Hopewell opened his *Congregation: Stories and Structures* by noting that "Christian congregations took me by surprise." Barbara Wheeler, in her editor's foreword to that book, recounts how Hopewell came to his surprising discovery of the congregation and how he developed his distinctive cultural/symbolic/narrative approach to it.[15] Together with other ethnographers Hopewell began to move congregational studies towards an approach that viewed these institutions as living subcultures or, as we suggested in *American Congregations: Portraits of Twelve Religious Communities*, local cultures.

A pivotal moment in the development of the field came in 1982 when Hopewell and a Committee for Congregational Studies (Jackson W. Carroll, Carl Dudley, Loren B. Mead, and Barbara Wheeler) convened, with the assistance of the Lilly Endowment, a national gathering of scholars, denominational leaders, and consultants to engage in an unprecedented interdisciplinary consideration of one congregation, which was given the pseudonym of Wiltshire Church. That meeting in Atlanta, Georgia, which drew several hundred participants, resulted in an important if somewhat imprecisely titled publication,

Building Effective Ministry: Theory and Practice in the Local Church, edited by Carl Dudley.[16] Equally important was the way it attended to the thick richness of life in one rather conventional mainstream Protestant Church and recognized the need for numerous perspectives to comprehend fully all that was going on within it. The promise and the difficulty of bringing sociologists, anthropologists, practical theologians, and organizational development experts into conversation were powerfully demonstrated.

The committee continued to collaborate, sharing results of individual projects like the study of the religious life of Hartford, Connecticut, by David A. Roozen, William McKinney, and Jackson W. Carroll. That project, which eventuated in their *Varieties of Religious Presence: Mission in Public Life* (1984), used congregations as a principal unit of analysis for studying the relationship of religion to the public life of a major American city. It also demonstrated the growing interdisciplinary character of congregational studies as it employed both ethnographic and more conventional social-scientific approaches. The committee evolved into the Project Team for Congregational Studies and produced a *Handbook for Congregational Studies,* edited by Jackson W. Carroll, Carl S. Dudley, and William McKinney (1986). The project team also became a means of interchange for the growing number of scholars who took up the study of congregations in the 1980s.[17]

Methodologically, ever since Brunner and Douglass, the social sciences have predominated among students of the congregation. Initially virtually all students of the congregation were sociologists. But, as David A. Roozen and Allison Stokes point out and as we have noted above, specialists in organizational development, anthropology, and sociology have contributed as well. Conspicuously absent from these efforts were the church historians. But, as *Portraits of Twelve Religious Communities* indicates, professional historians have at last added their distinctive voice to this conversation. But even if late, the historical contribution to congregational studies is a crucial one. As historian Jay Dolan has observed, "people can never understand who they are unless they understand who they were."[18]

Advancing the Study of the Congregation

This volume contributes to the expanding conversation about the congregation and seeks to advance it in several ways. First, it helps us assess the importance of congregational history for future congregational studies.[19] At their best, historians can highlight the changing character of congregations, the way the past shapes present realities and future possibilities, and the complexity of the relations between individuals, institutions, events, and environments, thus providing a much needed corrective to the more static images that can result from ethnographic and sociological research. Further, the intricate ways congregations interact with, shape, and respond to the larger historical, social, cultural, and religious context become more apparent. Long-standing truisms about the role of congregations in modern life give way before concrete evidence to the contrary.

Second, along with an appreciation for congregational history, the authors in this volume bring to the conversation their own distinctive disciplinary perspectives. Although half of the following chapters come from historians (Holifield, Marty, Bass, and Dolan), the other half represent disciplines from which historians often benefit but with which they seldom collaborate—sociology (Warner), theology (Gilkey and Browning), and ethics (Franklin). Alternating between the historical and other perspectives, these essays represent the flow of the Congregational History Project's conversation. This kind of conversation among methodological approaches, which includes frequent reference to the specific narrative histories in volume 1, places the congregation in broad, comparative context without losing sight of the particularity of religion as it is actually lived and practiced in local settings. As one of us has observed, the congregation is one of the few places in our culture where persons regularly engage in the enduring human attempt to relate to the holy or transcendent, and "the relationship of these universal human concerns to the particularities of one local place of worship is what makes congregational history so interesting."[20]

The eight essays in this volume constitute an interdisciplinary conversation about precisely this relationship. Assuming the importance of American congregational life, they reflect on this congregational reality by addressing three central sets of questions. First, where is the congregation located on the broader map of American cultural and religious life? How does it fit into the other, more carefully studied parts of our religious, social, political, economic, and cultural ecology?

Second, what are congregations and what do they do? Or to put it another way, what are the distinctive qualities, practices, tasks, and roles of congregations in the American story? What should they be?

Third, how are these institutions shaped and led? What patterns of leadership have characterized American religious life and how can they be improved upon?

The following essays do not, of course, answer definitively these questions. But they do suggest new approaches to important topics that have until now been superficially treated or ignored.

Part One: Congregations in Context

Given their persistent presence on the American landscape and their specific mailing addresses it seems redundant to ask about congregational location. Yet, the Congregational History Project set out to correct an enormous cartographic failure by both local congregational leaders and experts on religion to locate American congregations precisely. For more than half a century, it seemed as if virtually everyone was operating with a defective map. Often the problem was one of scale. Leaders of local congregations seemed to work with idiosyncratic local maps that extended no further than their property lines or perhaps ones that extended in diminishing detail into a nearby neighborhood or out towards one particular denominational mission field. Scholars of American religion and their colleagues in the social sciences and history employed maps drawn to a much larger scale, but these seldom contained any traces of local congregations.

The maps we are referring to are, of course, figurative. We are speaking of the religious, sociological, historical, theological, cultural, economic, and political contexts into which people incorporate their experience. The two types of mental maps—local and popular on the one hand and national and scholarly on the other—had no relationship. New maps that could relate the local zones of lived American religion and the larger patterns, trends, and dynamics of national life were needed.

The four essays in the first section of this book attempt to address this need. From distinctive vantage points, two historians, a sociologist of religion, and a theologian seek to relate local American congregations to much larger dynamics and processes. At the same time, their sensitivity to local congregational life enables them to redraw the larger interpretive maps employed within their particular scholarly disciplines.

Historian E. Brooks Holifield begins this effort by drawing a pioneering outline of a congregational history of America. In "Toward a History of American Congregations," he sketches an exploratory map of a huge uncharted territory, knowing that later cartographers will provide corrections and revisions. Nonetheless, Holifield helps us recognize the pervasiveness of American congregational life at the same time that he traces a pattern of development in all of the congregating that has taken place in the American story. Basing his work on recent research on church membership figures, Holifield asserts that "the primary extrafamilial form of community for much of the American population has been the religious congregation" and challenges conventional wisdom about patterns of growth and decline in congregational membership percentages. Throughout more than three hundred years of American life, 35 to 40 percent of the population, he claims, has regularly attended religious services and participated in congregational forms of community life.

Such steadiness and proportional significance are only part of the historical map he draws, however. As he traces congregational life over time he discerns four major stages in congregational development which reflect different understandings of community in America. Up to the time of the American Revolution, the congregational ideal was a *comprehensive* one. Despite differences from one colony to another, in general each congregation sought to embrace the entire community in which it was located. But such comprehensive congregations became impossible as the society became more ethnically and religiously diverse and complex, and the congregational community evolved into a *devotional* form in which each religious group nurtured its members according to its own lights and distinctive practices. Still later in the nineteenth century the *social* congregation attempted to provide a friendly environment and a broad range of opportunities in response to a changing society characterized more by cities and industries than by small towns and farms. Finally, around the middle of the twentieth century, Holifield suggests, a new *participatory* form of congregational life emerged, one in which members could participate, consumer-style, on their own terms. By sketching congregational history into the larger map of the American search for community, Holifield helps us understand that quest differently.

Sociologist of religion R. Stephen Warner draws a different kind of map in "The Place of the Congregation in the Contemporary American Religious Configuration." In the process he discovers a startling "convergence across religious traditions toward 'de-facto congregationalism'." Despite the diversity of religious traditions in North America, Warner describes an organizational uniformity that transcends differences of theology and polity. For example, Presbyterians and even

Roman Catholics, both of whose official polities place authority in "higher" bodies, behave in certain ways much like Congregationalists or Baptists. Presbyterians make their own congregational decisions, such as calling pastors, with little interference "from above." Increasingly Roman Catholics, like their Protestant neighbors, "float" from their neighborhood parish to one more to their liking, without bothering to seek official approval. In other words, American religion, at least in its local institutional forms, has increasingly assumed a congregational shape regardless of traditional distinctiveness or cultural diversity.

Oddly enough, as Warner notes, this organizational uniformity is closely related to the religious diversification of the American religious landscape. As immigrant religious groups proliferated, they adapted (and continue to do so) to the American reality around them, in order to survive, assimilate, and thrive. As several histories in the first volume of *American Congregations* demonstrate, assuming a congregational shape was an essential strategy employed by varying religious groups in order to maintain distinctive traditions while adapting to the American environment. Form, in a very real sense, has followed function, and to understand the way religion has developed in North America and influenced American society, one must understand the congregational form it has increasingly assumed. Warner's map provides a variety of other useful landmarks as he helps us spot ongoing movements beneath the surface of American religion, such as the decline in number of mainline congregations and the almost symmetrical upsurge in evangelical and other "new" types of congregations.

Langdon Gilkey draws a third kind of map, a religious or theological one, in his chapter, "The Christian Congregation as a Religious Community." Recent scholarship on religion in America has emphasized the decline since the 1960s of the mainstream Protestant establishment, leading many to wonder just what role, if any, these traditionally important religious groups will play in contemporary North American society.[21] Returning to themes he had taken up at the beginning of his theological career more than thirty years ago, Gilkey considers these matters, with particular attention to the distinctively religious character of congregations.

While it may seem self-evident that congregations are religious institutions, Gilkey's intentional posing of the question reminds us that congregations do more than play social roles or perform communal functions that interest sociologists and historians. They have, or at least ought to have, a religious genius or character. Drawing on his personal experience both within and beyond the Protestant establishment, Gilkey discerns a "religious vacuum" in many congregations which has resulted at least partially from their uncritical identification with the broader culture. Consequently, according to Gilkey, such congregations often have little of a distinctive nature to contribute either to the public moral order or to the individual religious lives of their members. Gilkey thus locates congregations, especially those formerly labeled as mainline, in a process of cultural accommodation that threatens them at their religious heart. Only as they recover their proper mission of theological reflection on their scriptures and traditions, provision of moral action and guidance, and the cultivation of piety can these congregations occupy their proper religious location in American society. Echoing his earlier argument, Gilkey joins Warner in noting an Americanization of religious life into congregational forms but wonders if the process must inevitably result in a loss of religious vitality and theological substance.

Historian Martin E. Marty concludes this mapping section by considering the congregation's existence on the problematic line between public and private life. In his chapter "Public and Private: Congregation as Meeting Place," Marty identifies three different scholarly perspectives on the congregation's relationship to this public/private dichotomy. As noted above in our discussion of congregational studies, observers like Gibson Winter and Peter Berger in the 1950s and 1960s found little to praise and much to condemn in the suburban congregations which dominated the American religious landscape. Such critics concluded that congregations had mistakenly settled in the private sphere of American life, and some called for new institutional initiatives truer to what they perceived to be the mandates of the Christian gospel.

In the next two decades scholars (including some, like Berger, who had drawn the first sociological map) began to revise their interpretation and speak of congregations as part of a class of "mediating structures" that bridged the two spheres.[22] While he is more appreciative of the second map than the first, Marty finds this one still too limited for understanding the complex role of congregations. He proposes instead that the congregation is "the meeting where public religious life begins." In this reading "congregations as aggregates and part of an aggregation are themselves publics and parts of a larger public. Members by taking part in them venture out of privacy into a zone of interactions" (p. 150). In congregations believers do many things that relate to both private and public spheres. But in the very act of meeting for these tasks, they constitute a distinctive type of public realm. Marty's map may be as much a guide for future direction in the American religious landscape as it is a reflection of past experience. As congregations enter the next millennium they are faced with key challenges concerning both their private and public dimensions and the relationship between them.

Taken together, these four essays present new ways to locate congregations on the American landscape. They also call into question many earlier attempts to map that territory. Finally, they provide vantage points for newer and more accurate maps to be drawn in the future.

Part Two: Congregations and Traditions

As the first volume of American Congregations clearly demonstrates, congregations gain much of their distinctive quality from the traditions that live within them. But congregations are also places where traditions (both sacred and secular) interact, collide, and converge. The discovery of this tradition-laden quality of American congregational life and the essential ongoing dynamic of revision and innovation taking place within them is one of the distinctive contributions that the study of congregational history offers.

Sadly, this creative, often subliminal, side of American congregational life has gone largely unnoticed. Historian Dorothy Bass, in "Congregations and the Bearing of Traditions," corrects this oversight as she locates congregations within the great religious traditions and then explores one of the congregation's most significant tasks—the transmission of those traditions from generation to generation. She notes that, as congregations embody and transmit a religious tradition, they also contribute to the shaping of that tradition in the process. Standing as they do on the border between past wisdom and present realities, congregations are inevitably caught between religious continuity and religious change. Building on Alasdair MacIntyre's concept of tradition as "an historically extended, socially embodied argument," Bass analyzes the contribution of congregations to what is essentially a dialectical process between individuals or families and the religious tradition of which they are a part.[23] In this process, "congregations impart to individuals and families a place in a tradition, and conversely, those same individuals and families, through congregations, give back to a tradition its own being and vitality, constituting and reconstituting it through time" (p. 174). To Bass, congregations and the practices they cultivate are essential links between the needs of individuals and families and the resources of great religious traditions. This crucial linking task helps explain both the persistence of congregations and their importance to the ecology of American religion.

As a practical theologian reflecting on the needs of contemporary congregations, Don S. Browning also confronts the problem of traditions in congregational life. Using different terminology than does Bass, he nonetheless emphasizes the way in which congregations stand between traditional religious pasts and the realities of life in the present. In his closely argued "Congregational Studies as Practical Theology," Browning employs a distinctive model of practical theology to describe and analyze the congregation's role as a community of practical theological reflection. Building on his previous attempts to articulate a fundamental practical theology, Browning revisits the classic congregational studies of Wiltshire Methodist Church and the Church of the Covenant in order to study their interpretive life, the ways these congregations actually undertake their theological work.[24] Their experience illuminates a process of practical theological reasoning that includes descriptive, historical, systematic, and strategic moments. In his view, a sensitivity to both congregational traditions and congregational history are essential to the practical theological task of every congregation. Moreover, congregational studies are useful to the discipline of practical theology precisely because they illustrate this process of reflection. Congregational studies, in turn, need to become more intentional about congregations' normative and interpretive theological dimensions.

Part Three: Congregations and Leadership

One of the greatest challenges facing American congregations throughout their history is that of securing adequate leadership. Although a large "how to" literature seeks to aid clergy and other religious leaders, relatively little scholarly attention has been given to the changing patterns of congregational leadership. By contrast the first volume of *American Congregations* illustrates both the internal struggle to maintain viable congregational leadership and the externally oriented impulse to provide religious leadership for the society.

Historian Jay Dolan attends to this dimension of American congregational life in his essay, "Patterns of Leadership in the Congregation." With reference to Protestant and Jewish as well as Roman Catholic congregations, Dolan summarizes the changing patterns of congregational leadership from 1607 to 1940. Highlighting three basic periods in congregational leadership (1700–1776, 1790–1840, and 1840–1940), Dolan discerns a surprising continuity within Protestantism, Judaism, and Roman Catholicism in the way that leadership developed. In the colonial period, he finds a certain tension between clericalism and a developing populism among believers, epitomized in the First Great Awakening. In the second period, democratization ruled, and lay influence increased in Protestant, Catholic, and Jewish congregations alike. From the mid-nineteenth to the mid-twentieth century, an increasing professionalization among clergy led to greater clerical control over Protestant churches and Jewish synagogues. In Roman Catholic parishes during this period, the influence of the laity declined, and the "priest took over control of the parish" (p. 242). In all three traditions, the nature of congregational leadership and the public role of the congregation were affected by geographical environment, the voluntary principle in religion, increasing professionalization, and the realities of gender and social class. In all of them "adaptation was the norm and diversity the central feature insofar as leadership in the congregation is concerned" (p. 226).

Ethicist Robert Franklin demonstrates how traditions and local cultures create a leadership matrix in congregations that clergy and other religious leaders ignore at their peril. In "The Safest Place on Earth: The Culture of Black Congregations" Franklin draws upon the distinctive experience of the African-American church to underline the dynamic relationship between strong pastoral leadership and vital congregational culture. Celebrating the central role played by the African-American church in creating vital local cultures, Franklin identifies a variety of leadership styles which can be effectively employed to maintain and mobilize black congregations as agents of social change. Without attempting to provide an exhaustive account of black church culture, Franklin describes several specific features which are "defining ritual practices found in the vast majority of black congregations" (p. 226). When these are drawn upon by a gifted leader, congregations can be places of enormous political, social, economic, and cultural creativity. His preliminary explorations of the nexus between leadership and congregational culture open up an important area for further inquiry by practitioners seeking to enhance congregational life and also by scholars interested in the study of American religious leadership.

These three sets of essays, then, participate in an unfolding conversation about congregational life in America. Our conversation partners recognize the significance of congregations in the North American story, and they encourage new partners to join the conversation about them and carry it further. Admittedly America's religious congregations have not been perfect. While they have provided shelter and community in a sometimes lonely and frightening world, they have frequently embodied patterns of exclusiveness and hostility. While they have nurtured leadership, they have often restricted the exercise of power to certain privileged groups. While some have courageously advocated reform, others have harbored intolerance and injustice. While they have brought together the riches of religious traditions and the contemporary needs of persons and families to shape new worlds of meaning, they have also failed to encourage other expressions of personal and communal identity to form. While they have contributed to public debate by providing a meeting that is itself a kind of public, they have sometimes been so exclusive that they have forced people either to keep their deepest convictions private or to express them in other settings. But whether congregations have worked for good or ill or both at the same time, they have been indispensable in shaping American society and the American character. It is our belief that awareness of their enormous impact on American life is beginning to dawn, promising for American congregations a more visible and valued place in our imaginations.

NOTES

1. David Tracy, *The Analogical Imagination: Christian Theology and the Culture of Pluralism* (New York: Crossroad, 1981), p. 101.

2. For an overview, see Allison Stokes and David A. Roozen, "The Unfolding Story of Congregational Studies," in *Carriers of Faith: Lessons from Congregational Studies*, ed. Carl S. Dudley, Jackson W. Carroll, and James P. Wind (Louisville: Westminster/John Knox Press, 1991), pp. 183–92. According to Stokes and Roozen, congregational studies has been "a story of pragmatic problem-solving," bringing together a concern for congregations and a reliance on a variety of social-scientific methods (p. 184). Another helpful discussion of the origins of congregational studies is Chapter 2 in James Hopewell, *Congregation: Stories and Structures*, ed. Barbara Wheeler (Philadelphia: Fortress Press, 1987). See also Barbara G. Wheeler, "Uncharted Territory: Congregational Identity and Mainline Protestantism," in *The Presbyterian Predicament: Six Perspectives*, ed. Milton J Coalter, John M. Mulder, Louis B. Weeks (Louisville: Westminster/John Knox Press, 1990), pp. 67–89.

3. On the contributions of Douglass and the Institute for Religious and Social Research, see Jeffrey K. Hadden, "H. Paul Douglass: His Perspective and His Work," *Review of Religious Research* 22 (September 1980): 66–88, and Edmund deS. Brunner, "Harlan Paul Douglass: Pioneer Researcher in the Sociology of

Religion," *Review of Religious Research* part 1, vol. 1 (1959–60): 3–16; part 2, vol. 1 (1959–60): 66. On the legacy of Brunner and Douglass for the sociological study of American religion, see Yoshio Fukuyama, "The Uses of Sociology by Religious Bodies," *Journal for the Scientific Study of Religion* 2, no. 2 (Spring 1963): 195–203.

4. H. Paul Douglass and Edmund deS. Brunner, *The Protestant Church as a Social Institution* (New York: Harper and Brothers, 1935), pp. v–vii, 3–30; quotation from p. 9.

5. Robert T. Handy, "The American Religious Depression, 1925–1935," *Church History* 29 (1960): 3–16.

6. The Church of the Savior's story is told in Elizabeth O'Connor, *Call to Commitment* (New York: Harper & Row, 1963); Sydney E. Ahlstrom, *A Religious History of the American People* (New Haven: Yale University Press, 1972), p. 1083; Douglas W. Johnson, "A Study of New Forms of Ministry" (New York: Department of Research, National Council of Churches of Christ in the U.S.A., 1969).

7. Loren Mead described early aspects of the emergence of congregational consultants in *New Hope for Congregations* (New York: Seabury Press, 1972).

8. H. Richard Niebuhr, *Radical Monotheism and Western Culture* (New York: Harper Torchbooks, 1970), p. 58.

9. Peter L. Berger, *The Noise of Solemn Assemblies* (Garden City: Doubleday, 1961); Gibson Winter, *The Suburban Captivity of the Churches* (Garden City: Doubleday, 1961); George W. Webber, *The Congregation in Mission* (Nashville: Abingdon Press, 1964), p. 13; Langdon Gilkey, *How the Church Can Minister to the World without Losing Itself* (New York: Harper & Row, 1964); *The Church for Others and the Church in the World* (Geneva: World Council of Churches, 1967); George W. Webber, "The Struggle for Integrity," *Review of Religious Research* 23, no. 5 (September 1981); Norman Goodall, ed., *The Uppsala Report, 1968* (Geneva: World Council of Churches, 1968). See Martin Marty's chapter in this volume for a fuller account of this period in congregational studies.

10. Will Herberg, *Protestant-Catholic-Jew: An Essay in American Religious Sociology* (Garden City: Anchor Books, 1955).

11. Martin E. Marty, *The New Shape of American Religion* (New York: Harper & Row, 1958), pp. 134, 125; *Christian Century*'s "Creative Churches" Series included eight articles which ran from December 5, 1956, to October 23, 1957; James M. Gustafson, *Treasure in Earthen Vessels: The Church as a Human Community* (1961; reprint ed., Chicago: University of Chicago Press, 1976). In *The Protestant Church as a Social Institution*, Douglass and Brunner observed that, at their best, objective studies of religion "may serve to confirm faith in the treasure of the spirit which lies within the earthen vessels of institutionalism and in those imponderable values which multitudes testify to, as more real to them than all objective facts" (p. 18).

12. C. Ellis Nelson, *Where Faith Begins* (Richmond: John Knox Press, 1967), p. 12.

13. In a letter to the editors of this volume J. Ronald Engel confirmed Adams's

frequent reference to the symbolic significance of the offering plate; Peter L. Berger and Richard John Neuhaus, *To Empower People: The Role of Mediating Structures in Public Policy* (Washington, D.C.: American Enterprise Institute for Public Policy Research, 1977); Parker J. Palmer, *The Company of Strangers: Christians and the Renewal of America's Public Life* (New York: Crossroad, 1981); Martin E. Marty, *The Public Church: Mainline-Evangelical-Catholic* (New York: Crossroad, 1981).

At the same time books by Johann Baptist Metz and Jürgen Moltmann continue to press the claim that congregations are captive to a bourgeois religion, a sign that the cultural-captivity argument still has potency. Moltmann and Metz both opt for new religious structures—in Moltmann's case the small circle which practices Christlike friendship, in Metz's the basic communities scattered throughout South America and, in a few anomalous cases, northern Europe and America. See Johann Baptist Metz, *The Emergent Church: The Future of Christianity in a Post-Bourgeois World,* trans. Peter Manns (New York: Crossroad, 1981); Jürgen Moltmann, *The Passion for Life: A Messianic Lifestyle,* trans. M. Douglas Meeks (Philadelphia: Fortress Press, 1978).

14. Michael H. Ducey, *Sunday Morning: Aspects of Urban Ritual* (New York: The Free Press, 1977); Samuel C. Heilman, *Synagogue Life: A Study in Symbolic Interaction* (Chicago: University of Chicago Press, 1976); Melvin D. Williams, *Community in a Black Pentecostal Church: An Anthropological Study* (Pittsburgh: University of Pittsburgh Press, 1974).

15. Hopewell, *Congregation: Stories and Structures,* pp. xi–xv, 1.

16. Carl S. Dudley, ed., *Building Effective Ministry: Theory and Practice in the Local Church* (San Francisco: Harper and Row, 1983).

17. David A. Roozen, William McKinney, Jackson W. Carroll, *Varieties of Religious Presence: Mission in Public Life* (New York: Pilgrim Press, 1984); Jackson W. Carroll, Carl S. Dudley, and William McKinney, *Handbook for Congregational Studies* (Nashville: Abingdon Press, 1986).

18. Jay P. Dolan, ed., *The American Catholic Parish: A History from 1850 to the Present,* 2 vols. (New York: Paulist Press, 1987), 1:1.

19. See James P. Wind, *Places of Worship: Exploring Their History* (Nashville: American Association for State and Local History, 1990) for a discussion of the craft of congregational history. See also James W. Lewis, *The Protestant Experience in Gary, Indiana, 1906–1975: At Home in the City* (Knoxville: University of Tennessee Press, 1992), for a recent example of congregational history, focusing on urban congregations.

20. Wind, *Places of Worship,* p. xix.

21. See, for example, Wade Clark Roof and William McKinney, *American Mainline Religion: Its Changing Shape and Future* (New Brunswick: Rutgers University Press, 1987); Robert Wuthnow, *Restructuring American Religion: Society and Faith Since World War II* (Princeton: Princeton University Press, 1988); William R. Hutchison, ed., *Between the Times: The Travail of the Protestant Establishment in America, 1900–1960* (Cambridge: Cambridge University Press, 1989).

22. Berger and Neuhaus, *To Empower People: The Role of Mediating Structures in Public Policy,* pp. 2–3.

23. Alasdair MacIntyre, *After Virtue* (Notre Dame: University of Notre Dame Press, 1981), p. 207.

24. These studies are found respectively in Dudley, *Building Effective Ministry,* and Nelle G. Slater, ed., *Tensions Between Citizenship and Discipleship: A Case Study* (New York: Pilgrim Press, 1989). See also Don S. Browning, *A Fundamental Practical Theology* (Minneapolis: Fortress Press, 1991).

ONE

Toward a History of American Congregations

E. Brooks Holifield

EARLY IN THE NINETEENTH CENTURY, when an American na[...]
Finley had a conversion experience, his first impulse w[...]
"Christian society." He had prayer meetings in the woods[...]
brother and a friend, but these were not enough. He wanted[...]
congregation: "I sighed for Church privileges," he said, "and[...]
nion with the people of God." He sought a community.[1]

With quite a different purpose, historians in America have[...]
dertaken the quest for community. Since the early twentieth [...]
they have returned to the theme of community—especially to th[...]
of its decline. They have described a communal ideal in seven[...]
century New England succumbing to individualism and mate[...]
interpreted eighteenth-century political movements—includin[...]
movement to ratify the Constitution—as signals of the collapse[...]
ganic communities; and described the transitions in nineteenth-ce[...]
American cities as transformations of communal spheres into bu[...]
cratic and impersonal societies. By the 1930s, some sociologists vie[...]
the rise of the impersonal metropolis as the final collapse of older [...]
munal ways of living.

Within the past four decades, other historians and sociologists h[...]
argued that communal forms persisted within impersonal social agg[...]
gates. The intimacy and face-to-face mutuality that Ferdinand Toenn[...]
called *Gemeinschaft* existed within and alongside the impersonal, a[...]
stract, rationalized, and bureaucratic patterns that he denoted with th[...]
term *Gesellschaft*. To numerous American scholars after 1930, the mod[...]
ern city and the international economy seemed permeated by primary[...]
groups—family, neighborhood, association—in which social experience[...]
retained its communal features. But few have noticed that the primary[...]
extrafamilial form of community for much of the American population[...]
has been the religious congregation.[2]

Congregations have changed. The comprehensive congregations o
e colonial period began in the early nineteenth century to be more
arrowly defined as devotional sanctuaries. By the end of the century,
owever, "social" congregations sought a different form of comprehen-
ve influence by providing not only worship but also recreation and
ocial services, and the participatory congregations of the twentieth cen-
ury expanded the social ideal by finding new ways to involve the laity
not only in worship but also in the planning and governance of the
church or synagogue. Once marked by relatively simple forms of internal organization, congregations have now often become complex: a
twentieth-century congregation can consist of multiple groups and a
complicated internal organization. The transitions and the increasing inner complexity of congregations are surface realities that suggest some
hidden depths.[3]

Continuities

Surveys of American religion often suggest that congregations flourished in early New England but then declined in cultural influence to
such an extent that by 1789 only 10 percent of Americans bothered to
join them. Only slowly, according to this view, did membership grow:
from 12 percent in 1800, to 22 percent in 1890, to the higher levels of
adherence that have appeared since 1950, when 50 to 60 percent of
Americans began to claim that they were members.[4]

This might be accurate, but it can mislead. From the seventeenth
century through the twentieth, participation in congregations has probably remained relatively constant. For most of the past three hundred
years, from 35 to 40 percent of the population has probably participated
in congregations with some degree of regularity.

The earliest congregations had a struggle. By 1642 in Maryland, for
instance, Catholic priests organized four churches and chapels—two for
settlers and two for missions—but religious tensions with Protestants
forced them to conduct most services in private, and the colony had only
six Anglican ministers before 1690. Quakers alone flourished, establishing twenty-one meetings by 1680, when the population had reached
about 20,000. Progress was equally slow in Virginia. By 1650, with a
population of about 12,000, the colony had around twenty active congregations, and a shortage of ministers meant that lay deacons often had
to lead the worship. Conditions improved by 1680, when thirty-four ordained ministers provided full or part-time service to all but one of forty-

PART ONE

CONGREGATIONS IN CONTEXT

eight parishes, but the geographical dispersion of the settlers made it hard for people to attend.[5]

Congregations were more successful in New Netherland, which in 1650 had nine Protestant churches for a population of perhaps 5,000. By the end of the century, the colony, renamed New York in 1664, had forty-eight Protestant churches and one Jewish synagogue for a population of 30,000. Domine Johannes Megapolensis reported that on Sundays "many hearers" were wont to "crowd into the church," even though they balked at paying his salary; but in New York, as in the Chesapeake colonies, only a small proportion of the population could have joined the crowds to which Megapolensis referred.[6]

Churches proliferated in New England, which in 1680 had 73 Congregationalist, 3 Quaker, 2 Baptist, and no Anglican churches. By 1700, the number increased to 146 Congregationalist, 1 Anglican, 6 Baptist, and at least 17 Quaker congregations. The 78 congregations of 1660 served a population of around 68,500, one congregation for every 878 colonists. By 1700 there were 170 New England congregations in a population of around 92,800, one for every 545 colonists. Settlement patterns in New England made it easier to attend a congregation there than in Maryland or Virginia.[7]

The colonial churches and synagogues had diverse understandings of membership. Calvinists in New England usually admitted to full membership—and communion in the Lord's Supper—only the "visible saints" who could offer a convincing narration of conversion. Anglicans in Virginia considered every properly baptized person in the geographical parish as a member. Early Jewish congregations embraced, in theory, every Jew in the community. Catholic churches included all properly baptized Catholic adults and children in the community.

In the New England Puritan congregations, the communicant membership remained small and exclusive. Already by 1649, communicants at the First Church in Boston represented no more than two-thirds of the town's families and less than half the adult male population. In Roxbury, 65 percent of the adult males were members in 1640, 45 percent in 1652. In New Haven, New London, Stonington, and Woodbury, only 15 percent of adult males were members by the end of the 1670s. Membership reports on 34 seventeenth-century congregations suggest that by 1660 less than 20 percent of the New England population held full communicant membership.[8]

By the end of the century, however, almost all Puritan churches also admitted halfway members, who were excluded from the Lord's Supper but were subject to church discipline and expected to attend faithfully. And when three congregations in Connecticut dramatically altered their criteria for membership after mid-century, allowing all who attended to join, the influx of new members suggested high rates of attendance.[9]

Colonial laws ensured that attendance would exceed membership. New England courts enforced mandatory attendance laws throughout the colonial period, and so did courts in other colonies. Even in Virginia, where as early as 1619 and as late as 1699 the Assembly imposed penalties on adults failing to attend some religious service, grand juries presented indictments throughout the century. By no means did everyone attend. In Virginia the population was too scattered; even in New England, people on the peripheries of settled areas could not reach a meetinghouse. But in stable communities the attendance was greater than the communicant membership.[10]

Substantial numbers continued to crowd into congregational gatherings in the eighteenth century. A computation from three standard sources indicates that by 1750 the colonists had formed at least 1,711 Christian and Jewish congregations, one for every 684 colonists, a number that rose to about 3,234 by 1780, one for every 859 Americans. Patricia Bonomi and Peter Eisenstadt have estimated that 80 percent of the white colonial population in 1700 should be counted as adherents of those congregations—a figure that fell to 59 percent in 1780. When we include the black population in the count, we find, using Bonomi and Eisenstadt's methods, that 71 percent of the population were adherents in 1700, 60 percent in 1750, 47 percent in 1780.[11]

Bonomi and Eisenstadt define adherents as attenders and their children. Not every member of an adherent family would have attended church on a given Sunday, but even if we assume that only half were present, an adherence rate of 70 percent would suggest that 35 percent of the population in 1700 might have attended with some regularity, though the number declined temporarily to 24 percent by 1780.

Numerous congregations distinguished communicant members, who received the Lord's Supper, from other parishioners who attended but did not receive the sacrament. This was a familiar distinction in New England, but selections from a 1724 report to the bishop of London by the rectors of eighty Anglican parishes also illustrate the differences: Christ Church in Maryland reported 200 to 300 auditors, 10 to 30 communicants; Christ Church in South Carolina, 70 attenders and 28 communicants; Abingdon Church in Virginia, 200 auditors, 60 to 70 communicants; St. Andrews, Staten Island, 100 hearers and 9 who received the sacrament. The Anglican minister Charles Woodmason, traveling in Carolina during the 1760s, wrote similar reports in his private journal.[12]

Awareness of that difference helps us interpret recent research on membership in the early nineteenth century. The federal census in 1850 found 38,061 congregations, one for every 611 Americans. Using extrapolations from census data, Roger Finke and Rodney Stark have argued that in 1850 the members of those congregations made up about 21 percent of the population.[13]

In Protestant churches, however, attendance still often greatly exceeded membership. When British traveler Andrew Reed toured the United States in 1835, he observed the difference: six congregations in Lexington, Kentucky, had 3,200 attenders and 900 communicants; two in Lexington, Virginia, had 800 attenders and 500 communicants; three in Danville, Pennsylvania, had 850 attenders and 325 communicants. In Danville, he found that 22 percent of the town were communicants but that 57 percent attended; Morristown had 29 percent communicants, 71 percent attenders. In the largest Congregational church in Northampton, Massachusetts, he counted 1,400 worshipers, while 300 more attended across town at the second church. His reports make it plausible that the 21 percent membership rate proposed by Stark and Finke entailed a substantially higher rate of attendance.[14]

We reach a similar conclusion when we extend the methods of Bonomi and Eisenstadt to the nineteenth century. If the average congregation in 1850 still ministered to eighty families—and that is at least plausible—then the rate of adherence, as defined by Bonomi and Eisenstadt, would have been 72 percent by mid-century; and if half of them attended on a given Sunday, the attendance rate would have been around 36 percent nationwide, a figure compatible with the conclusions of Stark and Finke.[15]

Other visitors from abroad noticed the high attendance. When Tocqueville arrived in 1831, "the religious aspect of the country" was the first thing that struck his attention. The English visitor Isabella Lucy Bird Bishop observed in 1859 that "the number of attendants on public worship is unusually large in proportion to the population, judging by the English standards," adding that "attendance at church is usually considered a necessary sign of respectability." She also provided one explanation for the discrepancy between attendance and full membership:

joining most Protestant churches, she said, was an "act of separation from the world," conditioned on "strict examination" and subjecting the member to "strict discipline." [16]

By 1890 the number of congregations rose to 165,297, one for every 381 Americans. Membership in those congregations also rose throughout the nineteenth century: Stark and Finke figure that the membership rate by 1890 stood at 33 percent and that the inclusion of the children of members would raise the rate further to 45 percent. But the meaning of membership had also shifted as large denominations relaxed their standards. Methodists, for instance, had once imposed lengthy probationary requirements, but in 1866 the southern branch eliminated them and before long the northern Methodists did the same. By 1887, Josiah Strong could survey thirty city congregations and find that only 56 percent of the members attended worship. In smaller communities attendance was higher, but the older pattern was reversing itself: the distinction between membership and attendance began to fade. It is plausible to conjecture that only 35 to 40 percent of the population still continued to attend churches and synagogues even though the number of members had risen. [17]

Federal censuses and other surveys show that after 1906 more than 50 percent of the population could be counted as members, rising to a high of 62 percent by 1980. Opinion polls confirm the high figures. In the twentieth century, however, attendance has invariably fallen below membership. Numerous polls have suggested that about 40 percent claim to attend regularly, though the claims might be exaggerations. It may be that except for a brief period in the late eighteenth century, the number has remained relatively constant since the late seventeenth century. [18]

All congregational statistics are suspect, and these are no exception. They consist of little more than informed guesses, heuristic and not conclusive. But they also suggest, however fragmentary and imprecise they might be, that the religious congregation has served as a source of community for substantial numbers of Americans for more than 300 years.

Comprehensive Congregations, 1607–1789

The meaning of community within congregations has undergone some transitions. The founders of the first congregations intended that they should comprehend the community: one congregation for each mission, village, town, or county. The ideal dissipated, but governmental coercion and geographical dispersion ensured that most colonists in the seventeenth century had access only to a single congregation. Even New England Puritans, who distinguished the congregation from the church (the visible saints who could receive the Lord's Supper), expected everyone in each town to attend a single congregation. The early congregations provided the only regular small-group activities that included every colonist—men, women, and children. And even after diverse congregations began to coexist, some variant of the ideal often remained: colonial Jewish synagogues, for instance, modeled themselves after the all-embracing synagogue communities (*kehillot*) of medieval Europe and identified the congregation with the entire Jewish community, for which the synagogue tried to furnish everything from worship and fellowship to kosher food and burial.[19]

In their internal organization these colonial congregations remained simple. In the leadership, a small lay group, such as the vestry in Virginia or the lay elders in New England, functioned alongside ordained clergy. By the 1720s some of the New England churches formed singing societies, but colonial congregations had none of the groups that would appear after the Revolution—Sunday schools, day schools, mission societies, sodalities, confraternities, or altar guilds. They had other ways of accomplishing their primary purpose.

The primary purpose was worship, and they assumed that everyone had an obligation to offer worship to an exalted God whose demands and mercies had been revealed in sacred scriptures. Many believed that their souls stood in perilous danger if they neglected such worship. The forms of worship varied: for Anglicans in the southern colonies, worship meant brief sermons accompanied by the weekly repetition of set words from the *Book of Common Prayer*, with sacramental communion four to six times a year. For New England Puritans it usually meant two sermons on a Sabbath day, lasting between one and two hours each, along with extemporaneous pastoral prayers, sung psalms, and periodic sacramental communion. Some eighteenth-century Baptists added other rituals, including the kiss of charity, the anointing of the sick, and the washing of feet. For Catholics worship meant homilies and public prayers that preceded the solemn celebration of the mass. For Jews it meant the repetition of traditional prayers and melodies with a cantor (*hazzan*) who sometimes conducted services every weekday as well as on the Sabbath and feasts.[20]

Whatever the form, congregations agreed that worship was their reason for being. When they fought among themselves, the source of conflict could usually be found in differing views of worship. Should infants be baptized? All infants or only the children of the godly? Should baptism be a communal act or a private ritual, as it often was in Virginia? Should the sermons be read or delivered extempore? Which rite should guide prayers in the synagogue? Should Christian worshipers sing hymns? How should they sing them? A bitter "Singing Controversy" agitated the churches of New England from the 1720s through the 1740s, with some members insisting that congregations sing by note and harmony and others decrying the new style as the onset of formalism. Dutch churches in New York argued about degrees of formality in worship; Anglicans in South Carolina worried about whether to sit or kneel at communion. Always the debates over worship turned on the same issues: some congregations tried to emulate the practices of the primitive church, others honored traditions that had accumulated over time, and still others thought that forms should be discarded if they stilled the spontaneous voice of the Spirit.[21]

Almost all agreed also that worship was the responsibility of the entire community. Because they believed that worship was a public, even civic, responsibility, moreover, colonial congregations not only sought governmental assistance but also subjected themselves to civic authority. In seventeenth-century New York, governors had to approve the ministers; in Connecticut, town meetings shared in decisions about ministerial salary and tenure; in Massachusetts, between 1636 and 1692, magistrates approved or disapproved the formation of new churches. In New England, moreover, the governors also invested public authority in the churches; Massachusetts until 1664 and New Haven until 1665 admitted only full church members to the status of freemen.[22]

Early colonial congregations usually depended on state financing. Only among Congregationalists in Boston and a few dissenters elsewhere did voluntary contributions maintain the churches. Several other Congregationalist churches tried voluntary maintenance of ministers, but they abandoned it. By the 1650s, most New England towns outside Rhode Island had discarded the voluntary system. In New York a trading company initially paid ministerial salaries, but after 1664 the governor empowered the church to tax the inhabitants. Virginia set aside glebes (farm lands) for ministers in 1619 and imposed church rates in 1623; churchwardens and sheriffs gathered the parish dues along with other taxes.[23]

In 1650, about 88 (79 percent) of the 112 colonial congregations probably received financial support from either trading companies or state taxation. But well-meaning laws did not ensure ministerial comfort: disputes between ministers and their congregations over the payment of legally prescribed salaries continually disrupted communities, and with the spread of dissent in the eighteenth century, state taxation receded as a substantial economic resource for the congregations. By 1750, probably about 674 congregations, or 39 percent of the total of 1,711, still received tax money. And after the passage of new state constitutions in the late 1770s and 1780s, eliminating public financial support for almost all churches outside New England, a plausible estimate would be that only 20 to 25 percent of America's 3,234 congregations drew from the tax collectors, though Anglicans in Virginia held on to their glebe land until 1802. By the time of the First Amendment, in 1791, most congregations had already weaned themselves financially from state support.[24]

The frequent salary disputes illustrated the control exercised by the laity. Lacking the hierarchical apparatus of the European churches, local churches and synagogues became accustomed to making their own decisions. Lay vestries in Virginia; town meetings and local selectmen in New England; and congregational leaders in the Middle Colonies hired their own ministers and set their own policies. This assertiveness troubled ministers. The Anglican commissary in Virginia, James Blair, complained that colonial churches treated ministers as mere "hirelings," and Gottlieb Mittelberger in Pennsylvania lamented that congregations there hired ministers by the year, "like cowherds in Germany." In New England, the ministers felt the need after the 1630s to reassert clerical authority, though the result was often stalemate. Even governors in Virginia, who had the right to induct parish ministers, had to accept the practice of parish vestries which extended probationary pastorates as a substitute for permanent induction.[25]

By the eighteenth century, ministers organized themselves—in presbyteries, synods, coetuses, ministeriums, and associations—and attained greater authority over local congregations, but local lay control never fully disappeared.[26]

The public status of congregations entailed public responsibilities. In Virginia, vestries kept the records of births and burials and handled relief of the poor and homeless; churchwardens oversaw orphans, corrected wayward parents, and looked into cases of child abuse. In New England, the towns assumed such duties, though congregations there and in the Middle Colonies sometimes set aside small amounts to help the poor. The sense of communal responsibility was especially visible when congregations disciplined members for wayward actions ranging from drunkenness and fornication to shoddy business practices. Anglicans in Virginia authorized their churchwardens to bring any transgressor in the parish before the congregation for public shaming. New England congregations assumed authority over only full or halfway members who had subscribed to the church covenant. In every region the congregations exercised discipline, though nowhere more than in New England; in six congregations in Massachusetts, Emil Oberholzer found an increase from 135 disciplinary cases between 1690 and 1729 to 260 between 1730 and 1769. In five other congregations between 1720 and 1760, he found a mean average of 40 hearings. Only after 1770 did he find the number declining—a subtle shift in the cultural meaning of religious practice—though in other regions (and sometimes even in other New England congregations) disciplinary practices continued.[27]

Just as congregations often embraced the whole community, so also did they reflect the community's social divisions. Their seating symbolized the social rankings: the best seats went to persons of highest status. Vestries and committees revised the seating plans every few years—a procedure known to create periodic disharmony. But presuming to take a seat beyond one's assigned station could be a mistake: When Richard Price in Virginia slipped into the pew assigned to a local justice, he found himself cited for an act "tending to the dishonor of God Almighty, the contempt of his Majesty and Mynisters, offence of the congregacion, scandall to religion, and evill example of others."[28]

Often men and women sat in separate sections. In New England after 1660, women joined the churches in greater numbers than men: one study of eighteen congregations found that women after 1660 constituted 54 to 65 percent of the members. Another study of twenty-eight churches found that women constituted 65 percent or more of the new admissions. On the rolls, at least, women assumed greater visibility as the percentages of men declined. But their seating depended on the status of their husbands; men of high standing and wealth could, by the mid-seventeenth century, seat their wives and children together with them in family pews, but most women still sat apart on benches arranged in accord with the status of men.[29]

Africans and Indians in New England sat in galleries, rear seats, or stairways, along with children. In the South, colonial congregations were not certain that they wanted even to include Africans. The Anglican missionary Morgan Godwin complained in 1680 about resistance to the baptism of African slaves for fear that the sacrament might affect either their temporal status or their opinions of themselves. Only after 1760 did sizable numbers of Africans begin to enter colonial congregations.[30]

Congregations reflected other ethnic divisions: immigrants clung to familiar liturgies in their own language. Well into the eighteenth century, linguistic divisions were tenacious, and they began to disappear only with the second and third generations. But even the ethnic coloration of congregations exemplified their comprehensive character— their embrace of a larger community, their function in preserving larger communal values.

By the middle of the eighteenth century even small towns sometimes had several congregations. The comprehensive ideal had required that a single congregation embrace a geographical region. It could not abide diversity. When diversity came, the social meaning of religion— and of community—in America changed.

Devotional Congregations, 1789–1870

A tide of settlers washed away the comprehensive congregation; denominational competition kept it from returning. Even in the Carolina backcountry, Charles Woodmason complained, competing sects had by 1767 "built upwards of 20 Meeting Houses" in every "Hole and Corner where they could raise Congregations." By 1774 Separate Baptists had formed fifty-four congregations in Virginia, some planted in the midst of the Anglican parishes. By the early nineteenth century, the congregation no longer served a unifying function in the communities. The diversity reached even the small towns: in 1841, Charleston, Indiana, with a population of a few hundred, had six competing congregations, some with only twelve to twenty-five members.[31]

Congregations proliferated at an unprecedented pace. In 1780 there were fewer than 3,000; in 1820, at least 10,904; by 1860, about 54,000—an increase outstripping population growth. The revivalism of the Second Awakening created thousands of permanent local institutions. A census survey in 1906 revealed that 3,637 congregations traced their beginnings to the period before 1800 but that 21,929 claimed to have been founded between 1800 and 1849. They also changed in style and social composition; by 1850 more than half the congregations in America were filled with Baptists and Methodists, whose boisterous worship raised the eyebrows of more staid competitors. The early nineteenth century was the halcyon era of congregational expansion.[32]

While congregations expanded in number, they lost autonomy and scope. The organizing of denominations meant that they more often felt the effects of decisions made at national and regional conventions and associations. They also existed alongside a bewildering array of other voluntary associations—Tocqueville said there were "associations of a thousand kinds"—that fulfilled functions the congregations had once monopolized: fellowship, charity, the dissemination of information, and concerted action for various causes. Some worked with the congregations; others, like the Freemasons, could compete with them for loyalty.[33]

Americans now led far more segmented lives than their forebears had led. The market economy created more towns and nurtured distinctions between townspeople and country folk; the change from the family-craft system to mercantile and factory capitalism meant that workers began to live in one neighborhood and work in another, that urban women increasingly assumed domestic roles rather than working in family-based production, and that economic classes viewed one another from greater social distances. The hardening of the slave system accentuated the distinctions between blacks and whites. Congregations felt all of these changes; in cities and towns, at least, they drew a segmented and self-selected clientele.[34]

Their primary purpose was still worship, but now they began to segment worship. In addition to the regular Sunday services, they formed prayer meetings, Bible classes, Sunday schools, devotional gatherings, and mission societies that brought people together in small groups, often organized by age and gender. "To give satisfaction" in the new congregation, wrote Heman Humphrey in 1842, ministers had to know how to conduct "private religious meetings," and Enoch Pond advised young ministers that they should expect to hold at least three "extra religious meetings" each week. Catholics introduced sodalities, confraternities, rosary societies, and special devotions. In Catholic churches in the Midwest between 1800 and 1860, more than 70 percent of all parish societies were devotional groups like the Confraternity of the Immaculate Heart of Mary, devoted to prayer for the conversion of sinners, or the Confraternity of the Sacred Heart, formed to nurture devotion to the suffering Christ. Among Jews the new devotionalism appeared around mid-century, when immigrants created a variety of fraternal societies, charities, clinics, and clubs and defined the synagogue more narrowly as a house of prayer and education.[35]

The early history of the Sunday schools illustrated the change within Protestant congregations. Appearing in the United States in 1787, the

Sunday schools at first offered classes in reading, writing, and religion for poor children and adults; free blacks were eager participants in the northern cities. Independent societies ran them; congregations were ambivalent, though some offered their buildings, and the early schools were not always linked to a congregation. By the 1820s, however, as free public schools expanded, the Sunday schools became religious societies for children within congregations. By the 1850s, most congregations had made the Sunday school a part of their ministry to church families—one more group for instruction and devotion within the congregation.[36]

A further dimension of the segmenting appeared in the widening diversity in styles of worship. Jews split into rite congregations, depending on their preference for Sephardic, Polish, or German ritual, and a tiny number of antebellum Reform congregations, probably no more than eight by 1860, suggested yet another ritual possibility. Catholics shared the same Latin mass, but they often divided into national parishes with distinctive styles of worship, the Germans promoting a pageantry unlike the solemn simplicity of the Irish. Protestants had always disagreed about "set forms" in worship, but the democratizing rhetoric of the early national era encouraged a revolt not only against formal liturgies but also against the refined sermons and dignified prayers of the older antiliturgical traditions. The groups that grew fastest incorporated gospel hymns sung to popular tunes, loud and exuberant shouting, and colorful colloquial preaching. Their services had little in common with those of fashionable urban churches that worshiped with the aid of organs, professional singers, trained choirs, and well-educated preachers.[37]

By the mid-nineteenth century, black churches offered a blending of Protestant and African ritual. A visitor in 1858 to the African Baptist Church in Richmond, which seated 2,000, described a closely-packed service, women on one side of the church, men on the other, in which even before the preacher arrived "the people were singing with mouths and eyes distended, and their feet beating heavily." A lay elder's prayer preceded the sermon, evoking from the worshipers a continuing litany of individual responses: "Amen," "Oh dear! Oh grant it! Oh Jesus!" The same responses greeted the minister's sermon, followed by two prayers and a spontaneous "outburst of loud but harmonious singing, which was continued until the shades of evening warned all to their homes."[38]

These varied Protestant congregations were far more homogeneous socially than their predecessors had been a hundred years earlier. The comprehensive congregations of the early colonial era had encompassed rich and poor, observing the social differences by seating people according to their rank. By the 1730s in the larger cities, the rich and the poor began choosing separate congregations; affluent Dutch worshipers in New York sometimes felt more comfortable in Anglican than in Reformed services; Dutch Pietists criticized the wealthy and attracted the poor. In the early eighteenth-century South it became a truism that "none of the rich or learned ever join" Baptist congregations. By the early nineteenth century, the pattern was set. Even within the popular denominations, some congregations within the larger towns attracted the affluent, others the working classes. And within the congregations themselves, the wealthy usually assumed the leadership: In New York City in 1820, over 75 percent of the Protestant lay leaders were men—or the male relatives of men—who appeared in Moses Beach's compilations of the city's men of wealth.[39]

Methods of church finance—and of seating—reinforced the social homogeneity. By the 1780s, New England towns began to dismantle the committees that assigned pews; instead they began to sell the pews by auction. They sold them to the highest bidders and taxed them as private property. Wealthy pewholders opened pews for poorer members, but the pews now belonged to their owners in accordance with the principle of market exchange. Sale or rental of pews, supplemented by subscriptions among the members, soon became standard means of economic support for congregations. But pew sales also caused contention: democratizing groups like the Methodists reached the poor by banning the sale of pews. And reformers within more respectable churches attempted similar bans: "Let us not be ashamed to copy from the Methodists," urged Presbyterian layman Lewis Tappan, who worried that pew sales had driven the poor away. But sales and rentals seemed to many, both Protestants and Catholics, to be the only way to augment the amounts that members raised through subscriptions, fairs, and collections. By mid-century, the practice appeared even among northern Methodists—a trend that in 1860 helped create a separate Free Methodist denomination.[40]

Congregations remained places of public gathering. And in the antebellum era they occupied a place within a larger religious ecology. At a time when other public institutions—school systems, voluntary societies, even governing bodies—conveyed a Protestant aura and ideology, local Protestant congregations could abandon the older parish ideal without feeling that they had surrendered comprehensive influence. Local congregations served, moreover, as the financial backbone for the denominational and voluntary societies that worked to maintain a public witness. Sometimes, as in the temperance movement, they themselves became local voluntary societies working toward a public policy.

They continued to exercise public influence by imposing discipline on their own members. William Warren Sweet wrote of western congregations as the moral courts of the frontier; it was not unusual that the Mt. Hebron Baptist Church of Leeds, Alabama, between 1819 and 1865 punished 55 of its 376 members. But discipline persisted also in eastern congregations: Center Church, New Haven, tried only two cases in the eighteenth century but thirty in the nineteenth. And a study of seventeen congregations in Massachusetts reveals thirty-nine disciplinary cases between 1800 and 1809, forty-four in the next decade, and eighty-two during the 1820s, after which the practice began to decline. Congregational discipline took congregations out of the sanctuary and into the streets.[41]

For some social groups, congregations were the public arena. Women continued to join congregations more frequently than men. In the eastern cities of Massachusetts between 1800 and 1835, for instance, women constituted 78 percent of new members. In Utica, New York, religious revivals depended on the initiative of women who joined churches and brought their families with them. And the congregations provided public leadership roles for women members. Sunday school teachers were usually young single women; other women in the congregations organized not only altar guilds and devotional societies but also societies for foreign and domestic missions. By 1827 Samuel Miller at Princeton warned the clergy that unless they could win the confidence of women they would not be "very acceptable or very useful." "The female part of every congregation have, in general," he said, "an influence which, while it cannot be defined, cannot, at the same time, be resisted." It was an influence that women held in no other public institution.[42]

The congregation had a distinctive public function for African Americans: it was the sole public institution in which they could assume leadership. Most black converts joined white congregations—already by 1820 over one-fifth of Methodist membership was black—but during the antebellum period they also worshipped in at least 931 separate black congregations, 563 in the South and 368 in the North. Though whites tried to supervise them in the South, even southern congregations could serve as agencies of black initiative, as when Morris Brown in Charleston in 1817 led an African congregation out of the Methodist Episcopal

37

Church and into the new African Methodist Episcopal denomination, or when the First African Church of Savannah in 1833 successfully defied the town's white Baptist church by calling Andrew Marshall as its pastor. The Bethel AME congregation in Baltimore built its own Romanesque church (a $16,000 building), formed an African Academy to educate black children, founded a mission church for work with poorer blacks, and established a literary and debating society. Further North, black congregations worked closely with temperance and abolitionist societies, often opening their meetinghouses for abolitionist rallies.[43]

Immigrants, especially Catholics from Ireland and Germany, were the third social group to expand the functions of antebellum congregations. Catholics by 1850 were already a large denomination, with slightly over a million adherents, but they had managed to form only 1,221 parish congregations, 3.5 percent of the total in America. These Catholic congregations had to serve numerous social purposes. Because they could not count on other institutions, they offered their members not only worship but also relief societies, insurance societies, militia groups (for both protection and entertainment), Societies of St. Paul for welfare and youth work, temperance societies, and schools. In 1842, 54 percent of the Catholic parishes in New York City had their own schools, and about 20 percent of the total school population attended them. The schools proved too expensive for most parishes, but they illustrated the desire of Catholics to use their congregations to create their own public order within the larger public order. The busy Catholic parish foreshadowed the future of the American congregation.[44]

Social Congregations, 1870–1950

"The Catholic Church keeps its house of worship open the whole week through," wrote a Protestant minister in 1890. "Protestants are coming to understand that it is a miserably wasteful use of the Christian treasure invested in the sanctuary to open the house for the benefit of the people only once or twice a week." The church, he suggested, should become rather a "social home" for its members. By 1890, such notions were commonplace. Older established congregations began to look more like the ethnic churches of the 1850s. Whether they were imitating each other or enacting a common vision, many of America's 165,297 congregations displayed an eagerness to develop new patterns. The result was the emergence of the social congregation.[45]

It is well to specify the limits of the generalization. Many congregations changed little in either their internal structure or their self-conception in the century between, say, 1850 and 1950. The religious census of 1926 found that 167,864 (72 percent) of the nation's 232,154 congregations could be found either in the open country or in villages of fewer than 2,500 persons. For some groups and regions, the rural character of congregational life was even more pronounced: in the South, 83 percent of the congregations were country churches; in the Midwest, 75 percent were in villages; 76 percent of all black congregations were rural. These small rural congregations struggled to maintain themselves, and many lacked full-time ministers. Even when towns with up to 5,000 inhabitants are added to the figures, only 21 percent of the town and country communities in 1926 had resident ministers.[46]

In many of those rural areas, community life formed around the congregation. This was especially true of black churches. One study found in 1923 that 58 percent of the black congregations offered some form of educational or cultural enrichment, though only 20 percent had social or recreational activities. But most rural congregations viewed themselves almost exclusively as places of worship, and for many of the members this made the church a social center. "What do we do for recreation? Why, we go to church," said one rural southern woman. Yet even the worship was infrequent: in the rural South, 80 percent of the churches in 1923 had only one or two services a month. On any given Sunday, about 27,000 southern rural churches were closed. And such conditions were not limited to the South: a comprehensive study of rural churches in Ohio painted a similar picture.[47]

In the larger cities, however, the congregation by 1900 often seemed quite different from its 1850 predecessor. Again some limits on the generalization are in order: a survey in St. Louis in 1924 found that at least a third of the congregations were much like the typical village or rural church. In the working-class churches of Muncie, Indiana—and presumably of other places—worship remained the main social function through the 1920s. But at the turn of the century, cities of over 25,000 people held 17,906 (8 percent) of the nation's 212,230 congregations, and many of the larger ones created a new congregational form.[48]

One observer in 1890 spoke of "a complete revolution" in the social life of American congregations, and the chief symbol of the change, he said, was the church parlor, which in any large church had often become "almost as necessary as a pulpit." In the late nineteenth century, thousands of congregations transformed themselves into centers that not only were open for worship but also were available for Sunday school concerts, church socials, women's meetings, youth groups, girls' guilds, boys' brigades, sewing circles, benevolent societies, day schools, temperance societies, athletic clubs, scout troops, and nameless other activities. The older tradition of religious societies still flourished; almost every Catholic church, for example, sponsored a women's Altar Society, to provide altar cloths and vestments, and a men's Holy Name Society, which met for mass and communion and offered service in the neighborhood. Between 1860 and 1900, sodalities and devotional societies still probably accounted for 60 percent of Catholic parish societies. But Henry Ward Beecher advised the seminarians at Yale to "multiply picnics" in their parishes, and many congregations of every variety proceeded beyond picnics to gymnasiums, parish houses, camps, baseball teams, and military drill groups, with one church report in 1897 asserting that "uniforms, guns, and equipment are as essential as the Bible and the Hymnal in the advance of our work."[49]

Proponents of change argued that the new congregational activities could overcome the impersonality of large churches and synagogues, eliminate class distinctions, attract children and their parents, provide wholesome amusement for young people, and draw men more actively into congregational work. Women still outnumbered the men: in 1906 about 61 percent of Protestants and 51 percent of Catholics were women, and they attended more faithfully than men. Some ministers argued that only "parish organization" could recapture the men.[50]

The social congregation bore heavy responsibilities within immigrant communities. In 1906 at least 13 percent of American congregations still conducted all or some of their activities in a language other than English. By then the national Catholic parish and the *landsmannschaft* synagogue, organized according to ethnic heritage, had become a familiar feature of congregational life. The ethnic congregations mediated between their members and the larger society by providing benevolent and mutual-aid groups for sickness and death benefits, along with adult education, reading rooms, and recreation. Among Catholics, both immigrant parishes and others invested especially in parochial schools: in the Northeast, 30 percent had a school by 1880, 56 percent by 1930, and often half the parish budget went to support the school. The ethnic congregation offered a refuge from an alien culture; it tried to provide an alternative community.[51]

Among American Jews, the social congregation flourished not so much among the first-generation immigrants as among their offspring who identified themselves as Conservative. The Orthodox *shul* resisted the expansion of activities; Reform temples also were initially suspicious of too much nonreligious activity at the synagogue. But especially after Mordecai Kaplan popularized the notion of Judaism as an evolving religious civilization, Conservative synagogues found their own justification for creating social congregations. By the 1920s, new synagogue centers offered a panoply of recreational and social programs along with Hebrew schools and other educational efforts.[52]

The new-style congregations used a rhetoric of equality, friendliness, and democracy. Apart from penalties still prescribed in the Catholic confessionals, they also ceased to discipline their members. "If the church should take up the case of every inconsistent member," wrote one theologian, "it could do nothing but discipline the year round." Better not to discipline at all, decided many. They sought more democratic forms of group behavior: Reform Jewish congregations abandoned separate seating for men and women early in the nineteenth century, arguing that families should worship together and that separate seating diminished women. By the 1920s Conservative congregations also introduced mixed seating, with the result that seating patterns came to symbolize the differences between Orthodoxy and the other two branches of Jewish tradition in America. Christian congregations still fretted about the benefits of selling and renting pews, with some arguing that the practice confirmed class distinctions at worship by creating "the rich man's aisle" and "the poor man's corner."[53]

The opponents of pew rentals sought better ways of financing the congregations. They resurrected time-honored methods: subscription drives, assessments, pledges, bazaars, and fairs. Pew rentals remained popular—Plymouth Church in Brooklyn scandalized other congregations with its opulent pew auctions—but advocates of "the free-seat, secret-envelope system" made headway. By the 1920s most congregations had abandoned pew sales in favor of weekly offerings in envelopes, though subscription drives and parish fund-raisers still remained popular. They also gave increasing amounts of money for purposes other than their own maintenance: both in the cities and in the country churches, Protestant congregations by 1923 gave 25 to 35 percent of their offerings to missions and benevolent causes, up from 14 to 18 percent at the turn of the century.[54]

The enlivening activity of congregations continued to be worship, but reformers worried that Protestant worship had become a matter of isolated preachers talking to an audience. By the 1880s even nonliturgical Protestants were calling for responsive readings, more congregational singing (in place of professional choirs), and public repetition of the Lord's Prayer and the Creeds. Many congregations discovered during the eighties that their members no longer attended midweek prayer services and balked even at the time-honored custom of two preaching services on Sunday. To the reformers the solution was "the largest possible participation in worship," so that members would cease to think of Sunday morning as a time to see "how well the actors, in pulpit and choir, will perform."[55]

In a different way, Catholics also worried about congregational participation. As the Catholic population grew, the churches multiplied the Sunday masses, sometimes holding as many as seven on Sundays and four each weekday morning—with the Sunday high mass an increasingly elaborate service. But they also found that nonliturgical and private devotions grew in popularity to such an extent that by the 1930s they overshadowed the mass. Catholics came loyally to mass, but they flocked to novenas (nine-day prayer services), triduums (three-day prayer services), Forty Hours devotions (individual adoration of the sacrament, which stood exposed for forty hours in the church), and Perpetual Adoration (in which worshipers kept watch over the sacrament all night). The experience was individual and emotional, not communal or liturgical, and Catholic liturgical reformers sought, like the Protestants, to enhance the quality of communal participation.[56]

Jews debated similar issues. By the 1880s, congregations in search of greater decorum were introducing robed choirs, sermons, cantors, and liturgical forms that shifted the focus to the leaders of the worship service, including star cantors who attracted large crowds. The effort was to encourage decorum without diminishing Jewish tradition, but Orthodox Jews contended that traditional forms of congregational participation were being lost.[57]

Some of the new-style congregations nurtured a sense of social responsibility among their members. The term "institutional church" was probably coined in 1893, though the reality preceded the name. These congregations represented one form of the social ideal, extending their activities to meet the social needs of their neighborhoods and regions. Such congregations as St. Bartholomew's Episcopal Church or the Catholic Church of St. James in New York or the African Methodist Episcopal Institutional Church in Chicago offered ethnic missions, industrial schools, kindergartens, employment bureaus, clinics, visiting nurses, legal service bureaus that handled thousands of cases yearly, workers' clubs, girls' boarding houses, circulating libraries, gymnasiums, and dozens of clubs and classes for the tenement dwellers in the surrounding neighborhoods. By 1906, New York City had at least 112 institutional churches, Chicago about 25, and every other major city at least one; most were northern, though several black congregations embodied the institutional ideal in the larger southern cities.[58]

The new social congregations were busy. They assumed functions that had never occurred to their antebellum predecessors. Earlier congregations had worshiped together; they had also exerted public influence through the exercise of discipline and through the host of institutions—public schools, colleges, even public laws—that propagated their values. By the late nineteenth century, the discipline was beginning to fade and the other institutions were often moving away from their alliance with congregational culture, but the desire for influence remained. Most congregations could no longer discipline a member for illicit forms of recreation, but they could still hope to maintain influence over recreational choices by providing their own picnics and parties. The late nineteenth century introduced new ways for congregations to realize the seventeenth-century ideal of comprehensive influence. If they could no longer comprehend a geographical region, they could still comprehend a wider spectrum of the activities of their members.

Participatory Congregations, 1950–90

By the late twentieth century, a number of congregations had come close to realizing the ideal of comprehensive influence. They monopolized the lives of their members: worship, recreation, education, child-care, family life, vocational decisions. Most congregations chose another path. But the ideal of the social congregation—offering not simply worship but an array of other activities and services—has maintained its hold in American religion. By 1990 the nation had at least 350,337 religious congregations. Whatever the number—no one knows for sure—they were markedly diverse. At one end of the spectrum stood the mega-churches: In 1982, First Baptist of Hammond, Indiana, claimed 74,000 members; Highland Park Baptist in Chattanooga, with sixty satellite chapels, claimed 57,000; ten others claimed over 12,000 members each. But close observers pointed out that fewer than 500 congregations had an average attendance of more than 1,000 and that the average Protestant congregation had fewer than 200 members and drew only 40 to 60 people to its worship services. Probably 60 percent were rural. But even many of the small congregations multiplied groups and programs, often because larger denominational organizations held up the social congregation as the ideal.[59]

In 1962 sociologist Gibson Winter deplored the emergence of what he called the "organization church," which tried to overcome the disorienting effects of residential mobility by involving its members in a network of interdependent activities and functions through which they would develop loyalty to the organization. It substituted committees for sacraments, bazaars for confession, and a collection of functions for community. During the same period, the rabbi Bernard Lander worried that the synagogue no longer nurtured prayer and piety as much as it sponsored sisterhoods, brotherhoods, parties, dances, and programs with a recreational and quasi-therapeutic aim. Some clergy complained about the expectation that they "run a show" in which congregations sought more to be entertained than edified.[60]

Viewed in longer historical perspective, these congregations could be viewed as bearers of the comprehensive ideal that undergirded colonial religious groups. This was clearest in fundamentalist Protestant congregations like the Southside Gospel Church in New England, which provided teen services, deacons' meetings, choirs, Bible institutes, ladies' visitation, senior fellowship groups, children's clubs, family outings, sports groups, and a Christian Academy where children could be educated from nursery school through high school. Southside's members, wrote sociologist Nancy Ammerman, spent "almost every spare minute" on activities related to church. The pastor of the fundamentalist First Baptist Church in Dallas, which occupied six downtown city blocks, explained his congregation's growth partly by its willingness to "meet felt needs" among the members; the church not only multiplied study and devotional groups but built a seven-story recreational center, with gymnasium, bowling, and skating, and offered courses in charm and modeling, cake decorating, millinery, leathercraft, and any other topics that could hold members within the congregational culture. Its comprehensiveness was not geographical, as in the seventeenth century, but cultural.[61]

Few congregations aimed for this much comprehensive reach: fewer had the resources to attain it even if they had wanted it. But congregations did flourish in the mid-twentieth century by offering programs that met a wide range of needs defined by their members: recreation, education, study, and child-care. Stephen S. Wise Temple in Los Angeles exemplified the "service synagogue" with a full staff of rabbis, cantors, educators, social workers, and executives administering day-care centers, schools, social-service bureaus, and a fleet of buses. Synagogue supplementary schools became the dominant form of American Jewish education, encompassing about 75 percent of the school-age children who received any form of Jewish education. Conservative synagogues in the suburbs often attracted young Jews by organizing as centers with social and recreational programs.[62]

For social and economic reasons, some time-honored activities receded in importance: in most regions of the country, Catholic parishes supported fewer parochial schools in 1980 than in 1930, but many partially compensated by accelerating religious educational programs for adults alongside a panoply of other activities. One analyst found that only about 18 percent of the Catholic parishes in the study offered merely the mass and religious education of the young; 37 percent were "incredibly busy," wrote historian Jay Dolan, and even the remainder had a "complex range of programs."[63]

The complexity could be ample even in small congregations: when Melvin Williams studied the ninety-one-member Zion Holiness Church, a black Pentecostal congregation in Pittsburgh, he found not only worship services but also dinners, choirs, plays, trips, picnics, gatherings for mutual assistance, and money-raising activities. The congregation provided an alternative form of cohesion and solidarity within a larger environment that was often hostile or indifferent.[64]

By the 1980s, a large congregation no longer constituted a single group. Like the urban social congregation of the late nineteenth century, though to a far greater degree, it was a group of groups, and its members tended to be active only in a select number. Clergy had begun to recognize, moreover, that the larger congregations contained several distinct "audiences," some seeking mainly fellowship, others valuing personal witness to the faith; some eager for study, others committed to social concerns, and still others who stressed two or three of the interests but not the rest. Even small congregations often comprised a set of smaller groupings.[65]

Much of this organizing was a pragmatic reflection of a cultural ethos; Gibson Winter saw it as a signal of religious captivity to the surrounding culture. But it also signaled an increasing demand by the laity for participation in the congregations on their own terms. In the earlier institutional churches, a leadership elite, usually clerical, had defined the direction of the organizational elaboration. In the later forms of the social congregation, lay groups took more initiative. The impulse toward new forms of participation could be called the hallmark of the congregation in the late twentieth century.

The change was most visible in Catholic congregations because the older Catholic parochial ideal assumed a monarchical image of the parish priest. Even before Vatican II this image came under scrutiny; the decrees of the council, along with a marked decline in the number of priests between 1963 and 1972, resulted in a new leadership role for laity in Catholic parishes. The chief symbol of the change was the "parish council," a lay group designed to share responsibility with the pastor, though parish councils have yet to establish a firm footing in most congregations. More telling has been the move of laity and nuns to the fore as teachers and directors of religious education. Such a change has opened leadership especially to women: the Notre Dame Study of Catholic Parish Life estimated that women constituted 58 percent of all parish leaders aside from the pastor.[66]

The expansion of lay participation has been equally visible in the way congregations conduct their worship—the regular activity that still constitutes their uniqueness. The Catholic liturgical movement reached American parishes after 1945, and by 1970 the older devotional Catholicism was giving way to a liturgical piety that allowed the laity to form committees to plan the worship. Throughout American congregations, worship changed its forms: Catholics, Protestants, and Jews all prepared new rituals that accentuated the theme of participation.

The architecture of congregational buildings increasingly suggested the image of the congregation as a gathering that invited participation. Even before the building boom of the 1940s, congregations began to move away symbolically from a conception of worship as a performance for passive observers. Protestant innovators pushed the pulpit to one side, elevated the communion table to the platform, placed a cross and candles on it, and had their choirs sit facing the table rather than the pews. Catholics in the 1940s initiated the move toward simple tables rather than elaborate altar structures. In Judaism, the *bimah*, the reading desk, had traditionally been located on a platform in the middle of the congregation. Reform had altered this architecture of worship, but the impulse toward participation prompted its recovery in Reform and Conservative congregations. By 1954, at least one out of every four new religious buildings was "modernistic" in design, and the modern buildings were designed to permit congregations to act together within liturgical spaces.[67]

For many congregations, participation in a common quest and worship came to seem more important than doctrinal uniformity. Pollsters often expressed surprise at the diversity of belief they found within modern congregations. Outside fundamentalist congregations, and sometimes even within them, the laity seemed inclined to select the religious ideas that made most sense to them and to ignore the rest. Even conservative Protestant congregations often lacked an elementary knowledge of the Bible. Yet the evidence still indicated that people joined congregations to seek a sense both of belonging and of meaning, and that congregations which made this a challenging and demanding quest seemed in the 1970s to flourish.[68]

Anyone who would understand either of these quests in America—for meaning or for belonging—will have to attend to the study of congregations. Just as the painstaking examination of New England towns and Virginia counties helped to alter our historical awareness of our seventeenth-century colonial past, so the equally painstaking examination of religious congregations promises to alter our perceptions both of religion and of community in America. To explore the congregation is to penetrate to the grass roots of American religious culture; the study of the congregation promises to illumine topics as wide-ranging as voluntarism, money, punishment, leadership, education, attendance, and countless others. Most of all, the study of the congregation clarifies an enduring dimension of community in America. More Americans have belonged to a church or a synagogue than to any other private association. That fact alone makes the congregation a resource for a deeper understanding of America.

NOTES

1. Anne Loveland, *Southern Evangelicals and the Social Order, 1800–1860* (Baton Rouge: Louisiana State University Press, 1980), p. 14.

2. Thomas Bender, *Community and Social Change in America* (New Brunswick: Rutgers University Press, 1978), pp. 17–167.

3. This essay expands an argument that I initially developed in "The Historian and the Congregation," in *Beyond Clericalism*, ed. Joseph G. Hough, Jr., and Barbara Wheeler (Atlanta: Scholars Press, 1988), pp. 89–101.

4. Milton V. Backman, *Christian Churches in America* (Provo: Brigham Young University Press, 1976), p. xv.

5. Evarts Greene and Virginia Harrington, *American Population Before the Federal Census of 1790* (New York: Columbia University Press, 1932), pp. 125, 136; Jon Butler, *Awash in a Sea of Faith* (Cambridge, Mass.: Harvard University Press,

1990), p. 53; Edwin S. Gaustad, *Historical Atlas of Religion in America* (New York: Harper and Row, 1962), p. 167; Philip A. Bruce, *Institutional History of Virginia in the Seventeenth Century*, 2 vols. (New York: Putnam, 1910), 1:189, 190; G. M. Brydon, *Virginia's Mother Church and the Conditions Under Which it Grew*, 2 vols. (Richmond: Virginia Historical Society, 1947–52), 1:225, 512; 2:43.

6. Randall H. Balmer, *A Perfect Babel of Confusion* (New York: Oxford University Press, 1989), p. 13; Richard W. Pointer, *Protestant Pluralism and the New York Experience* (Bloomington: Indiana University Press, 1988), p. 31.

7. Gaustad, *Historical Atlas*, pp. 3, 167; Bureau of the Census, *Historical Statistics of the United States* (Washington, D.C.: Government Printing Office, 1960), p. 756.

8. Darrett Rutman, *Winthrop's Boston* (New York: Norton, 1965), p. 147; Butler, *Awash in a Sea of Faith*, p. 62; Robert Pope, *The Halfway Covenant* (Princeton: Princeton University Press, 1969), pp. 105, 111, 119, 149, 236. I collected the reports on the thirty-four congregations from various sources.

9. Pope, *Halfway Covenant*, pp. 105–29.

10. Bruce, *Institutional History*, 1:28–37.

11. Gaustad, *Historical Atlas*, p. 23; Charles O. Paullin, *Atlas of the Historical Geography of the United States* (Baltimore: Carnegie Institution and American Geographical Society, 1932), pp. 245–86; F. L. Weis, *The Colonial Churches and the Colonial Clergy of the Middle and Southern Colonies, 1607–1776* (Lancaster, Mass.: n.p., 1939), pp. 17–18; Patricia U. Bonomi and Peter R. Eisenstadt, "Church Adherence in the Eighteenth-Century British American Colonies," *William and Mary Quarterly*, 3d ser., 39 (1982): 245–86. Pointer reached similar conclusions about New York: in 1700, he argues, 78 percent of the colonists there were church adherents; in 1775, the figure was 59 percent. Pointer, *Protestant Pluralism*, p. 31.

12. Bonomi and Eisenstadt, "Church Adherence," pp. 245–86; Rodney Stark and Roger Finke, "American Religion in 1776: A Statistical Portrait," *Sociological Analysis* 49 (1988): 42; Charles Woodmason, *The Carolina Backcountry on the Eve of the Revolution*, ed. Richard Hooker (Chapel Hill: University of North Carolina Press, 1953), pp. 21, 30, 48.

13. Roger Finke and Rodney Stark, "Turning Pews into People: Estimating 19th-Century Church Membership," *Journal for the Scientific Study of Religion* 25 (1986): 180–92.

14. Andrew Reed, *A Narrative of the Visit to the American Churches*, 2 vols. (New York: Harper, 1835), 1:49, 99–176, 253; 2:105–6, 283. Such numbers might seem exaggerated, but his count of full members corresponds to later scholarly estimates by Stark and Finke.

15. This assumes 5.5 members in a family. See Peter Laslett and Richard Wall, eds., *Household and Family in Past Time* (Cambridge: Cambridge University Press, 1972).

16. Alexis de Tocqueville, *Democracy in America*, 2 vols. (New York: Schocken, 1961), 1:365; Philip Schaff, *America* (Cambridge: Harvard University Press,

1961), p. 78; Isabella Lucy Bird Bishop, *The Aspects of Religion in the United States of America* (London: Sampson, Low, 1859), pp. 141, 169.

17. Finke and Stark, "Turning Pews into People," p. 187; George E. Smith, *The Life and Times of George Foster Pierce* (Sparta, Ga.: Hancock, 1881), p. 493; Washington Gladden, ed., *Parish Problems* (New York: Century, 1887), p. 346.

18. Dean R. Hoge and David A. Roozen, eds., *Understanding Church Growth and Decline, 1950–1978* (New York: Pilgrim, 1979).

19. Abraham J. Karp, "Overview: The Synagogue in America," in *The American Synagogue*, ed. Jack Wertheimer (Cambridge: Cambridge University Press, 1987), pp. 1–3.

20. See, e.g., Harry S. Stout, *The New England Soul* (New York: Oxford University Press, 1986), p. 4; Karp, "Overview: The Synagogue in America," in Wertheimer, *American Synagogue*, p. 4.

21. Randall Balmer, "The Social Roots of Dutch Pietism in the Middle Colonies," *Church History* 53 (1984): 187–99; Ola Winslow, *Meetinghouse Hill, 1630–1783* (New York: Macmillan, 1952), pp. 150–70; Laura L. Becker, "Ministers vs. Laymen: The Singing Controversy," *New England Quarterly* 55 (1982): 79–95; Stout, *New England Soul*, p. 159; Rhys Isaac, *The Transformation of Virginia, 1740–1790* (Chapel Hill: University of North Carolina Press, 1982), p. 63.

22. Balmer, *Perfect Babel*, p. 21; Pope, *Halfway Covenant*, p. 82; David Hall, *The Faithful Shepherd* (Chapel Hill: University of North Carolina Press, 1972), p. 125.

23. Hall, *Faithful Shepherd*, p. 148; Balmer, *Perfect Babel*, p. 12; Bruce, *Institutional History*, 1:91.

24. I calculated the percentages by analyzing Gaustad's counts of colonial congregations in the light of the establishment legislation in each colony, as summarized by Leonard Levy, *The Establishment Clause* (New York: Macmillan, 1986), pp. 1–62. The figure of 1,711 congregations in 1750 is based on Gaustad's count of 1,462 supplemented by Quaker meetings and Abraham Karp's count of six synagogues in Wertheimer, *American Synagogue*, pp. 2–5. The figure of 3,234 for 1776 comes from Paullin (*Atlas of the Historical Geography*, pp. 245–86) and includes the Quaker meetings, though I added six Jewish congregations to Paullin's total. The figure of 20 to 23 percent is derived from counting the Congregationalist churches in New England, subtracting the Boston congregations (which never accepted state financial support), estimating that Baptists had sufficient majorities in about twenty towns to qualify for tax support under the 1780 Massachusetts constitution, and dividing the result, 754, by 3,234. Outside of New England, only the Georgia state constitution allowed such financial support, and its ecclesiastical tax provisions might not have been implemented.

25. Bonomi and Eisenstadt, "Church Adherence," p. 247; Hall, *Faithful Shepherd*, pp. 93–120, 156–96.

26. Butler, *Awash in a Sea of Faith*, pp. 116–28.

27. Bruce, *Institutional History*, 1:85–87; Stephanie Grauman Wolf, *Urban Village* (Princeton: Princeton University Press, 1976), pp. 235–36; Rutman,

CHAPTER ONE

Winthrop's Boston, p. 217; Emil Oberholzer, *Delinquent Saints* (New York: Columbia University Press, 1956), pp. 238, 260, 261.

28. Robert J. Dinkin, "Seating the Meetinghouse in Early Massachusetts," *New England Quarterly* 43 (1970): 450–64; Darrett Rutman and Anita Rutman, *A Place in Time* (New York: Norton, 1984), p. 129.

29. Gerald F. Moran, "Sisters in Christ," in *Women in American Religion,* ed. Janet Wilson James (Philadelphia: University of Pennsylvania Press, 1980), p. 53; Mary Maples Dunn, "Saints and Sisters: Congregational and Quaker Women in the Early Colonial Period," *American Quarterly* 30 (1978): 582–601; Dinkin, "Seating the Meetinghouse," p. 465; Winslow, *Meetinghouse Hill,* pp. 146–47.

30. Dinkin, "Seating the Meetinghouse," pp. 450–64; Morgan Godwin, *The Negro's and Indian's Advocate* (London, 1680), pp. 19, 20, 36, 44, 124; Lorenzo Johnston Greene, *The Negro in Colonial New England* (New York: Atheneum, 1969), pp. 282–83; Butler, *Awash in a Sea of Faith,* pp. 129–63.

31. Woodmason, *Carolina Backcountry,* p. 240; Isaac, *Transformation of Virginia,* p. 173; Bishop, *Aspects of Religion,* p. 39; T. Scott Miyakawa, *Protestants and Pioneers* (Chicago: University of Chicago Press, 1964), p. 128.

32. Gaustad, *Historical Atlas,* p. 43; Bureau of the Census, *The Statistics of the Population of the United States, 1870* (Washington, D.C.: Government Printing Office, 1872), p. 506; Donald Mathews, "The Second Great Awakening as an Organizing Process, 1780–1830," *American Quarterly* 21 (1969): 23–43; *Bureau of the Census Special Reports: Religious Bodies: 1906,* 2 vols. (Washington, D.C.: Government Printing Office, 1910), 1:99; J. D. B. DeBow, *Statistical View of the United States (1850)* (Washington: Beverly Tucker, 1854), p. 136.

33. Richard D. Brown, "The Emergence of Voluntary Societies in Massachusetts, 1760–1830," *Journal of Voluntary Action Research* 2 (1973): 64–73.

34. Donald M. Scott, *From Office to Profession* (Philadelphia: University of Pennsylvania Press, 1978), pp. 5–70.

35. Stephen J. Shaw, "The Cities and the Plains," in *The American Catholic Parish,* ed. Jay Dolan, 2 vols. (New York: Paulist Press, 1987), 2:304; Jay Dolan, *The Immigrant Church* (Baltimore: Johns Hopkins University Press, 1975), p. 63; Heman Humphrey, *Thirty-Four Letters to a Son in the Ministry* (Amherst, Mass., 1842), p. 17; Enoch Pond, *The Young Pastor's Guide* (Bangor, Maine, 1844), p. 125; Jack Wertheimer, "The Conservative Synagogue," in Wertheimer, *American Synagogue,* pp. 111–49.

36. Anne Boylan, *Sunday School* (New Haven: Yale University Press, 1988), pp. 6–59; Jack Seymour, *From Sunday School to Church School* (Washington, D.C.: University Press of America, 1982), pp. 29–33.

37. Karp, "Overview: The Synagogue in America," in Wertheimer, *American Synagogue,* pp. 9–10; Leon A. Jick, *The Americanization of the Synagogue* (Hanover: Brandeis University Press, 1976), p. 173; Dolan, *Immigrant Church,* p. 80; Nathan Hatch, *The Democratization of American Christianity* (New Haven: Yale University Press, 1989), pp. 57–138.

38. Bishop, *Aspects of Religion,* pp. 109–13.

39. Balmer, *Perfect Babel,* pp. 102, 114; Rhys Isaac, "Evangelical Revolt," *William and Mary Quarterly,* 3d ser., 31 (1974): 363; Gregory Singleton, "Protestant Voluntary Organization and the Shaping of Victorian America," *American Quarterly* 27 (1975): 551.

40. Anne Rose, "Social Sources of Denominationalism Reconsidered," *American Quarterly* 38 (1986): 254; Reed, *Narrative of the Visit,* 2:351; Dolan, *Immigrant Church,* p. 49.

41. Wayne Flynt, "'A Special Feeling of Closeness': Mt. Hebron Church, Leeds, Alabama," in James P. Wind and James W. Lewis, eds., *American Congregations,* vol. 1: *Portraits of Twelve Religious Communities* (Chicago: University of Chicago Press, 1994), p. 115; Harry Stout and Catherine A. Brekus, "A New England Congregation: Center Church, New Haven, 1638–1989," in ibid., p. 40; Oberholzer, *Delinquent Saints,* p. 262.

42. Richard D. Shiels, "The Feminization of American Congregationalism, 1730–1835," *American Quarterly* 33 (1981): 61–62; Mary P. Ryan, "A Women's Awakening," *American Quarterly* 30 (1978): 602–23; Boylan, *Sunday School,* p. 105; Samuel Miller, *Letters on Clerical Manners and Habits* (New York: G. & C. Carvill, 1827), p. 339.

43. Hatch, *Democratization,* p. 157; Mechal Sobel, *Trabelin' On: The Slave Journey to an Afro-Baptist Faith* (Princeton: Princeton University Press, 1979), p. 222; Donald Mathews, *Religion in the Old South* (Chicago: University of Chicago Press, 1977), p. 203; Benjamin Quarles, *Black Abolitionists* (New York: Oxford University Press, 1969), p. 83; Larry Mamiya, "A Social History of the Bethel African Methodist Episcopal Church in Baltimore: The House of God and the Struggle for Freedom," in Wind and Lewis, *Portraits,* pp. 221–92; Albert Raboteau, *Slave Religion* (New York: Oxford University Press, 1978), p. 191.

44. Gaustad, *Historical Atlas,* pp. 78, 168; Dolan, *Immigrant Church,* pp. 81, 105; Joseph J. Casino, "From Sanctuary to Involvement," in Dolan, *American Catholic Parish,* 1:28; Roger Finke and Rodney Stark, *The Churching of America, 1776–1990* (New Brunswick: Rutgers University Press, 1992), pp. 112–13.

45. G. B. Willcox, *The Pastor Amidst His Flock* (New York: American Tract Society, 1890), p. 110; Henry K. Carroll, ed., *Report on Statistics of Churches in the United States at the Eleventh Census, 1890* (Washington, D.C.: Government Printing Office, 1894), p. xxx.

46. Bureau of the Census, *Religious Bodies: 1926,* 2 vols. (Washington, D.C.: Government Printing Office, 1930), 1:13–15, 69; H. N. Morse and Edmund deS. Brunner, *The Town and Country Church in the United States* (New York: George H. Doran, 1923), p. 41; Warren Hugh Wilson, *The Farmer's Church* (London: Century, 1925), p. 40.

47. Edmund deS. Brunner, *Church Life in the Rural South* (New York: Doran, 1923), pp. 33, 60, 72–73, 88; Charles Otis Gill and Gifford Pinchot, *Six Thousand Country Churches* (New York: Macmillan, 1919), p. 8.

48. H. Paul Douglas, *The St. Louis Church Survey* (New York: Doran, 1924), p. 101; Robert S. Lynd and Helen M. Lynd, *Middletown* (New York: Harcourt

Brace, 1929), p. 400; Bureau of the Census, *Special Reports, Religious Bodies, 1906,* 2 vols. (Washington, D.C.: Government Printing Office, 1910), 1:21, 69.

49. Willcox, *Pastor Amidst His Flock,* p. 101; Henry Ward Beecher, *Yale Lectures in Preaching* (New York: Fords, Howard, and Hulbert, 1892), pp. 155, 159; Jeffrey M. Burns, "Building the Best," in Dolan, *American Catholic Parish,* 2:41; Jay Dolan, "The Struggle to Serve," in *Transforming Parish Ministry,* ed. Jay Dolan, R. Scott Appleby, Patricia Byrne, and Debra Campbell (New York: Crossroad, 1990), p. 210; Ihna T. T. Frary, ed., *Village Green to City Center* (Cleveland: Euclid Avenue Church, 1943), p. 141; Casino, "From Sanctuary to Involvement," in Dolan, *American Catholic Parish,* 1:28.

50. E. Brooks Holifield, *A History of Pastoral Care in America* (Nashville: Abingdon, 1983), pp. 170–71; Gladden, ed., *Parish Problems,* p. 283; Dolan, "Struggle to Serve," in Dolan, *Transforming Parish Ministry,* p. 210.

51. Casino, "From Sanctuary to Involvement," *American Catholic Parish,* 1:29, 48; Dolan, "Struggle to Serve," *Transforming Parish Ministry,* p. 287.

52. Karp, "Overview: The Synagogue in America," in Wertheimer, *American Synagogue,* pp. 20–22; Wertheimer, "Conservative Synagogue," in ibid., p. 121; Paula E. Hyman, "From City to Suburb," in ibid., p. 187; Deborah Dash Moore, "A Synagogue Center Grows in Brooklyn," in ibid., pp. 297–326.

53. Willcox, *Pastor Amidst His Flock,* p. 175; Jonathan Sarna, "The Debate Over Mixed Seating in the American Synagogue," in Wertheimer, *American Synagogue,* p. 386; Gladden, ed., *Parish Problems,* pp. 102–4.

54. Altina L. Waller, *Reverend Beecher and Mrs. Tilton* (Amherst: University of Massachusetts Press, 1982), p. 101; Gladden, ed., *Parish Problems,* p. 104; Willcox, *Pastor Amidst His Flock,* p. 137; Burns, "Building the Best," in Dolan, *American Catholic Parish,* 2:28; Michael J. McNally, "A Peculiar Institution," in ibid., 1:161; C. Luther Fry, *Diagnosing the Rural Church* (New York: Doran, 1924), p. 72; H. Paul Douglass, *The Springfield Church Survey* (New York: Doran, 1926), pp. 113, 118; Morse and Brunner, *Town and Country Church,* p. 143.

55. Gladden, ed., *Parish Problems,* pp. 408, 412; Willcox, *Pastor Amidst His Flock,* p. 47. See James P. Wind, *Places of Worship* (Nashville: American Association for State and Local History, 1990).

56. Casino, "From Sanctuary to Involvement," in Dolan, *American Catholic Parish,* 1:51, 74; Burns, "Building the Best," in ibid., 2:38.

57. Wertheimer, "Conservative Synagogue," in Wertheimer, *American Synagogue,* p. 120; Leon A. Jick, "The Reform Synagogue," in ibid., p. 101; Karp, "Overview: Synagogue in America," in ibid., p. 21.

58. Ferenc M. Scasz, *The Divided Mind of Protestant America, 1880–1930* (University, Alabama: University of Alabama Press, 1982), pp. 48–55; Ralph E. Luker, "Missions, Institutional Churches, and Settlement Houses: The Black Experience, 1885–1910," *Journal of Negro History* 69 (1984): 108.

59. Constant H. Jacquet, Jr., and Alice M. Jones, eds., *Yearbook of American and Canadian Churches, 1991* (Nashville: Abingdon Press, 1991), p. 265; C. W. Zunkel, *Growing the Small Church* (Elgin: Cook, 1988), p. 1; John Vaughan, *The World's 20 Largest Churches* (Grand Rapids: Baker, 1984), pp. 283–84; Lyle

Schaller, *The Small Church Is Different* (Nashville: Abingdon, 1982), pp. 9, 11; C. R. McBride, *Protestant Churchmanship for Rural America* (Chicago: Judson, 1962), p. 39; James L. Carr, *Bright Future* (Richmond: John Knox, 1956), p. 17; Wade C. Roof and William McKinney, *American Mainline Religion* (New Brunswick: Rutgers University Press, 1987), p. 97; Jay Dolan and David Leege, *A Profile of American Catholic Parishes and Parishioners* (Notre Dame: Notre Dame Study of Catholic Parish Life, 1985), p. 6; Carl Dudley, *Making the Small Church Effective* (Nashville: Abingdon, 1978), pp. 66–67.

60. Gibson Winter, *The Suburban Captivity of the Churches* (New York: Doubleday, 1961), p. 92; Claire Cox, *The New-Time Religion* (Englewood Cliffs: Prentice-Hall, 1961), p. 174; Urban T. Holmes III, *The Future Shape of Ministry* (New York: Seabury, 1971), p. 153; James D. Glasse, *Profession: Minister* (Nashville: Abingdon, 1968), p. 13.

61. Nancy Ammerman, *Bible Believers* (New Brunswick: Rutgers University Press, 1987), pp. 35–37, 106 ("Southside Gospel Church" is Ammerman's fictional name for the congregation she studied); Vaughan, *World's 20 Largest Churches*, p. 130; Cox, *New-Time Religion*, p. 169.

62. Barry Chazan, "Education in the Synagogue," in Wertheimer, *American Synagogue*, p. 171; Wertheimer, "Conservative Synagogue," in ibid., p. 125.

63. Karp, "Overview: The Synagogue in America," in Wertheimer, *American Synagogue*, p. 129; Dolan, "Struggle to Serve," in Dolan, *Transforming Parish Ministry*, p. 304; Dolan and Leege, *Profile*, p. 5.

64. Melvin Williams, *Community in a Black Pentecostal Church* (Pittsburgh: University of Pittsburgh Press, 1974), pp. 82–109.

65. Dean Hoge and David Roozen, "Research on Factors Influencing Church Commitment," *Understanding Church Growth*, p. 64; Earl Brewer, *Protestant Parish* (Atlanta: Communicative Acts, 1967), p. 69.

66. Casino, "From Sanctuary to Involvement," in Dolan, *American Catholic Parish*, 1:95; Dolan, "Struggle to Serve," in Dolan, *Transforming Parish Ministry*, p. 275; Patricia Byrne, "In the Parish But Not of It: Sisters," in ibid., p. 190.

67. E. Brooks Holifield, "The Architect and the Congregation," *Faith and Form* 19 (1986): 37–41.

68. Victor Obenhaus, *The Church and Faith in Mid-America* (Philadelphia: Westminster, 1963), p. 74; Brewer, *Protestant Parish*, p. 66.

TWO

The Place of the Congregation in the
Contemporary American Religious Configuration

R. STEPHEN WARNER

AFTER A PERIOD OF NEGLECT by scholars and denominational leaders, the *congregation*—a term this chapter uses to speak of local religious assemblies in general—has returned to the spotlight. Despite neglect, the congregation remains the bedrock of the American religious system. It is in congregations that religious commitment is nurtured and through them that most voluntary religious activity is channeled. Indeed, with due respect for pluralism and caution about overgeneralization, I would maintain that the significance of congregations is *increasing*. In the United States today, we are seeing convergence across religious traditions toward de facto congregationalism, more or less on the model of the reformed Protestant tradition of the congregation as a voluntary gathered community.

This convergence toward de facto congregationalism is happening despite, indeed partly because of, the increasing divergence of religious cultures in the United States; it constitutes both assimilation to a deep-seated interdenominational American religious model and selective adaptation of normative elements contained in the various religious traditions that make up our pluralist mosaic. Purists within few, if any, of these traditions can wholly embrace the congregational model; yet neither is it totally foreign to any of these traditions. The model is at variance with the official ideals of some of the most Americanized of U.S. religious traditions—for example, the Presbyterian Church (U.S.A.) and the U.S. Roman Catholic church—but aspects of it suit the needs of some more recent, and more exotic, arrivals to this country—for example, Pakistani Muslims and Thai Buddhists. Although culturally specific, the growing convergence toward the American congregational model is not therefore a simple case of cultural imperialism or morphological fundamentalism, and those religious educators with an ecumenical calling need not shun it in the name of multiculturalism.

No mere book chapter could fully substantiate such a far-ranging thesis, and the evidence submitted in this chapter varies in quality and quantity, in depth and breadth. The chapter's best established but least extensive evidentiary base is *New Wine in Old Wineskins*, my ethnographic social history of Mendocino Presbyterian Church in the 1960s and 1970s, a California church whose pastors traversed the same trajectory from social justice to evangelicalism that much of American Protestantism followed in those turbulent years.[1] More extensive but less intensive are observations based on field trips to metropolitan Chicago places of worship that I have taken with my students since 1978 as exercises in the sociology of religion.[2] Building on these field trips, I have carried out more intensive research on Christian congregations within two radically different communities, Korean Americans and gays and lesbians, materials from which appear below.[3] Scholarly interest in congregational studies has been rapidly growing, and I therefore also draw upon recent literature on contemporary developments in the form of monographs, articles, conference papers, dissertations, theses, and the first volume of *American Congregations*.[4] Some developments, however, most notably the burgeoning of Latino Protestant congregations, are still seriously underresearched, and I have had to make use of stories in local newspapers and popular journals to document them. Throughout, my emphasis is on contemporary congregations.

Ecclesiastical Arithmetic

By various estimates, there are over three hundred thousand local religious assemblies in the United States today, about one for every four hundred Americans claimed as members of religious bodies. Research done in 1988 for Independent Sector, a Washington, D.C., clearinghouse for nonprofit organizations, counted 294,271 congregations (churches, synagogues, temples, and mosques) in the United States outside of Hawaii and Alaska.[5] The National Council of Churches (NCC) 1991 *Yearbook* reports, on the basis of "current" (1989 and 1990) and "noncurrent" statistics provided by denominations, that there are 350,337 congregations of Christians, Jews, Buddhists, and "miscellaneous" groups (mostly Unitarians) in the U.S.[6] Based as they are on Yellow Pages listings for the contiguous forty-eight states, the Independent Sector figure is clearly too low. The NCC count, however, includes some data over thirty years old and does not correct for some congregations' multiple denominational affiliations; it is probably too high.

The majority of these congregations go by familiar Judeo-Christian labels of European origin. As frequenters of country byways will suspect, the United Methodist Church and the Southern Baptist Convention are the largest groupings, each claiming over thirty-six thousand congregations. The Evangelical Lutheran Church in America, the Presbyterian Church (U.S.A.), and the Assemblies of God each claim over eleven thousand. Seven historically African-American Christian denominations (the African Methodist Episcopal Church, the A.M.E. Zion Church, the Christian Methodist Episcopal Church, the Church of God in Christ, the National Baptist Convention of America, the National Baptist Convention, U.S.A., Inc., and the Progressive National Baptist Convention, Inc.) together claim over sixty-six thousand congregations. In 1991, after some deep cutbacks, there remained 19,971 Roman Catholic parishes in the U.S., and, in 1990, 3,416 Jewish synagogues were reported. All of these figures are reported in the *Yearbook* of the National Council of Churches, whose communications office takes pains regularly to assemble denominational statistics.[7]

The profile of American congregations has changed in two remarkable ways since the watershed year of 1965 identified by Martin Marty in his chapter below, the year Watts exploded and the Vietnam War escalated, when the reforms of the Voting Rights Act of 1965 and the Immigration Act of 1965 were made law, the year when Vatican II concluded and decades of sustained growth in mainline Protestant church membership reversed. The first change in American congregations is apparent to the byways traveler (and is duly recorded in the *Yearbook*): the mushrooming of conservative Protestant congregations and the disappearance of mainline ones. According to recent figures reported by the NCC, nearly thirteen thousand fewer congregations of six mainline Protestant denominations (American Baptist, Episcopal, Lutheran, Methodist, Presbyterian, and United Church of Christ) existed in 1987 than had existed in 1965. Their numbers were replaced by more than thirteen thousand additional congregations of six conservative denominations (Assemblies of God, Church of God [Cleveland, Tennessee], Jehovah's Witnesses, Latter-day Saints, Nazarenes, and Seventh-day Adventist).[8] This shift is obvious in small towns all across America, whose outskirts are strewn with brand-new wood-frame houses of worship and adjoining parking lots for the local Assemblies, Kingdom Halls, and Mormon wards, and whose stately brick downtown Presbyterian and Congregational churches have been merged or recycled as community museums and professional office buildings.[9]

The *Yearbook* data tell only part of the story of the shift in congregational presence. For example, they do not report the 350 congregations of Calvary Chapel, or the 250 of the Vineyard, or the 210 of the Fellowship of Inner-City Word of Faith Ministries, three new Southern California–based protodenominations of charismatic Christian congregations, whose affiliates are now scattered all over the country.[10] The Independent Sector's study of congregations provides further insight into the conservative congregational shift. Of congregations existing at the time of the study (1987), the more recent the founding, the more likely they were to characterize themselves as conservative. Forty-seven percent of the congregations founded before 1900 called themselves "liberal" or "moderate," whereas 68 percent of those founded since 1970 labeled themselves "conservative" or "very conservative."[11]

The second recent change in the profile of congregations—especially noticeable in metropolitan America—is the flowering of immigrant religious centers. The abolition of country-of-origin quotas in the immigration law of 1965 has made it possible for very different, and often non-European, religious communities to get a toehold in the U.S., and many of these groups are sufficiently new and scattered to have escaped the purview of the NCC. The *Yearbook*, for example, includes data from only one Buddhist body, the century-old Japanese-origin Buddhist Churches of America (who report 19,441 members in sixty-seven congregations for 1989). From other sources, we hear of sixty-seven Korean Buddhist centers less than twenty years old, sixty Japanese Buddhist temples, over one hundred Southeast Asian Theravada "wats," and in all over five hundred Buddhist meditation centers. At last report, there were forty-some ecumenical Hindu temples and thirty-seven centers of the mostly Gujarati Swaminarayan sect. Estimates of Muslim centers, some of them designated mosques, range from three hundred to two thousand.[12]

In addition, about two thousand of the Protestant congregations listed by the NCC *Yearbook* are Korean ethnic congregations among the Southern Baptist, United Methodist, Presbyterian (U.S.A.), Assemblies of God, and other denominations. A new Korean Presbyterian denomination, the Korean Presbyterian Church in America, has more than two hundred local congregations nationwide. Another fast-growing category of Protestant congregations is that of the various Hispanic peoples in the U.S., now about 9 percent of the U.S. population (or 22.5 million), according to the surely undercounted 1990 census. The Gallup organization estimates that 20 percent of U.S. Hispanics claim a Protestant affiliation, and Hispanic Protestant congregations abound in cities such as New York, Chicago, and Los Angeles. Yet I know of no national enumeration or even an estimate of their numbers in the U.S. or their denominational affiliations.[13] The Church of God in Christ, the black Pentecostal denomination, claims 15,300 congregations, more than the Evangelical Lutheran, Episcopal, or Presbyterian (U.S.A.) churches. In short, the mix of American congregations, definitely including those of Protestants, is becoming at once more conservative and more multicultural.

When we speak of increasing pluralism in American religion, we usually have in mind the proliferation of denominations and religious movements. Nearly sixteen hundred different denominations are reported to exist in the U.S. and Canada, from tiny schismatic groups to the huge Roman Catholic church, and eight hundred nationally organized religious special-purpose groups, from the Fellowship of Christian Athletes to the Ecumenical and Evangelical Women's Caucus.[14] But when we speak of the grass-roots religious participation that visitors to the U.S. have always remarked on, we speak of people all over the country regularly gathering to worship together, at appointed times and places, in congregations by the hundreds of thousands.

Such ecclesiastical arithmetic tells us that the fortunes of congregations must be more uneven than those of the denominations with which most of them are affiliated. We know that denominations come and go—arising by schism and disappearing by merger[15]—and wax and wane,[16] but of necessity these vicissitudes will be visited upon the population of congregations with much greater frequency. The smooth growth-and-decline curves we can draw from the membership statistics of Protestant denominations obscure the ragged plots of the ups and downs of their constituent congregations.[17] When a major denomination reports the loss of a substantial proportion of its members, thousands of its constituent congregations may have ceased entirely to exist. Denominational decline means contraction at the national level—lower budgets and loss of jobs—but decimation—widespread congregational demise—at the local.

Moreover, denominational and congregational fortunes need not mesh. One conclusion of the Notre Dame Study of Catholic Parish Life conducted in the 1980s was that "relative to the life of the rest of the church, parishes seem to have a life of their own."[18] When a denomination is growing, planting new congregations and recruiting new members, some individual congregations will nevertheless be dying. When a denomination is declining, some congregations will be burgeoning. Sociologist Samuel Kincheloe's classic analysis of "the behavior sequence of a dying church" concerns an inner-city Chicago parish suffering from neighborhood change in the 1920s, when its parent denomination was thriving. My own history of Mendocino Presbyterian Church chronicles the similarly countercyclical phenomenon of rapid congregational growth at a time of sustained denominational decline.[19] As a matter of sheer statistics, then, the congregation is not the denomination writ small.

The Congregation in the Context of Other Religious Bodies

While both may be called "the Presbyterian church" and while they are organizationally linked, a world of difference lies between Mendocino Presbyterian Church and the Presbyterian Church (U.S.A.). That the first is a local assembly of persons and the second a national network of assemblies is the beginning of the matter, but that they go by the same name is equally important. Congregation and denomination are and do different things, but they are historically intertwined. The denomination owns rights to the logo that points the traveler to the local congregation a couple of blocks to the right or left off the state highway through town. Some other local congregation was the school that bred into the traveler the desire to seek out like-minded worshipers while on the road. Ideally and minimally, the denomination is an organization for the furtherance of religious commitments, whereas the congregation is a community for the nurturance of those commitments.

To the extent that the *denomination* exists—a reality that various primitivist Protestant groups have long fought and that some new immigrant groups are just starting to cope with—it serves several functions. It plants congregations (and accepts other self-started groups into its fold, which is how organized Presbyterianism first came to Mendocino in 1859). It trains, certifies, disciplines, nurtures, and pensions members of the clergy (more broadly, religious professionals). It provides leadership for congregations between pastors and financial support during lean times. It defines doctrine and carries out nonlocal mission.

The *congregation* is where members are recruited, baptized, catechized, confirmed, absolved, administered the sacraments, registered, received by letter, counted, asked weekly for their substance, mobilized for service, disciplined, and buried. As the local branch of the people of

God, it is the organizer of worship, religious instruction, community service, stewardship, and fellowship.

In comparison to religiously oriented or quasi-religious small groups like Alcoholics Anonymous chapters and home prayer meetings (which likely involve at least a fifth of the adult American population),[20] congregations and the denominations to which the majority of them belong have in common that they are relatively stable and institutionalized. Congregations and denominations alike may be chartered, commissioned, consecrated, dedicated, franchised, or incorporated, and they typically have addresses, offices, and phone numbers. But unlike religious special-purpose groups like Americans United for Separation of Church and State or Moral Majority, which also have offices and telephones, congregations and denominations typically provide for extensive participation. They are not segmental associations whose "memberships" are little more than lists of names in a computer. In contrast to religiously inspired social movements like the Women's Christian Temperance Union, the American Anti-Slavery Society, Operation Rescue, and Sanctuary, which also involve members deeply, congregations and denominations do not define themselves in terms of a single issue of public policy; they have multiple purposes.

Congregations and denominations differ in the chances that their members will encounter one another face to face. A substantial fraction, sometimes a majority, of the members of a congregation will see each other every week, whereas a tiny proportion of the members of a denomination (as many as three-tenths of a percent for the highly mobilized Southern Baptists) are in each other's presence at conventions held once a year or less, with members of regional judicatories falling somewhere between. Yet this does not mean that denominations therefore lack the personal element that gives congregations their rich, many-layered, and emotion-laden texture. To the contrary: the work of denominations is carried out by people who see each other often and are often intimately known to one another. Denominational organs—agencies, lobbies, seminaries, publishing houses—bring people together in ways that, if anything, accentuate the effect of congregating. Task-force meetings, seminars, and workshops, cafeteria conversations, summer institutes, and travel to conferences are some of the ways that bonds of solidarity and common outlooks are inculcated at the denominational level.[21]

Sociologically, the most important contrast between denominations and congregations (as well as between, on the one hand, religious special-purpose groups and seminaries and, on the other, religious small groups and social movements) is that the former are staffed by religious professionals—those who earn their living in the field of religion—and the latter are constituted by religious amateurs who spend their time, and some of their money, in the name of religion. The Bakkers and the Rajneeshes aside, religion is not a sure way to get rich, and religious professionals must be in it for more than the money, as a true vocation. Parishioners, for their part, have typically mixed motives, some of which can be quite venal. The professional-amateur distinction is not a contrast in religious purity, but it is fundamental.

Congregations are by definition local assemblies, whereas denominations are regional, national, or international organizations, and each of the two levels is suited for different activities. Sociologist Phillip Hammond has proposed a general rule for appropriate allocation of ministry activities to ecclesiastical levels. He classified activities from an "expressive" pole to an "instrumental" one and ecclesiastical levels from that of the congregation to that of the national board. Hammond placed worship at the expressive end and legislative lobbying at the instrumental, with home visitation, help with welfare agencies, and building retirement homes arrayed between. Hammond's rule was this:

> The more instrumental the orientations required by the activity, the more effectively can it be carried out by a regional, national, or specialized ministry; but the more expressive the orientations required, the more effectively can the activity be carried out by a local parish ministry.[22]

We can expect, therefore, that congregations are typically groups of amateurs spending disproportionate time on activities that are hard to define, whereas denominations will have professionals devoted to articulated goals.

Accordingly, when we look at the congregation from the point of view of the denomination, and vice versa, we can appreciate the misgivings each body seems to have about the other, even as they depend on each other. The congregation, from whose tithes and offerings the denomination derives the bulk of its income, too often appears from above to be a social club whose members neglect the calling of their faith in favor of the pleasure of one another's company. The denomination, from which the congregation typically derives its leadership, its hymnody, and its confessional identity, too often appears from below to be a bureaucracy serving officials' career interests and heterodox agendas. At worst, congregations and denominations regard each other as means and themselves as ends.

Scholars of religion have tended to share these one-way points of view, as participants in this project have documented. The chapters by Langdon Gilkey and Martin Marty in this volume shed light on the historiography of recent American Protestant thought and its appreciation of the congregation. It seems that the dominant voices in American Protestantism at midcentury, influenced by both prewar social gospel and postwar existentialism, took for granted the local religious nurture on which their praxis depended and relegated congregational life to the discredited private sphere. Mainline Protestant congregations were cajoled by theologians and judicatories to look outward for missions to carry out, and they were held up for praise when and if they tried to make a difference in the lives of precisely those who were not their own members.[23] Concentration on the life of the congregation itself was attributed to "the sin of 'morphological fundamentalism.'"[24]

Even Donald Metz, in one of the few sociological books of the 1960s concerned with congregational life, shared this systematic externalist bias. Writing about six newly founded congregations in suburban California communities, he cautioned: "Aside from such *privatized* family troubles as juvenile lawlessness or marital difficulties, there is not much that could be termed social problems in the community. The congregation in this situation may have to look hard for an *outlet* for such intentions of service as it might have. . . . [T]here is a distinct *danger* that the new congregation will be satisfied to *internalize* its activities" (emphasis added).[25] In such an intellectual climate, it is no surprise that many clergy of serious purpose felt they could be prophetic in direct proportion to their distance from the local congregation.[26]

Recently, the pendulum has swung away from the denomination's point of view. The statistical decline of the mainline denominations that set in after 1965 caused introspection at headquarters. Feminists questioned the good faith of formal organizations in general and clerical hierarchies in particular. Journalists turned their attention to such cross-denominational newsmakers as the electronic church. Laity got involved with such paradenominational movements as evangelicalism, charismatic renewal, *Cursillo de Cristiandad* (a spiritual renewal movement of lay Roman Catholics) and Walk to Emmaus (its Protestant analogue),

Marriage Encounter, liturgical renewal, *havurot* (home-based Jewish prayer and study groups), and Sanctuary.

For the time being, many observers agree that the congregation is worthy of attention and respect. In the Mendocino Presbyterian Church, the social activist pastor Peter Hsu had told his elders in 1963, "basically, our church exists for mission," leaving no doubt that mission meant international peace and racial justice. A decade later, Larry Redford, the evangelical chairperson of the church's pastor-search committee, insisted that "the mission of the church is the church," meaning the Mendocino congregation; and the vitality and faithfulness of the congregation under the pastor the committee chose made his redefinition of mission itself seem prophetic.[27]

The Congregation as a Voluntary Community

The typical American congregation is a voluntary religious community. To say that the congregation is a *religious* community is to say that it is ordinarily a face-to-face assembly of persons who together engage in many activities, all of them somehow understood as having "religious" meaning, few of them lacking emotional significance. To say that the congregation is a *voluntary* community is to say that mobilization of members must rely on idealism or personal persuasion rather than coercion or material incentives, but *voluntary* also signifies, particularly in the U.S., that the congregation cannot assume the loyal adherence of its members as if they were all part of the same tribe; it must actively recruit them.

Using the terms of Talcott Parsons's sociological theory, the American congregation is a collectivity-oriented, functionally diffuse, affective, and particularistic social grouping but essentially an "achieved" rather than an "ascribed" one. *Collectivity orientation* means that members are enjoined to concern themselves with the welfare of the group, not only with their own interests (which is *self-orientation*). When an interpersonal relationship or social institution is *functionally diffuse*, as opposed to *functionally specific*, the burden of proof rests with those who would exclude a potential activity as illegitimate, and the relationship or institution will tend to absorb activities that are feasible given available resources and the default of alternative agencies. *Affective* relations are those that are in themselves emotionally satisfying; the opposite—typically the "businesslike" orientation—is *affective neutrality*. Expectations

63

that parties to a relationship should be bound by their common membership in a particular category (for example, religion, place of residence, ethnicity, family) are *particularistic;* expectations that persons should transcend such categories in their dealings with others are *universalistic.* Statuses into which we are born (sex, race, national origin) are *ascribed;* those we have discretion over (which have come in modern society to include occupation and education) are *achieved.*[28] The communalism and voluntarism of the American religious system chronically frustrate efforts to make congregations over into finely tuned instruments of divine mission, and they persistently require congregations to look inward to the sources of their sustenance. We can see the significance of this when we consider some widely recognized and approved activities of congregations—worship, education, mission, and stewardship—before turning to what may be the master function of congregations in such a pluralistic society as the United States: fellowship.

Worship

To congregate is, as Martin Marty points out, to meet, and this is particularly salient in worship. Indeed, for many believers and traditions, collective expression is normatively essential to religious experience.[29] Protestant hymns generally have parts for four voices. Catholics pass the peace through the hands of those around them. Jews need a minyan of ten for certain prayers and two *gabbaiim* to oversee the reading of the Torah. Muslims join in prayer every Friday and are expected once in a lifetime to come together (now by the millions) in Mecca.

Moreover, worship is sensual. One's faculties and senses are mobilized to attend to the light streaming through stained glass (and a shadow across the soloist's face), the sound of the choir (and of a crying child), the grip of the greeter's hand (and the hardness of the pews), the scent of incense (and of someone's aftershave), and the taste of communion wine. Islam tries to avoid sensuality in worship, but its very ethic of plainness is itself a high aesthetic, bringing its own pleasure in the contemplation of Islamic architecture, Arabic calligraphy, nonrepresentational decoration, and hand-loomed rugs. Moreover, one cannot fail to be moved by the sound of communal prayer, when, in response to the imam's Arabic chant, masses of bodies accomplish sacred calisthenics in perfect unison.

With the richness of the human surroundings and the sensory input, worship always carries as much in the way of diffuse connotation as in doctrinally pure denotation. No matter how high-toned the worship, worship itself is affective and diffuse, and worship is only the beginning of congregational life.

Religious Education

In our highly mobile society, a good deal of attention is paid to religious education, as the structure of denominations and paradenominational agencies attests. Seminaries offer degrees, and congregations hire specialists in Christian education. Sunday school curricula are constantly reworked and competitively advertised. Adult education materials are available in bewildering variety from denominational agencies and mail-order catalogs. Yet effective education requires the translation of standardized materials into the idiom of the student body. In the world of churches, therefore, educators, including preachers and teachers, must learn the local culture, as the evangelical pastor Eric Underwood did in Mendocino in the 1970s.[30] Drawing on the work of James Hopewell, a pioneer in congregational studies, religious educator Barbara Wheeler writes, "The task of the leader . . . is to harvest the local knowledge that the congregation cannot express or judges to be unimportant, to bring it to consciousness and give it shape."[31] The religious educator can be truly effective only by bearing in mind the unique body of stories that members of a congregation tell about their common experience.

Hopewell worked with Anglo-Saxon Protestant congregations in relatively traditional American settings. How much greater is the need for the teacher to be fluent both in religion and in the setting of the congregation (Christian theologians might say "in both Christ and culture") when the congregation is one of immigrants! Effective education is inescapably particularistic.

Mission

From the congregation's point of view, mission can mean little more than collecting and sending financial contributions to denominational agencies, but most likely it involves one or more of a bewildering array of activities undertaken by members of the congregation—visiting, cooking, driving, cleaning, tutoring, building, studying, debating, leafletting, letter-writing, picketing—where sharing the activity is part of its meaning. Because of the diverse human resources of those serving any given mission project (as well as other sources of unpredictability), a committee set up for one purpose easily develops new ones. In some churches, women's rights groups find themselves taking up the issue of homosexuality within a few meetings. A support group for an overseas orphanage becomes as well a study group on the issue of transracial adoption. The Church and Community Project at McCormick Seminary in Chicago documented how congregational mission projects, even under professional guidance that is oriented to articulate social theory, often have results unintended by their initiators.[32] Mission, which we often think of as purposive, goes off in many directions and is thus another source of functional diffuseness in congregations.

Stewardship

Every religious organization in a formally voluntary religious system must have some way of acquiring and allocating material resources. For most congregations, this is done by volunteers who (at worst) get saddled with the job or who (at best) are called to it by reason of their skill and inclination. Professional religious critics suspect that such volunteers carry out their tasks to the detriment of prophetic values, and professional religious managers that they do so by complying with small-town, small-business norms of logrolling and back-scratching. But volunteers' particularistic skills (or local knowledge) are evidently effective, for local congregations garner $40 billion in individual gifts each year and an average of ten hours per month of volunteer time on the part of 10 million of their laity, as estimated by the Independent Sector survey.[33] Without this money and time, not only local congregations but also denominations and seminaries would be out of business.

The inherent functions of the congregation are carried out, in short, in a largely unbureaucratic, noninstrumental manner, which is remarkable when we consider the immense size of our society's religious sector and the increasingly bureaucratic character of most of our organizational lives. It is likely that their communal character, along with their public nature, is part of the attraction that congregations hold for their members. In the congregation, one can feel at home as a member of a large family in a huge living room. Of course, not only sweetness and light pertain in congregations, any more than in families. But congregations and families fight over many things, not just questions of public policy. A study of local church conflicts in even such a politically aware community as the neighborhood of the University of Chicago shows that only a minority of conflicts take place along a liberal-conservative axis; congregational conflict, too, is diffuse and particularistic.[34]

Fellowship

The U.S. is a nation of joiners with a puritanical, individualistic ethos, and its intellectuals talk of sociability most often with a bad conscience, a fact that inhibits the study of religion. Social scientists have mapped the profound link between religion and social integration, but this is a link that is suspect to theologians. Peter Berger, a sociologist as well as a Protestant existentialist theologian, articulated the suspicion a generation ago in *The Noise of Solemn Assemblies*. All religions serve to socialize individuals to the norms of their group, however narrow these may be, and endow them with a good conscience about their limitations, how little justified that conscience may be, and this is particularly true when religion occupies the conspicuous place that it does in the U.S. "Suffice it to say here that a religious establishment such as ours is highly conductive to 'bad faith,'" wrote Berger.[35] In the pluralist society that is the United States, fellowship is both the most typical and the most problematic function of congregations.

Yet fellowship is inherent to congregating. The contemporary meaning of congregation is contained in the word's Latin derivation, an "assembling" (flocking, herding, gathering) together of people. It is appropriate that this volume and the project that produced it use the term *congregation* for the local religious unit, for it is meeting with other men and women that is the heart of the American congregational experience. *Parish*, on the other hand, has Greek roots referring first to the neighbor (the *oikos*, or household nearby) and second, with further spatial reference, to the district under the supervision of an elder. Parish has valuable connotations, particularly in reminding us that a common residence often means a common fate, which the congregational spirit too readily obscures. But it is a different concept.[36]

Thomas Day, satirizing Protestantization in Roman Catholic church music, invidiously contrasts the Catholic parish ideal to the Protestant congregational one. He likens the congregation to a chartered bus returning from a hobbyist's convention, filled with contented, like-minded people, whereas the parish is like a city bus crawling through crowded streets, open to anyone who has the modest fare. The congregation may be made up entirely of people who subscribe to the same selection of highbrow magazines, whereas the parish has to deal with the "whole magazine rack." The congregation is an exclusive "private club," whereas the parish is a "human zoo," made available as a "public utility for everybody."

> Four thousand people who call themselves Protestant and live in the same area will take themselves to a variety of places on Sunday morning: the fundamentalist Baptist church, the Quaker meeting house, the High Church Episcopalian establishment, the Salvation Army, and so on. Four thousand people who call themselves Roman Catholic and live in the same neighborhood will find themselves in the same parish. Seated in the same pew will be the union leader, the union-busting employer, the nun with a degree in theology, and the saintly man who puts a dollar underneath the statue of the Infant of Prague for good luck.[37]

Day's vision of the parish is an appealing one, but he knows that it historically depended for its realization on government support, financial endowment, or noblesse oblige. If the proletarian, the capitalist, the woman theologian, and the superstitious man occupy the same pew today in the United States, it is because they are somehow *drawn* to be there together. They do not *have* to be.

The practices of congregation and parish briefly converged in the experience of the early New England Puritans. Those who had come together across the Atlantic, and even further into the wilderness to places like New Haven, did so to escape religious decadence and to found a new order. They established parishes on these shores that were in the first generation also congregations, because the territory they encompassed was coextensive with the white population that had migrated together. Thus *congregation* and *parish* are conflated in the usage of the American Congregational tradition, and many a New England town still has its "First Church" on the green with "United Church of Christ" in small print within parentheses underneath.

But the New England "parishes" ceased to carry binding obligations early in our national history, and the use of the term by Protestants has been an archaism ever since, as both the Baptist and Roman Catholic traditions recognize. For Catholics a congregation is a collegium, as it is for Protestants, but a worldwide one with its meeting place in the Vatican. For strict Baptists (and they abound), congregational autonomy requires that territorial bodies can be only "conventions" and those who deliberate in them only "messengers." In this view, the denomination is emphatically a social network, not an authority. For better or worse, the American Protestant congregation (and increasingly the Catholic parish, as I argue below) is an assembly of people who choose to be together.

Sociological theorist Allan Silver traces the prominence of fellowship in American public life to congregationalism, which constituted, he claims, "the core religious culture in America during its formative period . . . , the most influential religious 'deep structure'" in our heritage. "In congregational doctrine, there is something sacred and irreducibly ultimate about the moral texture of face-to-face relationships organized as local congregations. . . . On this view, the church is composed of compacts made among freely choosing persons." In contrast to European ecclesiology and sociology, which stress the role of hierarchy and territoriality in the constitution of the parish, the American ideal is that "the congregation is created by the consent of individuals not merely to join it, but to create it continuously by their continuous consent."[38] Historian Timothy Smith goes further to argue that the congregational ideal of a "worshiping brotherhood" rooted in souls, not soil, was developed in all of the colonial Protestant communions regardless of their previous theories of church polity.[39] The gathered congregation has an ancient, ecumenical heritage as a social form in the United States.

Contemporary sociologists of religion have determined that denominations grow when they found new congregations and decline when they do not. It may be that new church development itself causes denominational growth or that robust denominations have the confidence to plant congregations whereas dispirited ones think they cannot or should not.[40] Whatever the direction of causation, it is plausible that one reason for the correlation is the dynamic of friend-seeking among religious Americans. Mobile Americans implicitly recognize that new congregations are places where new friends can effectively be sought out. Research by sociologist Daniel Olson has shown that when a congregation is settled, its members tend to have all the friends they have room for, and they have less incentive to seek out new recruits. New and growing congregations make more room for those who seek fellowship.[41] This is probably why suburban churches have grown faster since World War II than urban or rural ones. As Phillip Hammond proposes, "(*a*) people in fractionated society need centers of community, and (*b*) local parishes may provide such centers."[42]

In a society of immigrants, it was perhaps inevitable that religious gatherings would serve as places of fellowship. In the religious assembly, immigrants gathered at least in part to speak the language of the old country and to celebrate its festivals. The congregation was a *Gemein-schaft* in the midst of the alien *Gesellschaft*. There immigrants did not have to contend with the demands of the new society but could relax in an atmosphere of relative familiarity. The post-1965 surge in immigration has extended the ecumenical reach of the fellowship functions of religion. In his survey of religious adaptations of immigrants from South Asia, religion scholar Raymond Williams observes, "In the United States, religion is the social category with clearest meaning and acceptance in the host society, so the emphasis on religious affiliation and identity is one of the strategies that allows the immigrant to maintain self-identity while simultaneously acquiring community acceptance."[43]

Korean Americans, who number around eight hundred thousand, avail themselves of the congregational form as a Korean world within the American world. In a recent major study of Chicago-area Korean Americans, sociologists Won Moo Hurh and Kwang Chung Kim found that an astonishing 77 percent are involved in churches. Church affiliation itself was found to be conducive to the mental health of women; holding a church office, which 23 percent of church affiliates did, was similarly healthy for the men. "The Korean ethnic church seems to play an important role in satisfying the needs for social status, prestige, power, and recognition within the immigrant community," Hurh and Kim observed. "These needs would be particularly strong for those male immigrants who are expected to 'succeed' in the new country but cannot penetrate into the mainstream of the dominant group's social structure."[44]

Immigrant Muslims seem to derive similar benefits from their religious participation. According to historian Yvonne Yazbeck Haddad and sociologist Adair Lummis, "There is no question that for a considerable number of Muslims today the mosque plays an important role in social integration. This is particularly true for women whose lives may be isolated and lonely and for whom events at the mosque provide a welcome opportunity to interact with others of the community."[45]

But it is not only immigrant newcomers who enjoy the benefits of American religion as a private-public space, a meeting ground whose virtual owners are privileged to define the terms of discourse. The decline of the historic mainline denominations has prompted reflection on the extent to which they long served to enshrine values that we now recognize as those of an elite minority. Only a generation ago, observes sociologist William McKinney, such congregations nurtured a "belief in an innate hierarchy in which social values, values of taste, moral values and intellectual values all combine in a self-evident pattern," a "feeling of being right and open-minded at the same time, of being at once well-bred and progressive."[46] Whether we regret or welcome the demise of such a confident belief system, the perspective of time and fortune makes clear both its partiality and the role of mainline congregations in its former dominance.

Because religious affiliation is presumptively legitimate in American society (if no longer socially obligatory for the metropolitan upper middle class) and religious pluralism taken for granted, the local congregation has long served as a site for many activities that are not necessarily religious, from English-language instruction for immigrants to wholesome entertainment for teens. The imperative for such ancillary activities typically being prescribed not by the broader religious tradition but by the situation of the local congregation, congregations within the same denomination are as greatly varied as the localities within which they exist. As Barbara Wheeler has noted, "More than seminaries or denominational structures, which play a part in constructing traditions but which have privileges that insulate them from some of the consequences of doing that, congregations are the places . . . where the struggle to find religious meaning in a chaotic world occurs in the most complete and complicated way."[47]

The sociocultural aspect of congregational life, the extent to which congregationalism permits groups to celebrate their culture, should not be disdained. The congregation is not only a place where suburbanites can make friends and foreigners can avoid speaking English. It is not only a place where one's parochial prejudices can be affirmed out of earshot of unwelcome strangers (or a demanding ethic can be proclaimed to a faithful remnant). It is also one of the few places in our society where the oppressed can predictably expect to find encouragement. One of the most powerful expressions of American congregationalism is found in African-American churches, and it was African-American churches in the South that formed the organizational nucleus of the civil rights movement. In the black congregation, ingredients for a successful challenge to segregationist society were assembled: respected leaders, membership rosters, meeting spaces, financial systems, and the presence of a powerful God.[48]

Religious associations encourage the weak by invoking powers that outsiders respect, give lip service to, or merely tolerate. Thus church is one of the few places in rural America where girls from patriarchal households can go on their own without prompting suspicion of their intentions.[49] Members of black churches are serious about the power of the same God white society claims to revere, expecting God "to help them cope with joblessness, poverty and discrimination by transforming their despair into hope," in the words of pastor James Henry Harris.[50]

Besides being an acceptable form of association, religious gatherings are also relatively free from scrutiny. As sociologist Aldon Morris describes the atmosphere of Southern black churches, "Behind the church doors was a friendly and warm environment where black people could be temporarily at peace with themselves while displaying their talents and aspirations before an empathetic audience."[51] Religious association is "private" in the sense that church is like family: just as passersby don't ordinarily drop in for dinner, they don't ordinarily walk into your church. That means that confidences can be shared, confidences like the need to overcome both internal temptation and external oppression. Thus lower-class black churchgoers are told by their pastors to avoid some temptations in their environment—partying, drinking, drugs— even as they celebrate other aspects of their culture—gospel music, chanted sermons, colorful dress—and chastise their oppressors.[52]

Congregations can function as protected enclaves in a hostile world. Middle-class white parents have a good chance of protecting their children from harm by their freedom to choose desirable neighborhoods, but black families are more likely to be segregated into neighborhoods with high rates of pathology. Religious communities can help them to guide their children. A feminist student on my campus, an American black woman raised as a Muslim, had this to say about her seemingly paradoxical commitment to a patriarchal religion:

> In the MSA [Muslim Students' Association], no one *expects* me to fail. . . . Blacks give lip service to the importance of education, but if you are black and a good student while growing up, you do not get encouragement, at least not from anyone besides your parents. "There she is with that book again," they'd say. But Muslims expect me to be educated and to question things, so that I can use my education to live and spread Islam.[53]

Congregations of the Metropolitan Community Church are also enclaves: here gay men and lesbians can meet and pray for each other, hold their partner's hand at the communion rail, mend bad habits, heal psychic wounds, volunteer home care for persons with AIDS, meet political candidates, and organize demonstrations.[54] In this way, church can be a place for people to develop a morale with the power to transform not only the world outside but also themselves inside, without risking the attention of the dominant society, which would be ready to use what the oppressed tell each other as an excuse to blame the victim.

Insofar as all Americans are minorities today—I emphatically include religious liberals of the old mainline—the congregation, with its diffuse, affective, and particularistic nurturing capacity, can help them resist their own particular temptations from the surrounding culture and nourish their higher aspirations.

De Facto Congregationalism and the Declining Significance of Denominationalism

The congregational form of local organization is the sanctioned, official norm among only a few of America's religious communities, notably Baptists and Jews (see the chapters by Wayne Flynt and Karla Goldman and Jonathan Sarna in the first volume of *American Congregations*, as well as the unmerged Congregationalists, the Christian Churches, Friends, and Brethren. Formal congregationalism is doctrinally foreign to most of the prominent American denominational traditions—the Catholic, Episcopal, Presbyterian, and Lutheran lineages as well as the Methodists and their many offshoots. Nonetheless, the congregational mentality has great practical force as an unofficial norm in American religious life.[55]

To be sure, formal polity matters. Religious organizations, more or less by definition, are ideological organizations, and organizational forms are typically prescribed by ideology. Organizational ideals (for example, "apostolic succession" and "the priesthood of all believers") do count for some purposes.[56] In particular, the less congregational the constitution of a denomination, the more likely it is that church pastors can take controversial stances on local issues, because they cannot formally be fired by their congregations.[57] This does not mean that congregationalism always conduces to conservatism, however. A recent controversial example is that of providing "sanctuary" from U.S. Immigration authorities for Central American refugees. The chances that a local religious assembly will declare itself a sanctuary are greatly enhanced by formal congregational polity, perhaps because only independent congregations have the freedom to risk government seizure of their property.[58]

Yet regardless of formal polity, the history and current situation of religious communities in the U.S. have a communal and congregation-

73

alist bias at the local level and an organizational and bureaucratic one at the national. George Papaiouannou's study in the first volume of *American Congregations* of a Greek Orthodox parish reminds us that the highly episcopal Greek Orthodox Archdiocese of North and South America was begun at the local level by congregations of self-made business-men.[59] On the other hand, the formally congregational Baptists have spawned great national bureaucracies.[60] Over the past generation, Protestant denominations have experienced the waxing and waning of hier-archy—of effective presbyterianism and episcopalianism—but the end result, as Donald Metz intuited over twenty years ago and sociologist Robert Wuthnow has recently analyzed, has been the "declining signifi-cance of denominationalism" for church members, for congregations, and for the society at large.[61]

Throughout the 1950s and 1960s, mainline Protestant denomina-tions buried old differences through mergers and federations in order better to carry on what they saw as God's work. The northern Presbyter-ians merged with the more conservative United Presbyterians, the old New England Congregationalists with midwestern German Calvinists, and the Anglo-Saxon-origin Methodists with the German-origin Evan-gelical United Brethren. Lutheran bodies with German, Norwegian, and Swedish roots came together, and they began to talk of reuniting with the Catholics. Mainline denominations formed the National Council of Churches, and several of them shared its headquarters building on Riv-erside Drive in New York. Eventually, it became easier to recognize mainline Protestant leaders by their opinion on public affairs than by their theology, and it became difficult to discern what, other than a com-mon label, connected the various leadership cadres to the grass roots.[62]

The concept of the "declining significance of denominationalism" has several aspects. Denomination as a sociological variable has decreas-ing explanatory power in sociological research on beliefs and behavior of the laity, no doubt in part because so many Americans switch denomi-national affiliation during their lives.[63] Denominations that were historic antagonists have increasingly similar policies and structures. Congre-gations within the same denomination vary wildly in theology, lit-urgy, and social values. Amidst the clamor over centralized bureaucracy, mainline Protestant denominational agencies as well as the professional staff of the National Council of Churches have been cut back, and the denominational structures are internally divided between bureaucrats and judicatories (what sociologists call "staff" and "line").[64] Wuthnow argues that the impact of religion on public affairs is increasingly mediated not by denominations (or federations of denominations like the National Council of Churches) but by "special-purpose groups," whose members are typically individuals who share some focused concern.[65]

One reaction to denominational and interdenominational liberal ecumenism was the growth of a cross-denominational conservative reaction that further blurred historic identities.[66] Each of the mainline denominations has at least one outspoken theologically or politically conservative pressure group within, groups that seem to be in contact with each other through paradenominational conferences and publications.

A kind of local ecumenism also links the grassroots conservatives, but it is cultural more than policy-oriented, and it bypasses the denominations. Anthropologist Melinda Wagner, in her recent study of nine Christian grade schools located near each other in an Appalachian valley, found that the schools preached a generic conservative Christian faith and required group prayer but did not stress finer points of doctrine or ritual, despite the fact that the schools were sponsored by congregations affiliated with denominations of very different kinds: from new charismatic, evangelical, and fundamentalist to old Holiness and Pentecostal. School administrators played down their denominations' particularities, and many teachers looked forward to the establishment of an "all-Christian" high school in the central town, for which they would collectively serve as feeders.[67]

At the present time, in seeming response to unrest at the local, regional, and paradenominational levels, mainline Protestant denominations are decentralizing. The United Church of Christ and the Presbyterian Church have moved their headquarters from New York closer to their heartlands. As conservative opinion within their communions has been mobilized, liberal Episcopal and Presbyterian church leaders have tried to preserve room for maneuver as well as to avoid schism by accepting permissive rather than mandatory resolutions on such controversial issues as gay rights and consecration of women bishops. Much the same dynamic seems to be operating within the Reform and Conservative branches of American Judaism.[68] When liberal policies were hegemonic, liberal church leaders took advantage of episcopal and presbyterian structure. In a conservative time, decentralization is a fallback position for liberals, but it gives headquarters less leverage to enforce uniformity—on whatever issue—across congregations.[69] On matters of "lifestyle," congregations increasingly go their own way, so there are diametrically opposed "Bible-believing" congregations and "reconciled" ones (those who are accepting of gays) in all the mainline churches.

"Walk-in closets," parishes widely known but not officially acknowledged to welcome homosexual men, are a widespread feature of the Anglo-Catholic wing of the Episcopal Church, whatever the current policy of that denomination on the legitimacy of homosexual expression.[70]

De facto congregationalism implies that congregations can chart their own religious course despite their denominational ties. For example, many Presbyterian congregations use the popular evangelical hymnal, *Hymns for the Living Church*, instead of one of the denominational hymnals. Although they must comply with denominational pastor-search procedures, many have chosen ministers trained at the independent evangelical Fuller Theological Seminary rather than at one of the denominational seminaries. The label *Presbyterian* on the door no longer conveys a great deal of information to the first-time visitor to a local church.[71]

De facto congregationalism also means that the local church is effectively constituted by its members, not by geography. In a city like Chicago, the mobility of congregations and the stability of edifices are often evident in building cornerstones and carved inscriptions. A former synagogue in Greek revival style is now owned by a Puerto Rican Pentecostal church. Another synagogue is now a Greek Orthodox church. A German Lutheran church built at the turn of the century is now owned by Hispanic Seventh-day Adventists. What was built as an Anglo-Saxon Presbyterian church and was later sold to a Korean congregation now houses an Orthodox church for Arab Christians, many of whom came from a town where their families had been settled for a dozen generations.[72]

De facto congregationalism is seen across the American religious spectrum. Despite the conservative ascendancy in the Southern Baptist Convention, which may mean that nonconforming seminary faculty stand to lose their jobs, "local church autonomy was not just a symbol,"[73] and congregationalism is robust in the SBC. Lay involvement is strong, and the gathered-church ideal encourages local group homogeneity. The average tenure of Southern Baptist pastors is thirty months, and the denomination is increasingly multicultural, with ethnically distinct congregations worshiping in eighty-seven different languages and dialects.[74] Southern Baptist churches have structural similarities with Orthodox Jewish synagogues, which place the greatest emphasis on rabbinical authority but at the same time need rabbis least, because the laity are so active.[75]

Korean Presbyterians provide an instructive example of the declining significance of denominationalism among Protestants and the increasing pressures toward de facto congregationalism.[76] There are approximately three hundred ethnic Korean congregations in the Presbyterian Church (U.S.A.), and they represent the fastest-growing sector of that denomination. One of these congregations, in fact the oldest Korean-American church, recently succeeded in withdrawing from the denomination and legally taking along its property, for which it had paid. The judge held that the congregation, the Korean United Presbyterian Church of Los Angeles, clearly never meant to comply with the denomination's rule that the congregation holds property only in trust for the denomination. "We are pleased that the issue of whether the Presbytery has the ability to determine who is the rightful congregation has finally been addressed by the court," said the congregation's lawyer as the judge's decision in the four-year lawsuit was announced. "We hope that the Presbytery will not carry the case any further and will allow the Korean church to worship as it pleases."[77] Here the liberal secular American language of rights was invoked to argue for the religious autonomy of a largely immigrant congregation.

Presbyterians constitute a plurality of Christians in Korea, and they were accustomed in their homeland to practices that contravene PCUSA rules and customs, including life terms for ruling elders, exclusion of women from ordination, and a relatively literal reading of the Bible. The fact that 200 congregations have joined the Korean Presbyterian Church in America (as well as about 1,500 congregations enrolled in other American denominations) represents an option for Korean immigrants of which American Presbyterian leaders are very much aware. One response has been the establishment of a nongeographical, ethnic judicatory within the PCUSA, Han Mi Presbytery, expressly for Korean Americans. The denomination wants to hold on to its congregations, but the result is that Presbyterianism becomes structurally more diverse.

A form of de facto congregationalism seems to be rising among American Catholics. Two congregational processes, both likely related to the rising social status of American Catholic laity, seem to be taking place. One is the greater role for laity and women religious in the ritual and administration of the parish, a development that can claim both the virtue of Vatican II sanction and the necessity of addressing the priest shortage. There are many studies of this process.[78] The other process—the "floating" of laity from parish to parish in search of a spiritual home—is widely acknowledged by clergy and laypeople, but I know of no large-scale systematic studies of it.

It is no secret that many lay Catholics have a proprietary attitude toward their parishes to which they are not canonically entitled.[79] It seems plausible that the history of national ethnic parishes and changing neighborhoods in American cities combines with lay Catholics' transportation resources to create among them a sense of entitlement to parishes suited to their own liking. Meanwhile, since midcentury, Catholics have been secure in their Americanness and middle-class standing. No longer does the parish have to be a refuge from a hostile world; it can now be more a vehicle for expression.[80]

I see impressionistic evidence of de facto congregationalism in widely varied sources. Journalist Andrew Sullivan observes that Catholic laity are aware of

> the shifting emphasis from parish to parish and priest to priest on the fundamentals of the faith: the balance of fact and metaphor in scriptural interpretation, the shift from the sacrament of confession to the dominant role of the Eucharist, notions of social responsibility, of community-based worship, of scriptural rather than theological catechism, of obligation to the poor, witness to the unborn, the old, and the emergence of both charismatic and old-style devotional traditions.[81]

Sociologist Melissa Ray studied a midwestern parish whose members "identified themselves and their faith in terms of the specific parish of St. Alicia first and only then in terms of the larger institutional church." She calls their attitude one of "partial alienation," but it is part of what I mean by de facto congregationalism.[82]

In a study of a Catholic diocese in the upper Midwest, Donald LaMagdeleine and John Glesser report that the present bishop "has not hindered the development" of "ideologically homogeneous parishes" to meet the needs of diverse constituencies.[83] As one of my Catholic neighbors told me about the attitude of the hierarchy in the Chicago archdiocese, "they'd *like* you to go to the parish where you're registered, but they would rather you went to some other Catholic church than none at all." Father Thomas Propocki, vice-chancellor of the archdiocese of Chicago and a canon lawyer, had this to say on the matter in an interview: "Because of the social mobility of our current society it makes sense to let people choose parishes."[84]

Such church officials may be relying on a liberal interpretation of a revision of Catholic canon law effective since 1983. Canon 518 provides:

As a general rule a parish is to be territorial, that is it embraces all the Christian faithful within a certain territory; whenever it is judged useful, however, personal parishes are to be established based upon rite, language, the nationality of the Christian faithful within some territory or even upon some other determining factor.

Thus canon law says that the norm is that parishes are to be territorial, with boundaries determined by the bishop, but that exceptions are now formally permissible.

The official comment on the change is this: "Following Vatican II, the First Synod of Bishops (1967) recognized the need to constitute personal jurisdictions although it confirmed the principle of territoriality in church organization. This meant that territory no longer is considered a constitutive element but only a determining element of the community of the faithful. . . ." Four exceptions were recognized by the bishops: Eastern rite parishes; common-language parishes; national-origin parishes (which may now be established by the bishop—a change from the 1917 law, which required permission from the Vatican for such parishes); and the fourth:

Various other groups could include college and university personnel, military forces, charismatic groups, etc. Following Vatican II a number of bishops . . . allowed certain experimental parishes to develop under their supervision. They did this to meet the spiritual needs of various groups. . . . Some hold that strictly territorial groupings of the faithful are frequently artificial and deadening as the territorial principle as a norm for parish affiliation becomes increasingly obsolescent. . . . Although the territorial principle makes for good order, the needs of modern Christians have become so varied and their styles of commitment have expanded so much that a new approach today is important.[85]

In the spring of 1991, sociology student Carol Biesadecki interviewed a cross-section of twenty-five Chicago-area Catholics who identified themselves in response to her advertisements as those who attend mass at a parish other than the one they live in. She called them "floaters," and they gave many reasons for venturing from their home parish. Some went for a particular priest and his homilies, or for the cultural style they perceived among the parishioners. Some went to experience intimacy, others majesty. Some wanted an elaborate liturgy, others an abbreviated one. Some wanted a more convenient time, while others were sorely inconvenienced by the miles and hours that their floating took. Some who had moved to the suburbs returned to the urban parish of their youth. No single reason for floating dominated, yet there were some patterns: women and younger persons were slightly more likely to cite the particular priest, younger people to be drawn to the cultural style of fellow parishioners, and older people to be drawn by nostalgia for the past and a sense of intimacy in their chosen parish. In other words, floating does not mean that Catholics agree on one liturgical, musical, architectural, theological, or political style, but rather that they feel increasingly free to find the style that does suit them. As Biesadecki put it: "If the parish environment does not provide an atmosphere for a productive spiritual life, it makes sense to find one that does."[86]

The experience of a new African-American parish in the Chicago archdiocese seems to be a tacit concession to the concept of the local church as a gathered community. Saint Benedict the African, in the South Side neighborhood of Englewood, represents a consolidation of five preexisting parishes into a new building. The consolidation was necessary because Englewood had lost most of its white (particularly Irish-American) population in the last generation, the people whose ancestors built many of these churches. "Where Englewood residents were once Catholic in large proportions, they are now maybe 2 percent Catholic," observes reporter Grant Pick, and the rest, he says, are predominantly Baptists, Methodists, and Pentecostals. The heritage of St. Benedict's parishioners shows in the design of the building, whose main architectural focus is a stone baptistry pool twenty-four feet in diameter and three-and-a-half feet deep, which, says Pick, is "reminiscent of the Baptist tradition in which countless Englewood Catholics were raised." In the words of one parishioner, "This church was built for us, in our time. Our old churches were built for other people, who abandoned those churches. Now we have a feeling of ownership."[87]

Structural convergence toward the American model of congregational life seems to be taking place also among Muslims in America, as Earle Waugh observes in the first volume of *American Congregations* and as other students of the Muslim experience in America agree.[88] The mosque, established in Islam as a place for prayer, has become in Alberta an educational and service center to meet the needs of the Muslim community, a kind of church, with adult classes, potlucks, and coffee-hours. The imam, who according to Islamic practice should be expected only to lead prayers, is asked on this side of the Atlantic to celebrate marriages, counsel families, visit the sick, conduct funerals, and represent his people among the local clergy, modeling himself in the process on priests, pastors, and rabbis. This might be called a form of assimilation, but it is done not only to meet immigrants' secular needs but also to help them perpetuate their religion. At the same time that old-country traditions weaken, the religious significance of the mosque increases.[89]

Muslims in Toledo, Ohio, have developed organizational patterns on the congregational model, according to the research of Islamicist Frederick Denny. They have instituted membership, with annual dues, and they hire their imam as an employee of the corporation. They have a council of elders comparable to those of Presbyterians, but the council "has supreme authority over the affairs of the center. At this point the analogy with Presbyterian polity breaks down, for in the case of the Toledo Islamic Center there is no official transcendent authority like Presbyterianism's synod and general assembly."[90]

Similar processes are going on among Asian-origin Buddhists. The Korean Buddhist Kwan Um Sa temple in Los Angeles occupies the opulent second story of a former Masonic temple catercorner from the headquarters of Han Mi Presbytery, and the Buddhist leaders are well aware of the Christian model and competition. The temple's abbot told an interviewer that "church membership increased rapidly after he initiated several social service and family counseling programs, including marriage and youth counseling, hospital arrangement, hospital visits, arrangement for Social Security benefits, etc. The church's van provides transportation for elderly members."[91] Japanese-American Jodo Shinshu Buddhists use the word *church* for their places of worship, which also are used to stage elaborate, American-style weddings and to host ethnic food bazaars. To judge from appearances, these Buddhists do not sit on mats but on pews purchased from American church-supply houses.[92]

At the Sri Lankan Buddhist *viharas* of New York and Washington, lay involvement centers on scheduled events, festivals, and special occasions, with most of the observances occurring on Sundays. "This scheduling is a concession to the demands of American society, which has traditionally reserved Sundays for religious observances," observes religious historian Anne Blackburn. Those who live at long distances from the viharas are able to come only for such events as Sinhalese New Year, in April, and Vesakha, commemorating the Buddha's birth, enlightenment, and death, in May. At such times, congregants can enjoy the rare pleasures of speaking Sinhalese with nonfamily members and sharing others' home-cooked traditional foods. Instead of being immersed in a taken-for-granted Buddhist environment, these Sri Lankans must organize to enjoy the benefits of religious ritual, devotions, and instruction for their children.[93]

Sociologists Paul DiMaggio and Walter Powell have invented the term *institutional isomorphism* to label the general process of modeling that produces the particular convergence I call de facto congregationalism. They argue that "organizations that copy other organizations" have a "competitive advantage" and contend that "in most situations, reliance on established legitimated procedures enhances organizational legitimacy and survival characteristics."[94]

Because of post-1965 immigration, Los Angeles is reported to have the greatest variety of Buddhisms in the 2,500-year history of that faith, and Buddhist leaders there are confronting unprecedented challenges and opportunities for institution-building and ecumenical cooperation. The Dalai Lama recently gave this advice to the Buddhist Sangha Council of Southern California, which comprises members of a dozen ethnic groups: "Another thing we should consider is that our Christian brothers and sisters, and also some Jewish and Hindu organizations, take a very active role in social work, in social welfare, in education, in health. But Buddhist monks, Buddhist traditions, are somewhat lacking in that. . . . We could have more activity in these areas of social service."[95] As Los Angeles becomes more culturally diverse, more religious organizations that take the form of American congregations are likely to grow within it.

Beyond Tribalism to Voluntarism: From Ascription to Achievement in Religion

Not all denominations are declining in significance, nor are all congregations going their own separate ways. Mormon wards resemble each other closely, as we are informed by the research reported by Jan Shipps, Cheryll May, and Dean May, in the first volume of *American Congregations*, and the parent denomination, the Church of Jesus Christ of Latter-day Saints, is formidable. Moreover, sociologists know that the category "Mormon" carries predictive power in social surveys. But this should remind us that denominationalism, when denominations were communities more than organizations, historically helped people to understand who they were, to forge their cultural identity.[96] In other words, there is no intrinsic religious contradiction between *denomination* and *congregation*. The contradiction, when it exists, is organizational.

Under what circumstances can Americans' insistence on having their own churches be reconciled with the churches' being something more than flattering cultural mirrors for their members? Or, to put the question another way, how can the commitments of religious traditions be made the commitments of the local laity?

It needs to be said that there are costs to congregationalism, de facto and otherwise. The local group can go off on its own idiosyncratic way, which in the case of Jim Jones's People's Temple was well off the deep end.[97] Years before Jones's trek to Guyana and the subsequent mass suicide, the People's Temple ranch near Ukiah, California, was already a negative symbol of "Lone Ranger Christianity" for a post-hippie charismatic Christian fellowship I studied in 1976, whose leaders fitfully sought out "spiritual covering" in lieu of affiliation with one of the mainline denominations they scorned as temples of "churchianity." They eventually aligned with the "spiritual shepherding" movement of Bob Mumford and Dennis Peacocke, the guiding principle of which was that "everyone should know who is over you and who is under you in the Body."[98]

More likely than spiritual idiosyncrasy, however, is the opposite pattern, where the congregation conforms excessively to its local environment, becoming a spiritualized replica of secular parochialism. The more congregational the local church, the more responsive and vulnerable it is to its local environment. Not only does narrow parochialism offend transcendent religious values, it also religiously disadvantages those who are socially disadvantaged in the parochial environment, for example, those women and youth whose religious involvement is entailed by the patriarchal families in which they are bound.

Denominations can help otherwise subordinated voices be heard. For example, denominational (and otherwise cross-congregational) ties have helped African-American women achieve practical influence in the affairs of such officially male-dominated churches as the Church of God in Christ, as sociologist Cheryl Townsend Gilkes has shown.[99] The Camp Ramah movement, a youth-oriented network in the U.S. and Canada closely connected to Conservative Judaism and the Jewish Theological Seminary, has provided an atmosphere where classical Jewish texts "could spring to life without the obtrusiveness of either familial background or urban distractions." On the basis of intense camp experiences, Ramah alumni later became catalysts for change in Conservative synagogues, particularly in participatory and feminist directions.[100] It should be noted that such conferences and summer camps derive part of their power from an even more radical application of the gathered-community principle than the one exemplified by the local congregation: they bring women and young people together across, rather than within, circumscribed geographic locales.

Denominational bonds can transcend congregational cultures. Early in its career as a denomination, the Universal Fellowship of Metropolitan Community Churches, whose founding congregations were overwhelmingly composed of gay males, made a conscious commitment to sexual equality. The UFMCC now claims the highest proportion of female clergy in any Protestant denomination.[101] Some Korean-American Presbyterian church leaders argue that staying within the mainline American denominational fold is essential to maintain the commitment of second-generation youth. An autonomous Korean-American denomination, they fear, would be utterly dominated by the first-generation patriarchal culture that American-reared young people often want to flee.[102] Leaders of the fledgling interethnic American Buddhist Congress were treated to the following observation made at Wat Dhammaram, a Chicago-area Thai Buddhist temple, by one of their number. He complained that Wat Dhammaram's leaders are so obsessed with maintaining old-country customs and language that they failed to notice their own children speaking English among themselves during a special ceremony—conducted in Thai—in the children's honor! In effect, the ABC is applying the principles of the American-style church federation in order to overcome cultural captivity.[103]

We should be careful, however, not to phrase the cultural conflict between the presumably cosmopolitan denomination and the equally parochial congregation in stark terms of sexism, ageism, or racism. Even if we assume that the denomination represents less compromised religious teachings than the congregation represents, it does not follow that religious leaders face the choice of either abject capitulation to, or radical conversion of, a presumed primordial local culture. The local cultures that congregationalism builds upon are not simple givens, to which the craven church-growth specialist merely accommodates.[104] Local cultures are more protean than that, and they can be turned to religious purposes.

The pastorate of Eric Underwood in Mendocino is an example. Educated in business administration at UCLA and in Bible and homiletics at Fuller Theological Seminary, Underwood was a first-rate evangelical preacher who instantly appealed to one sector of the congregation he came to pastor in 1973: the born-again ex-hippie Christians that Jesus-movement evangelists had left in the wake of their revivals on the Mendocino coast. But Underwood intuited another, albeit inchoate, cultural ideal more widely shared in his congregation than the vocabulary of southern-style revivalism, an intuition that began with the simple observation that Mendocino's population swarmed with newcomers from very diverse backgrounds. Listening to their elaborate life-stories and overhearing their casual conversations, Underwood discovered how far they had come to get to Mendocino and how much their decision to take up residence in a small town cost them. Because his own ethical principles stressed the virtues of face-to-face relationships ("structural sin" was a concept foreign to him), he could identify with his parishioner's stories. In his sermons, he reframed these stories in biblical terms and helped even the near secularists in his congregation understand the relevance of Christianity for their lives, even as he prodded them to acts of humility, decency, and generosity. In the end, his congregation prospered materially and spiritually and contributed heavily to its parent denomination.[105]

The Universal Fellowship of Metropolitan Community Churches provides another example. This 200-congregation denomination began with a gathering of twelve persons in Troy Perry's living room in 1968. Perry felt called to share with other gay men (and eventually lesbians) a conviction that he later used as the title for his first autobiography: "The Lord is my shepherd and He knows I'm gay." From his own experience, including a five-year immersion in Los Angeles's gay underground and a lifesaving vision of having been created gay by a benevolent God, Perry knew how profound were feelings of unworthiness among his acquaintances but also how surely evangelical faith could overcome those feelings. On such grounds he founded his church. His first followers were a mixed lot—former Roman Catholics and former Baptists predominated—but Perry preached from the outset a message that spoke to their need for redemption in the face of social stigma. Over time Perry arrived at an eclectic liturgy that suited the group; his first sermon, for example, was on Job's dispute with interlocutors. The Metropolitan Community Church communion offers a choice of Catholic wine or Baptist—and teetotaler—grape juice. When the AIDS crisis hit, death did not spare the UFMCC, but congregations pulled together as places of help and hope.[106]

Mendocino Presbyterian Church and the congregations of the Metropolitan Community Church that I know of are genuine communities: they are characterized by diffuse, affective, particularistic, and collectivity-oriented relations. But they are not communities into which one is born. Few people in the Mendocino church in the mid-1970s had grown up there, and in 1968 no one had been brought up in the UFMCC.[107] These churches, in other words, are not communities by social ascription but by choice. Moreover, such choices are not necessarily conservative. The members of Unitarian-Universalist churches are predominantly so by reason of adult conversion, not upbringing. Unitarianism is an achieved faith.[108] For this reason, the church-growth movement's "homogeneous unit principle" is not equivalent to tribalism. The identities and experiences on the basis of which religiously relevant cultural communities form are not necessarily those with which we are born: they are as likely to be matters of "lifestyle" (more typically an orientation to hearth and home than to homoerotic relationships) as of race.[109] Or, like deafness, they may crosscut (rather than mirror) social structural divisions.[110] Contingent or not, they are given meaning in the name of religious ideals that themselves are understood as perennial.

I used to be wryly amused when my contemporaries complained that stagnation had settled in after the social changes we tried to introduce in the 1960s. Didn't they realize, I wondered, how rapidly our world continued to change after the protests died down? Didn't they see that whole ways of life were disappearing? that the American industrial working class had reproduced its last generation? that the "family wage" was gone? that each child was being raised by more different people? that the WASP was becoming a minority? that there was a greater variety of persons of color in the United States than ever before? that organizations we used to take for granted—"the phone company," Pan-American World Airways, Pacific Stereo—had vanished? that it was getting steadily more difficult to become a home-owner or a college graduate?[111] Without even thinking of changes in the Amazon Basin, Southeast Asia, the Middle East, and Eastern Europe, were not these changes plenty to confront?

We live in "interesting times." Few of us carry out plans our parents made, nor can our children afford to heed our detailed worldly advice.[112] That with which we were born is seldom that with which we will die. To assume that religious identity is not problematic in these circumstances—that church members do not need to be convinced to be church members—has been the basic error of mainline Protestant planning over the past generation. Somehow, it was thought to be beneath the dignity of the Presbyterian Church to tell people they ought to be Presbyterians. It seemed enough to tell them, given their Presbyterianism, what their social obligations were. Today, even Jews, whose identity tends to be far more ascribed than is that of Protestants, have to be told what it means to be Jewish; at least many of their leaders think so. Older recipes have lost their relevance, and older identities their draw.

But not everything that is sacred has melted away. We are not yet a nation of monads. Americans are still religiously inclined, and the congregational form of organization is robust. When Americans need the support of others to become better persons, they form congregations, places where people recognize each other and pay attention to each other in the sight of whatever they take to be ultimate. Some de facto congregations are found in and around seminaries: whatever the theory of congregation, students as well as the people back home feel the need for the interpersonal affirmation that congregations provide.[113] Post-sixties Jewish youth began another kind of congregation, *havurot*, "small intimate fellowships for study, prayer, and friendship . . . [which] allowed for individual participation and spontaneity."[114] Many large local churches make use of weekly "house-church" meetings to give their otherwise anonymous members the benefit of true congregational life. The new denomination called the Vineyard does this, as do, my informants tell me, Korean mega-churches. (The Korean Methodists call their smaller meetings *Sok Hoe*, or "classes.") Another extensive category of de facto congregations are the thousands of twelve-step groups that have sprung up to help people cope with everything from alcoholism to their own propensity to violence, with the support and criticism of like-minded others in the sight of God as she or he is imaged.[115]

A few years ago, I went with my sociology of religion class to the regular weekly meeting of Dignity-Chicago, the local chapter of the national organization for gay Catholics. The meeting—really an unauthorized mass—took place on Sunday evening at Second Unitarian Church on the North Side, where the group took refuge after being expelled under Vatican pressure from the parish hall where their meetings had been held for fifteen years. I assumed it was not an oversight that the name of the priest celebrant was not announced, but everything else about the mass was in order. There was a procession, a six-person choir accompanied by guitar, a psalm and epistle read by lay lectors, the alleluia, the Gospel reading and a ten-minute homily by the priest, plenty of lay eucharistic ministers, and the dismissal, all in just under an hour. The sex ratio was highly skewed—indeed four of the five women present were members of my class—and the Lord's Prayer was recited using inclusive language, but the most unusual thing about the mass, my class agreed, was how enthusiastically the whole group of about eighty sang the hymns. We weren't used to that among Catholics.[116]

Afterward, we were greeted by one of the officers, and when we remarked on their singing, he had a ready answer. "We have chosen to be here," he said. "We are a congregation."

NOTES

I owe all of the stimulus for this paper, and many of the observations in it, to the Congregational History Project and my fellow seminar participants, some of whose work is cited herein. I am also deeply indebted to my students for their research and their initiative on field trips. The writing was supported by my home institution, the University of Illinois at Chicago, by the courtesy of the Department of Sociology at Northwestern University, and by a fellowship from the National Endowment for the Humanities. Fred Kniss and Daniel Olson commented on an earlier draft when it was presented to the fall 1991 meeting of the Chicago-Area Group for the Study of Religious Communities, and Allan Silver and James Wind provided written critiques of the same draft. Their comments were of great help in the process of revision.

1. R. Stephen Warner, *New Wine in Old Wineskins: Evangelicals and Liberals in a Small-Town Church* (Berkeley and Los Angeles: University of California Press, 1988); see also R. Stephen Warner, "Mirror for American Protestantism: Mendocino Presbyterian Church in the Sixties and Seventies," in Milton J Coalter, John M. Mulder, and Louis B. Weeks, eds., *The Mainstream Protestant "Decline": The Presbyterian Pattern* (Louisville: John Knox, 1990), pp. 198–223 and 250–53; and R. Stephen Warner, "Oenology: The Making of *New Wine*," in Joe Feagin, Anthony Orum, and Gideon Sjoberg, eds., *A Case for the Case Study* (Chapel Hill: University of North Carolina Press, 1991), pp. 174–99.

2. For example, see R. Stephen Warner and James S. Pappas, "Seeing the Word," *Christian Century* 110, no. 20 (June 30–July 7, 1993): 663–65.

3. R. Stephen Warner, "The Metropolitan Community Church as a Case Study of Religious Change in the U.S.A." (paper presented at annual meeting of the Society for the Scientific Study of Religion, Salt Lake City, 1989); R. Stephen Warner, "The Korean Immigrant Church in Comparative Perspective" (paper presented at colloquium on "The Korean Immigrant Church: A Comparative Perspective," Princeton Theological Seminary, February 16–18, 1990).

4. For a survey of this literature, see R. Stephen Warner, "Work in Progress toward a New Paradigm for the Sociological Study of Religion in the United States," *American Journal of Sociology* 98 (March 1993): 1044–93.

5. Virginia A. Hodgkinson, Murray S. Weitzman, and Arthur D. Kirsch, *From Belief to Commitment: The Activities and Finances of Religious Congregations in the United States* (Washington, D.C.: Independent Sector, 1988).

6. Constant H. Jacquet, Jr., and Alice M. Jones, eds., *Yearbook of American and Canadian Churches, 1991* (Nashville: Abingdon Press, 1991), p. 265.

7. Kenneth B. Bedell, ed., *Yearbook of American and Canadian Churches, 1993* (Nashville: Abingdon Press, 1993). The count of congregations for the African Methodist Episcopal Church is taken from the 1991 *Yearbook*.

8. *Yearbook of American Churches, 1967* and *1968*, edited by Lauris B. Whitman (New York: National Council of Churches, 1967 and 1968); *Yearbook of American and Canadian Churches, 1989*, edited by Constant H. Jacquet, Jr. (Nashville: Abingdon, 1989).

9. I have received this impression during travels all over the United States. The pattern was documented for Oswego, New York, by W. Seward Salisbury in "Continuity and Change in the Organization and Practice of Religion in a Small City in One Generation, 1951–1984" (paper presented at annual meeting of the Society for the Scientific Study of Religion, Louisville, 1987).

10. James T. Richardson, "Calvary Chapel: A New Denomination?" (paper presented at the conference on Evangelicals, Voluntary Associations, and American Public Life, Wheaton [Ill.] College, June 14, 1991); Randall Balmer, *Mine Eyes Have Seen the Glory: A Journey into the Evangelical Subculture in America* (New York: Oxford University Press, 1989), pp. 12–30; Robin Dale Perrin, "Signs and Wonders: The Growth of the Vineyard Christian Fellowship" (Ph.D. diss., Washington State University Department of Sociology, 1989); Les Parrott III and Robin D. Perrin, "The New Denominations," *Christianity Today* 34 (March 11, 1991): 29–33; John Dart, "Themes of Bigness, Success Attract Independent Churches," *Los Angeles Times*, July 20, 1991; "First FICWFM Convention a Huge Success," *Ever Increasing Faith Messenger* 12 (Fall 1991): 4.

11. Hodgkinson et al., *From Belief*, p. 10.

12. Tedsuden Kashima, *Buddhism in America: The Social Organization of an Ethnic Religious Institution* (Westport, Conn.: Greenwood Press, 1977); Tetsuden Kashima, "The Buddhist Churches of America: Challenges for Change in the 21st Century," *Pacific World: Journal of the Institute of Buddhist Studies*, n.s. no. 6 (1990): 28–40; Eui-Young Yu, "The Growth of Korean Buddhism in the United States, with Special Reference to Southern California," *Pacific World*, n.s. no. 4 (1988): 82–93; Donald K. Swearer, "Expatriate and Refugee: Theravada Buddhism in America" (paper presented at conference on Minority Religious Experience in America, Connecticut College, 1989); Don Morreale, ed., *Buddhist America: Centers, Retreats, Practices* (Santa Fe: John Muir Publications, 1988); Raymond Brady Williams, *Religions of Immigrants from India and Pakistan: New Threads in the American Tapestry* (Cambridge: Cambridge University Press, 1988), pp. 56, 179; John Y. Fenton, *Transplanting Religious Traditions: Asian Indians in America* (New York: Praeger, 1988), p. 178; Yvonne Yazbeck Haddad and Adair T. Lummis, *Islamic Values in the United States: A Comparative Study* (New York: Oxford University Press, 1987), p. 4; M. Arif Ghayur, "Muslims in the United States: Settlers and Visitors," *Annals of the American Academy of Political and Social Science* 454 (March 1981): 150–63; Yvonne Yazbeck Haddad, Introduction to *The Muslims of America* (New York: Oxford University Press), p. 3.

13. Robert Suro, "Switch by Hispanic Catholics Changes Face of U.S. Religion," *New York Times*, May 14, 1989, pp. 1, 22; Jorge Casuso and Michael Hirsley, "Wrestling for Souls," *Chicago Tribune*, January 7–9, 1990; Lynn Smith and Russell Chandler, "Catholics, Evangelical Christians Battle for Latino Souls," *Los Angeles Times*, December 2, 1989; Lawrence A. Young, "Hispanic Disaffiliation from the U.S. Roman Catholic Church" (paper presented at the annual meeting of the Association for the Sociology of Religion, Cincinnati, 1991); Kevin J. Christiano, "The Church and the New Immigrants," in Helen Rose Ebaugh, ed., *Vatican II and American Catholicism: Twenty-Five Years Later* (Greenwich, Conn.: JAI Press, 1991): pp. 169–86; Alex D. Montoya, *Hispanic Ministry in North America* (Grand Rapids: Zondervan, 1987); *Religion in America—1990* (Princeton: Princeton Religious Research Center), pp. 30, 79. One source gives a figure of 687 Hispanic Protestant congregations for Los Angeles County in 1987 (Justo L. Gonzáles, *The Theological Education of Hispanics* [New York: Fund for Theological Education, 1988], p. 3), and another reports 157 Hispanic Protestant churches in the San Francisco Bay area (Stewart Stout, *Las Historias: A Guide to Hispanic Protestant Churches in the San Francisco Bay Area* [Pasadena, Calif.: IDEA, 1988], p. 10). Given the census and Gallup figures and assuming further that only half of U.S. Hispanic Protestants are members of ethnic congregations serving as many as 1,000 persons each, we could make the extremely conservative guess that there are some 2,000 Hispanic Protestant congregations in the U.S., many of them affiliated with such historically Anglo denominations as the Southern Baptists, Disciples of Christ, Assemblies of God, Seventh-day Adventists, and Mormons, many of them outposts of Latin-American-based denominations, and many independent. I know of no monographic case studies of any such congregation, however.

14. J. Gordon Melton, *The Encyclopedia of American Religions*, 3d ed. (Detroit: Gale Research, 1989); Robert Wuthnow, *The Restructuring of American Religion: Society and Faith Since World War II* (Princeton: Princeton University Press, 1988), pp. 107–12.

15. Robert C. Liebman, John R. Sutton, and Robert Wuthnow, "Exploring the Social Sources of Denominationalism: Schisms in American Protestant Denominations, 1890–1980," *American Sociological Review* 53 (June 1988): 343–52.

16. Dean R. Hoge and David A. Roozen, eds., *Understanding Church Growth and Decline, 1950–1978* (New York: Pilgrim Press, 1979).

17. Compare Dean M. Kelley, *Why Conservative Churches Are Growing*, 2d ed. (San Francisco: Harper and Row, 1977), chaps. 1–2, with Warner, *New Wine*, fig. 5, p. 26.

18. Joseph Gremillion and Jim Castelli, *The Emerging Parish: The Notre Dame Study of Catholic Life Since Vatican II* (San Francisco: Harper and Row, 1987), p. 47.

19. Samuel C. Kincheloe, *The Church in the City: Samuel C. Kincheloe and the Sociology of the City Church*, ed. Yoshio Fukuyama (Chicago: Exploration Press, 1989), chap. 3; Warner, *New Wine*.

20. In a 1990 Gallup survey 29 percent of a representative sample of adult Americans said they were currently involved in small support groups that met

regularly, and 60 percent of those reported that their group was linked to a church or synagogue; other reports estimate that there exist some 150,000 "twelve-step" groups currently meeting in the U.S. Robert Wuthnow, "Small Group—Key to Spiritual Renewal?" (Princeton: George H. Gallup International Institute, 1990); Randolph G. Atkins, Jr., "Twelve-Step Groups as Modern Forms of Religious Life" (paper presented at the annual meeting of the Society for the Scientific Study of Religion, 1991).

21. The social life of religious agencies seems to be an underresearched topic. The preceding sentences draw upon Nancy Ammerman, *Baptist Battles: Social Change and Religious Conflict in the Southern Baptist Convention* (New Brunswick: Rutgers University Press, 1990), Jeffrey K. Hadden, *The Gathering Storm in the Churches* (Garden City: Doubleday, 1969), Paul M. Harrison, *Authority and Power in the Free Church Tradition* (Princeton: Princeton University Press, 1959), Sherryl Kleinman, *Equals Before God: Seminarians as Humanistic Professionals* (Chicago: University of Chicago Press, 1984), George Marsden, *Reforming Fundamentalism: Fuller Seminary and the New Evangelicalism* (Grand Rapids: Eerdmans, 1987), and Henry J. Pratt, *The Liberalization of American Protestantism: A Case Study in Complex Organization* (Detroit: Wayne State University Press, 1972), as well as on my own observations at 475 Riverside Drive and other religious sites.

22. Phillip E. Hammond, "Aging and the Ministry," in Matilda White Riley, John W. Riley, Jr., and Marilyn E. Johnson, eds., *Aging and Society*, volume 2, *Aging and the Professions* (New York: Russell Sage Foundation, 1969), pp. 293–323, quotation at p. 315.

23. Warner, *New Wine*, p. 97.

24. George W. Webber, *The Congregation in Mission: Emerging Structures for the Church in an Urban Society* (Nashville: Abingdon Press, 1964), p. 13.

25. Donald L. Metz, *New Congregations: Security and Mission in Conflict* (Philadelphia: Westminster Press, 1967), p. 36.

26. "Certainly, most denominational officials regard the growth of bureaucracy and increasing social distance as benefits. The officials are allowed to posit and pursue new programs with a minimum of traditional interference. They are more protected from sticky confrontations with nonprofessional church members. They are able to recruit innovative staff members who are more anxious to serve the denomination's 'Southeast Asia desk' or its 'campus ministry' than a suburban pulpit." N. J. Demerath III and Phillip E. Hammond, *Religion in Social Context: Tradition and Transition* (New York: Random House, 1969), p. 187.

27. Warner, *New Wine*, pp. 97, 164, 274–81. Liberal sociologist Wade Clark Roof articulates the mood of ecclesiastical reevaluation: "It was not until the 1950s that liberal intellectuals decided that the laity's preoccupation with personal faith encouraged self-absorption at the expense of theological and social issues. Perhaps it is time for a more balanced perspective. . . . Our preoccupation with universals often blinds us to sources of strength found in the particular. . . . Universality arises out of the particular, not the other way around." Wade Clark Roof, "The Church in the Centrifuge," *Christian Century* 106 (November 8, 1989): 1013–14.

28. Adapted from Talcott Parsons, *The Social System* (Glencoe, Ill.: The Free Press, 1951), chap. 2; see also Warner, *New Wine*, pp. 52–53.

29. Emile Durkheim, *The Elementary Forms of the Religious Life* (New York: The Free Press, 1965), p. 62.

30. Warner, *New Wine*, pp. 86–87, 170, 204–8.

31. Barbara G. Wheeler, "Uncharted Territory: Congregational Identity and Mainline Protestantism," in Milton J Coalter, John M. Mulder, and Louis B. Weeks, eds., *The Presbyterian Predicament: Six Perspectives* (Louisville: John Knox, 1990), at p. 87; James F. Hopewell, *Congregation: Stories and Structures* (Philadelphia: Fortress Press, 1987), esp. chap. 7.

32. Carl S. Dudley, "From Typical Church to Social Ministry: A Study of the Elements Which Mobilize Congregations," *Review of Religious Research* 32 (March 1991): 195–212.

33. Hodgkinson et al., *From Belief*, chap. 4. The 1993 *Yearbook* (p. 258) gives the figure of $17.2 billion in total 1991 or 1992 contributions for 36 reporting denominations comprising 44.7 million members (which amounts to $384 per capita). These reports include most of the old "mainline" churches but, unfortunately, do not include any of the historic African-American churches, the Churches of Christ, the major Pentecostal churches, the Mormon churches, the Roman Catholic Church, most Eastern Orthodox churches, or any non-Christian bodies; in other words, the recent *Yearbook* figures exclude approximately two-thirds of U.S. church members.

34. Penny Edgell Becker, Stephen J. Ellingson, Richard W. Flory, Wendy Griswold, Fred Kniss, and Timothy Nelson, "Straining at the Tie that Binds: Congregational Conflict in the 1980s," *Review of Religious Research* 34 (March 1993): pp. 193–209.

35. Peter L. Berger, *The Noise of Solemn Assemblies* (Garden City: Doubleday, 1961), p. 102.

36. Based on *The Compact Edition of the Oxford English Dictionary* (New York: Oxford University Press, 1971), pp. 516–17, 2079.

37. Thomas Day, *Why Catholics Can't Sing: The Culture of Catholicism and the Triumph of Bad Taste* (New York: Crossroad, 1991), p. 103; also pp. 79, 122, 87.

38. Allan Silver, "The Curious Importance of Small Groups in American Sociology," in Herbert J. Gans, ed., *Sociology in America* (Newbury Park, Calif.: Sage, 1990), pp. 61–72; quotations from pp. 61–63.

39. "Denominations" were later brought into being by such congregations to strengthen and support them, according to Timothy L. Smith, in "Congregation, State, and Denomination: The Forming of the American Religious Structure," *William and Mary Quarterly* 25 (April 1968): 155–76; see also Donald G. Mathews, "The Second Great Awakening as an Organizing Process, 1780–1830: An Hypothesis," *American Quarterly* 21 (Spring 1969): 23–43.

40. Penny Long Marler and C. Kirk Hadaway, "New Church Development and Denominational Growth (1950–1988): Symptom or Cause," in *Research in the Scientific Study of Religion*, ed. Monty L. Lynn and David O. Moberg (Greenwich, Conn.: JAI Press, 1992), 4:29–72.

41. Daniel V. A. Olson, "Networks of Religious Belonging in Five Baptist Congregations" (Ph.D. diss., University of Chicago, Department of Sociology, 1987); see also Phillip Barron Jones, "An Examination of the Statistical Growth of the Southern Baptist Convention," in Dean R. Hoge and David A. Roozen, *Understanding Church Growth and Decline*, pp. 170–72, and Wade Clark Roof, Dean R. Hoge, John E. Dyble, and C. Kirk Hadaway, "Factors Producing Growth or Decline in United Presbyterian Congregations," in ibid., p. 202.

42. Hammond, "Aging," p. 319n.

43. Williams, *Religions of Immigrants*, p. 11.

44. Won Moo Hurh and Kwang Chung Kim, "Religious Participation of Korean Immigrants in the United States," *Journal for the Scientific Study of Religion* 29 (March 1990): 19–34, at p. 31; see also Sang Hyun Lee, "Korean American Presbyterians: A Need for Ethnic Particularity and the Challenge of Christian Pilgrimage," in *The Diversity of Discipleship: The Presbyterians and Twentieth-Century Christian Witness*, ed. Milton J Coalter, John M. Mulder, and Louis B. Weeks (Louisville: Westminster/John Knox, 1991).

45. Haddad and Lummis, *Islamic Values*, p. 55; see also the study of Lac La Biche by Earle Waugh in James P. Wind and James W. Lewis, eds., *American Congregations*, vol. 1 (Chicago: University of Chicago Press, 1994), chap. 10.

46. William McKinney, "Revisioning the Future of Oldline Protestantism," *Christian Century* 106 (November 8, 1989): 1015.

47. Wheeler, "Uncharted Territory," p. 87.

48. Aldon D. Morris, *The Origins of the Civil Rights Movement: Black Communities Organizing for Change* (New York: The Free Press, 1984).

49. Elaine Lawless, *Handmaidens of the Lord: Pentecostal Women Preachers and Traditional Religion* (Philadelphia: University of Pennsylvania Press, 1988), pp. 72, 86.

50. James Henry Harris, "Practicing Liberation in the Black Church," *Christian Century* 107 (June 13–20, 1990): 599.

51. Morris, *Origins*, p. 6.

52. Frances Kostarelos, "First Corinthians Missionary Baptist Church: An Ethnography of an Evangelical Storefront Church in a Black Ghetto" (Ph.D. diss., University of Chicago, Department of Anthropology, 1990).

53. From an interview by Brook E. Lake, student at the University of Illinois at Chicago. Reported in a sociology of religion term paper, fall quarter 1989.

54. Warner, "The Metropolitan Community Church."

55. Silver, "Curious Importance."

56. Gary P. Burkart, "Patterns of Protestant Organization," in Ross P. Scherer, ed., *American Denominational Organization: A Sociological View* (Pasadena: William Carey Library, 1980), pp. 36–83.

57. James R. Wood, *Leadership in Voluntary Organizations: The Controversy over Social Action in Protestant Churches* (New Brunswick: Rutgers University Press, 1981), pp. 59–83. See also N. J. Demerath III and Rhys H. Williams, *A Bridging of Faiths: Religion and Politics in a New England City* (Princeton: Princeton University Press, 1992), p. 182.

58. Michael D. Matters, "Some Structural Correlates of Congregational Participation in the Sanctuary Movement: Research in Progress" (paper presented at annual meeting of the Association for the Sociology of Religion, Cincinnati, 1991).

59. Theodore Saloutos writes, in *The Greeks in the United States* (Cambridge: Harvard University Press, 1964): "Each church community was a democracy unto itself. It was governed by a board of trustees or directors, many of whose members were small independent businessmen, marked by that commanding proprietary air so often found in the self-made man. Authority was vested in these laymen; and many a clergyman discovered, much to his astonishment, that if democracy was diverting or rewarding for his parishioners, it was not exactly so for him. Despite the shortage of qualified priests, laymen remained in unquestioned control of church administration. They displayed a zeal for detail that confounded the clerics. There was little danger of clerical domination in the Greek church communities of the United States" (p. 129).

60. Ammerman, *Baptist Battles*; Harrison, *Authority and Power*.

61. Wuthnow, *Restructuring*, chap. 5 "[D]ifferences in denominational activity are most visible in the structure of ecclesiastical government. At the congregational level there appears to be a minimal difference between denominations in what are considered to be appropriate activities" (Metz, *New Congregations*, p. 22).

62. Daniel V. A. Olson and Jackson W. Carroll, "Religiously Based Politics: Religious Elites and the Public," *Social Forces* 70 (March 1992): 765–86; Hadden, *Gathering Storm;* Douglas W. Johnson, "Program Dissensus Between Denominational Grass Roots and Leadership and Its Consequences," in Scherer, ed., *American Denominational Organization*, pp. 330–45; K. Peter Takayama, "Strains, Conflicts, and Schisms in Protestant Denominations," in ibid., pp. 298–329; Mark Chaves, "The Intradenominational Power Struggle: Declining Religious Control of Protestant Denominational Organization" (paper presented at annual meeting of the Association for the Sociology of Religion, Cincinnati, 1991).

63. Wade Clark Roof and William McKinney, *American Mainline Religion: Its Changing Shape and Future* (New Brunswick: Rutgers University Press, 1987), chaps. 2 and 5. As a variable, denomination still has predictive power for the attitudes of religious professionals (see Daniel V. A. Olson, "Restructuring Among Protestant Denominational Leaders: The Great Divide and the Great Middle" [paper presented at the annual meeting of the Association for the Sociology of Religion, Cincinnati, 1991], which I suspect is due to the role of denominations in clergy careers).

64. Mark Chaves had made a similar distinction between the "agency structure" and the "religious authority structure." See his "Segmentation in a Religious Labor Market," *Sociological Analysis* 52 (Summer 1991): 143–58.

65. Wuthnow, *Restructuring*, chap. 6.

66. Mark A. Noll, "The Eclipse of Old Hostilities Between and the Potential for New Strife Among Catholics and Protestants Since Vatican II," in R. N. Bel-

lah and F. E. Greenspahn, eds., *Uncivil Religion: Religious Hostility in America* (New York: Crossroad, 1987), pp. 86–109.

67. Melinda Bollar Wagner, *God's Schools: Choice and Compromise in American Society* (New Brunswick: Rutgers University Press, 1990); idem, "The Demise of Denominationalism and the Rise of Ecumenism Inside Christian Schools" (paper presented to the Institute for the Study of American Evangelicals, Wheaton, Ill., June 1991).

68. David Heim, "Sexual Congress: The Presbyterian Debate," *Christian Century* 108 (June 26–July 3, 1991): 643–44; Julia Duin, "Episcopalians Fail to Resolve Sexuality Issues," *Christianity Today* 35 (August 19, 1991): 46–47; Jack Wertheimer, "Recent Trends in American Judaism," in David Singer, ed., *American Jewish Yearbook 1989* (New York and Philadelphia: American Jewish Committee and Jewish Publication Society, 1989), pp. 63–162, at pp. 124–39.

69. Similarly, denominational rigidity can become a resource for temporarily triumphant conservatives, as the Southern Baptist Convention is now finding. (See Ammerman, *Baptist Battles*, chap. 7.) Similarly out of character, it might seem, Orthodox Jewish leaders used civil courts to enforce the use of the *mehitza* to segregate men's and women's seating. See Wertheimer, "Recent Trends," p. 72, and Lawrence J. Schiffman, "When Women and Men Sat Together in American Orthodox Synagogues," *Moment* 14 (December 1989): 40–49.

70. Although I have visited such churches and informants have told me of others, I know of no scholarly studies of them. On the affinity of Anglo-Catholicism and aspects of gay culture, however, see David Hilliard, "UnEnglish and Unmanly: Anglo-Catholicism and Homosexuality," *Victorian Studies* 25 (Winter 1982): 181–210; and John Shelton Reed, "'Giddy Young Men': A Counter-Cultural Aspect of Victorian Anglo-Catholicism," *Comparative Social Research* 11 (1989): 209–36.

71. Morgan F. Simmons, "Hymnody: Its Place in Twentieth-Century Presbyterianism," in Milton J Coalter, John M. Mulder, and Louis B. Weeks, eds., *The Confessional Mosaic: Presbyterians and Twentieth-Century Theology* (Louisville: Westminister/John Knox, 1990), pp. 162–86 and 293–95, at pp. 181–82; Marsden, *Reforming Fundamentalism*, pp. 265–66; Warner, *New Wine*, passim; Warner, "Mirror"; R. Stephen Warner, "Visits to a Growing Evangelical and Declining Liberal Church in 1978," *Sociological Analysis* 44 (Fall 1983): 243–53.

72. R. Stephen Warner, "Starting Over: Reflections on American Religion," *Christian Century* 108 (September 4–11, 1991): 811–13.

73. Ammerman, *Baptist Battles*, p. 271.

74. Ellen M. Rosenberg, *The Southern Baptists: A Subculture in Transition* (Knoxville: University of Tennessee Press, 1989), pp. 103, 112.

75. Wertheimer, "Recent Trends," p. 109.

76. Lee, "Korean American Presbyterians."

77. John H. Lee, "Judge Rules Korean Church, Not Presbytery, Owns Property," *Los Angeles Times*, January 11, 1990; see also John H. Lee, "Koreans Sue Presbytery, Allege Bias, Deceit, Theft," *Los Angeles Times*, February 5, 1989, part II, pp. 1–2.

78. Dean Hoge, *The Future of Catholic Leadership: Responses to the Priest Shortage* (Kansas City, Mo.: Sheed and Ward, 1987); Gremillion and Castelli, *The Emerging Parish*, chap. 6; William D'Antonio, James Davidson, Dean Hoge, and Ruth Wallace, *American Catholic Laity in a Changing Church* (Kansas City, Mo.: Sheed and Ward, 1989), chap. 5; Ruth A. Wallace, *They Call Her Pastor: A New Role for Catholic Women* (Albany: State University of New York Press, 1992).

79. Timothy L. Smith, "Lay Initiative in the Religious Life of American Immigrants," in Tamara K. Hareven, ed., *Anonymous Americans* (Englewood Cliffs: Prentice-Hall, 1971), pp. 214–49; Jay P. Dolan, *The American Catholic Experience: A History from Colonial Times to the Present* (Garden City: Doubleday, 1985), chap. 6.

80. Gremillion and Castelli, *Emerging Parish*, chap. 2; Eugene Kennedy, *Tomorrow's Catholics, Today's Church* (San Francisco: Harper and Row, 1988), chap. 4.

81. Andrew Sullivan, "Incense and Sensibility: The Spiritual Confusions of American Catholicism," *The New Republic* 203 (September 24, 1990): 33–38, at p. 34.

82. From "Religious Organizations, Organization Theory and Social Theory" (paper presented at annual meeting of the Association for the Sociology of Religion, 1991), p. 9; based on Melissa Ray, "Blest Be the Ties That Bind: Interpretive Appropriation of External Mandates in an Organizational Culture" (Ph.D. diss., University of Wisconsin—Madison, Department of Sociology, 1991).

83. "Crumbling Pillars: Diocesan Leaders' Perceptions of Catholic Institutional Change" (paper presented at annual meeting of the Association for the Sociology of Religion, 1990), p. 14.

84. From an interview conducted by Carol Biesadecki and reported in "Why Do Catholics Float?" (B.A. honors thesis, University of Illinois at Chicago, Department of Sociology, 1991).

85. Canon law citation and commentary from Joseph A. Janicki, "Parishes, Pastors, and Parochial Vicars (cc: 515–552)," in James A. Coriden, Thomas J. Green, and Donald E. Heintschel, eds., *The Code of Canon Law: A Text and Commentary* (Commissioned by the Canon Law Society of America, New York, N.Y., and Mahwah, N.J.: Paulist Press, 1985), chap. 6, at pp. 418–19. I am indebted to Carol Biesadecki for this reference.

86. Biesadecki, "Why Do Catholics Float?," p. 45.

87. Grant Pick, "Resurrection," *Chicago Reader*, August 9, 1991, pp. 1, 20–28.

88. Haddad and Lummis, *Islamic Values*, pp. 54–59.

89. Waugh, "Reducing the Distance: A Muslim Congregation in the Canadian North," in Wind and Lewis, *Portraits*, chap. 10.

90. Frederick Denny, *Islam and the Muslim Community* (San Francisco: Harper and Row, 1987), p. 113. In a later paper, Denny observes that "Muslim legists are having to demonstrate, to themselves and their co-religionists, that such developments are Islamically acceptable." Frederick M. Denny, "Church/Sect Theory and Emerging North American Muslim Communities: Issues and Trends" (paper presented at annual meeting of the Society for the Scientific Study of Religion, 1990), p. 2.

91. Yu, "The Growth of Korean Buddhism in the United States," p. 90; author's field notes, December 4, 1989.

92. Kashima, *Buddhism in America,* pp. 184–89, 130, 135–37; author's field notes, September 4, 1991.

93. Anne Blackburn, "The Evolution of Sinhalese Buddhist Identity: Reflections on Process" (Bachelor's thesis, Swarthmore College, 1987), quotation from p. 71. John Fenton notes that "in America, Hindu temples tend to become like other American voluntary associations, and in time they will begin to resemble American synagogues and churches" (*Transplanting Religious Traditions,* p. 179). My own observations as well as those of my students suggest that Sunday is becoming the busiest day at Muslim centers in the U.S.

94. Paul J. DiMaggio and Walter W. Powell, "The Iron Cage Revisited: Institutional Isomorphism and Collective Rationality in Organizational Fields," *American Sociological Review* 48 (April 1983): 147–60, at p. 155.

95. *Changing Faces of Buddhism in America: The Dalai Lama Meets the Buddhist Sangha Council of Southern California, July 5, 1989* (Los Angeles: Buddhist Sangha Council of Southern California, 1989), p. 19.

96. William H. Swatos, Jr., "Beyond Denominationalism? Community and Culture in American Religion," *Journal for the Scientific Study of Religion* 20 (September 1981): 217–27.

97. John R. Hall, *Gone From the Promised Land: Jonestown in American Cultural History* (New Brunswick: TransAction Books, 1987); David Chidester, *Salvation and Suicide: An Interpretation of Jim Jones, the People's Temple and Jonestown* (Bloomington: Indiana University Press, 1988).

98. Warner, *New Wine,* chaps. 5, 6, 10, 11, and epilogue, quotation at p. 240; Peacocke appears under the pseudonym "Gary Armstrong." See also Sara Diamond, *Spiritual Warfare: The Politics of the Christian Right* (Boston: South End Press, 1989), chap. 4.

99. Cheryl Townsend Gilkes, "'Together and in Harness': Women's Traditions in the Sanctified Church," *Signs* 10 (Summer 1985): 678–99.

100. David Wolf Silverman, "A Word from the Editor" [introducing four articles on Ramah] in *Conservative Judaism* 40 (Fall 1987): 3–66, at p. 3; Wertheimer, "Recent Trends," pp. 127–30.

101. Troy D. Perry with Thomas L. P. Swicegood, *Don't Be Afraid Anymore: The Story of the Reverend Troy Perry and the Metropolitan Community Churches* (New York: St. Martin's Press, 1990), chap. 7; author's interviews in Los Angeles with Rev. Elder Donald Eastman (August 15, 1989) and Rev. Elder Nancy Wilson (December 3, 1989). The UFMCC has an increasing proportion of women among its membership, estimated by Rev. Eastman as 30 percent, and a number of congregations with lesbian majorities.

102. Sang Hyun Lee, "Called to be Pilgrims: Toward an Asian-American Theology from the Korean Immigrant Perspective," in S. H. Lee, ed., *Korean American Ministry: A Resourcebook* (Princeton: Princeton Theological Seminary, 1987), pp. 90–120; Young Pai, Deloras Pemberton, and John Worley, *Findings on Korean-American Early Adolescents and Adolescents* (Kansas City: University of Missouri School of Education, 1987); Warner, "Korean Immigrant Church"; see also

Mark R. Mullins, "The Organizational Dilemmas of Ethnic Churches: A Case Study of Japanese Buddhism in Canada," *Sociological Analysis* 49 (Fall 1988): 217–33.

103. William K. Bartels in the registrants' booklet for the American Buddhist Congress convocation (November 17–19, 1989), held at Wat Dhammaram in Bridgeview, Illinois; author's interviews with American Buddhist Congress leaders, Los Angeles, December 4, 1989, and August 29, 1991.

104. This is evidently the view of Ellen Rosenberg in her book, *Southern Baptists:* "There is a marketing philosophy behind it [Southern Baptist Convention growth]: find out who the congregation really is, not what you think it is or would like it to be, and set about meeting its needs" (p. 108). James H. Smylie finds such a church-growth strategy "troublesome biblically, theologically, and ethically, . . . because it fails to deal seriously with the identity of the Christian community as a community that is inclusive and that transcends the prejudices of race" ("Church Growth and Decline in Historical Perspective," in Hoge and Roozen, *Understanding Church Growth and Decline,* pp. 69–93, at p. 82).

105. Warner, *New Wine,* especially chaps. 7–9 and 12.

106. Troy D. Perry, *The Lord Is My Shepherd and He Knows I'm Gay* (Los Angeles: Nash, 1972); Perry and Swicegood, *Don't Be Afraid Anymore;* Kittredge Cherry and James Mitulski, "We Are the Church Alive, the Church with AIDS," *Christian Century* 105 (January 27, 1988): 85–88; Warner, "The Metropolitan Community Church."

107. Gay activists argue, indeed, that no one is raised to be gay; they differ mightily on whether people are born gay, with gay Christians for the most part affirming that they are (see Warner, "The Metropolitan Community Church"). A recent analysis of the controversy is found in Andrew Sullivan, "The Politics of Homosexuality," *The New Republic* 208 (May 10, 1993): 24–37.

108. Robert B. Tapp, *Religion Among the Unitarian Universalists: Converts in the Stepfather's House* (New York: Seminar Press, 1973).

109. See R. Stephen Warner, "Congregating: Walk Humbly at Rock Church," *Christian Century* 109 (October 28, 1992): 957–58.

110. Warner and Pappas, "Seeing the Word."

111. In *Brave New Families: Stories of Domestic Upheaval in Late Twentieth Century America* (New York: Basic Books, 1990), Judith Stacey analyzes the impact of such changes in the lives of Silicon Valley women of the working class and the role of their religious involvements in helping them reorganize their lives. See also Dan Morgan, *Rising in the West: The True Story of an "Okie" Family from the Great Depression through the Reagan Years* (New York: Alfred A. Knopf, 1992).

112. These ideas were stimulated by Deborah Sherman, "Becoming Workers: From High School to Work Among Black and White Workers" (Ph.D. diss., University of Illinois at Chicago, Department of Sociology, 1991).

113. I have in mind Rosemary Radford Ruether, *Women-Church: Theology and Practice of Feminist Liturgical Communities* (San Francisco: Harper and Row, 1988).

114. Wertheimer, "Recent Trends," p. 150; Riv-Ellen Prell, *Prayer and Community: The Havurah in American Judaism* (Detroit: Wayne State University Press,

1989); Shirah W. Hecht, "Religious Congregation in a New Mode: Tradition, Social Change and the Public Expression of Diversity" (paper presented at the annual meeting of the Society for the Scientific Study of Religion, 1990).

115. William Madsen, "A.A.: Birds of a Feather," chap. 9 in *The American Alcoholic* (Springfield, Ill.: Charles C. Thomas, 1974).

116. Thomas Day remarks, in *Why Catholics Can't Sing*, "I have heard a congregation of fifty elderly Episcopalians produce more volume that three hundred Roman Catholics" (p. 1).

THREE

The Christian Congregation
as a Religious Community

LANGDON GILKEY

The Problem

IN THIS ESSAY'S TITLE, "The Christian Congregation as a Religious Community," the important word is *religious*. Most contemporary studies of the congregation emphasize the last word, *community*, and ask about its structural forms (its polity); its increases and decreases; its social context and constituents (sociology); its modes of communal interrelation; its history; its peculiar narrative, images, and myths; its beliefs; its moral expectations, standards, and habits; and its most significant rituals and rites. These are all fundamental, even necessary, to its understanding. They are, however, not sufficient; the congregation as a church or embodiment of a church is of necessity a *religious* entity as well as a sociological one, a locus of the sacred or the holy as well as an embodiment, however unique, of communal relationships. If, therefore, we are to understand the congregation as a representative of the church, we must also reflect on how it is a religious entity, or, in special Christian language, how it is that God or God's grace acts in, is present to, or empowers this community.

The question of the religious nature of the congregation constitutes the discipline or subject named *ecclesiology*, a subject strangely ignored in most contemporary studies of the church. In most seminaries, for example, courses on theories of the church are now largely on polity, the inquiry into the structural form of the church: congregational, synodical, episcopal, and so on. Clearly what we term "ecclesiology" represents an inquiry relevant to every form of religion that is communal, for almost all religions assume some relation of their communities to the divine, the ultimate, or the holy. Our discussion here will confine itself to Protestant mainline congregations; nevertheless, even in this one stream we find lively and very significant disagreements about how God (or Christ or the Holy Spirit) is related to and present in the congregation. It is important, then, to consider this relatively neglected question: what is or might be the religious center of the mainline Protestant congregations in America, communities that are, according to all relevant signs, immersed in a "time of troubles"?

Paul Tillich, I believe, was the first to raise a troubled question about the religious reality of the Protestant churches in the modern West. In his well-known essay "The End of the Protestant Era?" (1925) he made a prophetic analysis whose accuracy in the American context has become fully apparent only since 1960. The church, he said, ideally combines a "Catholic substance," the presence of the divine in the community, with the "Protestant principle," a self-critical principle leading to a stance of repentance that "pointed the community beyond itself" to its divine ground.[1] Without the Protestant principle, the Catholic tradition, aware of its unity with the divine, points to itself as the embodiment of grace and is therefore in danger of idolatry. Correspondingly, without the Catholic substance, continued Tillich, the Protestant churches, bearing only the religious principle of prophetic criticism, are vulnerable to an inner emptiness and hence to a capitulation to the surrounding culture, that is, to receiving from bourgeois culture their sacred substance, namely, nationalism, capitalism, patriarchalism, rationalism, and a middle-class ethos. It was the actuality of this danger in Europe, and its possibility elsewhere, that made Tillich wonder if our epoch did not represent "the end of the Protestant Era."

Many an American in the 1950s, and I among them, felt the weight of this Tillichian analysis of the 1920s and asked if denominational Protestantism was not too vulnerable to its cultural matrix to be able to be fully the church. In *How the Church Can Minister to the World Without Losing Itself*, which I wrote in the late 1950s,[2] I expressed my sense of the vagueness, not to mention the elusiveness, in contemporary Protestant churches of what Tillich called "the Catholic substance" (I preferred to call it "the holy," on the inspiration of Ernst Troeltsch and Rudolf Otto).[3] At that point, with Protestant churches apparently everywhere expanding, this potential vacuum at the center seemed more to threaten the *authenticity* of the church than it did its *existence*, or even its social success. Now that the evidence since roughly 1960 indicates an unquestioned "external," that is, numerical and social, decline of the mainline Protestant churches, this point about religious substance, the reality or lack of it, or of some principle of the holy in the churches, appears in a new context: is this "religious vacuum," if there be one, *also* an important factor in the purported decline of the mainline congregations along with the well-documented demographic, sociological, historical, political, and moral factors?

It may be well at the start to summarize some of the objective evidence for this so-called decline of the mainline denominations.[4] Scholars generally agree that in the years 1900–1960 there existed what can fairly be called a "Protestant Establishment"; or, because the last two-thirds of the nineteenth century also represented a Protestant Establishment, this might be called "The New Protestant Establishment" (or possibly "the last" one). In any case, from 1900 to 1960 the memberships of these Protestant churches represented the ruling economic, political, and social elite of the northern U.S. They represented the owners and executives of most industrial and commercial properties; they were sovereign indirectly if not directly over most important political structures (except in the cities). They financed and managed the majority of private academic centers; most private universities provided, if they did not require, Protestant chapel services; and virtually all guaranteed clerical representation on their ruling boards. Finally, Protestants certainly dominated the majority of elite circles from coast to coast. The ruling classes in the United States, in other words, were mainline Protestants of one form or another.

Correspondingly their churches dominated the national religious scene, especially after their "victory" in the public eye over fundamentalism in the Scopes trial of 1925. It was the voices of mainline preachers that were heard in newspapers, magazines, and over the air wherever religion was represented; it was their preachers whose names were universally recognized across the nation; it was their leaders who managed the "important" religious bureaucracies and their volunteers who flooded (10 to 1) the mission stations abroad.[5] Two figures illustrate this dominance: in 1900, 50 percent of all college students attended Protestant colleges (the number today is roughly 15 percent); and in 1931, of 16,000 entries in the national Who's Who, 7,000 were either Episcopalian or Presbyterian, 2,000 were Congregationalists, and 1,500 were American Baptists; only 750 were Roman Catholic.[6] As historian William Hutchison has pointed out, particularly symbolic of this dominance was the now incredible "old-boy network" linking the nation's economic, political, professional, academic, and religious leaders into a closely knit, mutually respectful, and cooperative community, in effect a WASP oligarchy ruling economic, academic, ecclesiastical, and in the end political matters. Ivy League and Episcopalian-Presbyterian in the northeast, this network changed its denominational tone as it moved west, northwest, and southwest—but the WASP dominance remained from Boston all the way to Los Angeles.

Although the gradual dissolution of this clear pattern of Protestant dominance certainly begins, albeit hiddenly, in the 1920s and 1930s,[7] it is not until the sixties (there being the appearance of a strong religious "revival" in the fifties) that objective signs of mainline Protestant decline appear. Membership numbers in the mainline denominations not only level off but are steadily reduced; age levels creep up as younger members recede; Protestant prominence in media reports on religion vanishes; mainline Protestant dominance of the airwaves ceases and never even reaches the starting line on TV; and in education, church colleges steadily sever their ties with parent denominations, and large universities cease to nominate clergy for their boards of trustees, much less elect them to administrative posts.[8] Across the board mainline ("liberal") Protestant sovereignty over national cultural life comes to an end; by 1990 the Protestant domination just sketched seemed as distant and as incredible as was the social dominance of the churches prior to the Enlightenment, or the centuries-long Western imperial dominance over the entire Third World.[9] Clearly we live in a quite different era.

Basic of course to this dramatic shift in Protestant economic and social power—and so to the outward decline of its forms of religion—are changes in the economic and sociological status of Protestant groups. Protestants simply ceased to dominate American economic, professional, and academic life as they once did. Thus sociologically the Protestant middle or center collapsed. Other national, ethnic, and hence religious groups have moved into comparable if not superior roles of leadership in American society. First Jews (in the 1920s and 1930s) and then Catholics (after 1945) began to appear as participants and then as leaders in the most significant economic, professional, academic, and intellectual roles, and hence Protestants became only *one* group, often even a minority, in a much more *plural* social situation[10]—one now made even more complex with the upward movement of Hispanic, black, and most recently Asian Americans. The primary cause of the decline of mainline Protestantism is the vastly increased pluralism of American society in the social, economic, and political realms and so the presence of other than mainline Protestant groups at the various centers of American life. Protestants no longer dominate these centers but share them (as should be the case) with an ever widening diversity of religious, national, and ethnic groups—except, one must add, in the southeast and southwest, where the older Protestant sovereignty still remains, a sovereignty exercised, however, not by "liberal" mainline Protestants as much as by an unreconstructed and even resurgent evangelical Protestantism.

As America has become what its own principles long promised it should be, Protestants, who long dominated its life, have lost their central role and moved from the center to the periphery. As I have implied, this economic, social, and political pluralism represents a genuine moral and spiritual progress, a movement to a better, healthier society, one certainly more truly "American" (if the liberal tradition be right about America). Ironically, however, these same changes toward a more diversified and a more liberal society have given a new status—as a "minority voice"—and a "time of troubles" to those churches whose leadership, if not the majority of their constituents, largely championed precisely such a social movement into increased liberalism.

Clearly, then, the mainline Protestant decline is connected to the sharp dissolution of Protestant dominance in the economic, social, and political structures of American life. It is equally clear, however, that more is afoot here than merely a relatively "external" decline. There seems also to be an inner loss accompanying this reduction in external position and role. It is as if, now that they can no longer see themselves as the central nurturers and irreplaceable guardians of the nation's moral and spiritual health, they are now not at all sure who they are, what as communities they represent, and what their role in the wider community may be—as if, granted that their former sociological role is gone, no other sort of role, no "minority" task, is open to them. Assuming that this may be so—and data strongly imply that it is[11]—we need to give attention to this apparent diminution in the spiritual power of these denominations.

First, pluralism or diversity has implications beyond the mere loss of dominance of the former leaders. It also connotes directly an increase in what sociologists call *individualism:* as the number of competing groups increases and the relative status of each equalizes, the relation of an individual to any given group becomes less a matter of familial "givenness," of participation in a traditional status, and more a matter of personal choice.[12] Inherited and so unavoidable social ties to given communities recede, and self-direction in all issues of membership increases. Communal membership becomes a preference, not a matter of social or family destiny; it is contingent on choice and not on inherited necessity. Correspondingly, the grounds for such choices become inescapably those of self-fulfillment—what contributes to one's personal growth and well-being. The denominational community is in the deepest sense transformed into a contractual community constituted by the preferential choices of its individuals. Inescapably, therefore, not only does the community lose authority in doctrinal and ethical matters; it ceases to function as the supportive, nurturing, and rescuing community the churches have always been, even in sectarian Protestant history. Held together only by positive preferences, such communities are vulnerable to negative preferences—and in the vicissitudes of history, few communities can remain vital and creative under these conditions.

Second, the mainline denominations since around 1900 have represented religious groups interested in making major accommodation to "progressive" modern culture, accommodation in their modes of authority, their doctrines, their major ethical motifs (socially liberal: peace-loving, racially and ideologically tolerant, universalist, and so on), in a nonsupernatural liturgy, and perhaps most important, in their moderate, bourgeois, or possibly suburban lifestyle. Thus they reflected the moderate, democratic, rationalistic, autonomous, tolerant, and yet responsible middle-class culture that informed most of their members. Except for their theistic worldview (itself by no means to be taken for granted), they were in their liberal social conscience, their responsible good works, their (in principle) self-controlled personal habits, almost indistinguishable—except for their churchgoing—from the responsible, moral, humanistic, "secular" culture around them. To move from participation in such communities into a secular lifestyle represented a very small step, probably making a discernible difference only on Sunday morning. Thus as the possibility of these secular options became more widely recognized, and as the mood of preferential choice of communities grew, these groups tended more and more to lose members to the wider secular world. As the churches became in their fundamental ethos—if not in pulpit theology[13]—more secular, this slippage, especially with the passing of generations or with spatial and social mobility, became more apparent. Data indicate that the major losses in members of these churches were losses to the secular world.[14] If one assumes that the culture as a whole was also steadily becoming more secular—as most of liberal culture and most sociologists have done—then the problem with these churches is that they remained *too* religious to persist in an increasingly secular society.

During the 1960s radical changes took place in the general ethos of the country. Suddenly, from somewhere, new—or new on a wide scale—moral values became prominent, and older ones receded, especially among the student generation. "Make love not war" typified this shift, as did the sudden disgust with the materialistic, nationalistic, and racist culture inherited from the recent American past (the musical *Hair* and the film *The Graduate* provide two examples) and above all the sudden dedication on the part of many students to the task of morally refashioning the world's social institutions. The more liberal elements of the clergy had long supported these new values and this sort of social action; many more now continued to do so. But despite some important shifts in middle-class America as a whole, probably most of the older denominational membership did not share these new values. A noticeable gulf—apparent already on other issues in the McCarthy era—appeared not only between the generations but also between pulpit and pew, as integration, peace in Vietnam, and a more permissive personal lifestyle became widely championed. Note the total breakup, even reversal, of the older sectarian ethic: sexual permissiveness now joined with nonviolence; antivice legalism now sided with materialism and militarism.

The Protestant church communities thus no longer represented and mediated a common set of "American" values. What those American values in fact *were* now became (and still is) an issue of important national controversy, a debate that ran right through most Protestant congregations, separating the leadership of the mainline denominations from the remaining Protestant social and economic elite. Important parts of the churches were now openly critical of America and its mores; other equally important parts were increasingly defensive. Almost without warning the leading segments of the churches did not so much represent the dominant establishment as embody an anticultural *sectarian* ethos; they saw themselves almost as alienated "advance units" committed to the revolutionary movements of liberation from the oppressive elements of the culture as a whole. Union Seminary and the pulpit of Riverside Church, for example, not to mention Harvard Divinity School, ceased to represent the spiritual and intellectual wings of the American establishment (as they did even in the days of radical socialist Harry Ward and the young Reinhold Niebuhr), and seem now to have become centers of an almost revolutionary passion, concentrating their major efforts on themes of radical social liberation: black, feminist, Third World. The same could be said, I believe, of faculty and students in many less prominent Protestant seminaries. This is certainly an important sign of spiritual vitality for a "minority" church; but in representing a new and sharper division between clergy and laity, it is also a signal of trouble to come.

As a consequence, one feels that since roughly the 1950s the mainline churches have been riven by deep inner tensions: separations of generations, of laity and clergy, of congregation and church leadership. Instead of being a community that represents and nurtures a common religious and ethical ethos, a supportive and therefore needed communal "home" for its individuals, the church illustrates the tensions and controversies of the world. As a result, many congregations, unwilling to articulate these deep splits in a "Christian" community, repressed all this and thus represented, stated, articulated, and resolved nothing. To the hypothetical religious vacuum is added the relative silence in the congregation itself about these deep divisions—and since the 1980s is also added a deepening split, even in these churches, between a symbolic and literal interpretation of Scripture and so between an evolutionary and a traditional-fundamentalist interpretation of the Creation, the Fall, and Providence. The "conspiracy of silence" on important political, social, moral, and even scientific issues facing the nation, a silence that has characterized the communities most responsible for serious reflective discourse on these issues, really begins here.

We should note, furthermore, that churches are by nature middle-class-to-elite communities; they are moderate, rational, moral, and autonomous, like the class they represent. Their modes of thought, of decision, of worship, of song—of being—are moderate, self-disciplined, courteous—and unrevealing. Apparently it is hard for the Holy Spirit to penetrate into communities like these—as the vivid contrast with black Protestant churches, even middle-class ones, shows. Such people—and I am surely one of them—tend to form an "audience" in church, to listen, appreciate, and criticize, to keep their vices and problems strictly to themselves—as they would in a classroom or at the club. Only to the secular analyst, and possibly to the pastor privately as counselor, is the hair let down, are the onslaughts of anxious finitude, of regularly committed and so accepted sins, the abuses of body and of person, and the hostilities of the home allowed to surface. The mainline church community is probably the last place these are allowed to be visible—and yet all are unquestionably present; and certainly the church should deal with these issues if any community should. At this point one might note that the denominational church is too secular, too much like its surrounding middle-class culture, not religious or redemptive enough—if religion is to provide, as it traditionally has, the arena in which our finitude, our fatedness, our sin, and our death are brought to the surface, honestly looked at and confessed, and dealt with. Perhaps the moral silence on national ethical issues overlaps and unites with a religious silence on the pressures of the human condition, and in this combination the lack of a spiritual center becomes lethal.

I am voicing here the suspicion that in some respects the mainline churches are not so much losing people to an ever progressing secular order (as sociologists Wade Clark Roof and William McKinney seem to believe) as failing to rescue them from that order. Indeed, probably *both* currents are at work. The secular world of the West—scientific, technological, industrial, commercial, urban, professional, democratic, and humanitarian (the "secular order" of which the academy still dreams)— remains very powerful, especially to the educated professionals, the economic leaders, and the intellectuals of our world. To them the churches are at best a pale rendition of this world; what *assets* the churches may have for the wider culture are really secular (or "natural") in origin, whereas the *liabilities* of the churches for secular life are the effect of the remaining religious elements. Insofar as middle-class people come to view the world in this light (seeing religion as part of the *problem*), the liberal churches will lose them to one form of secular lifestyle or another—and there is now little in the traditions of church life, as we noted, to keep them there.

But another current seems also to be at work. The "secular" picture of a secular order now free from the former ravages of religion is a dream. Present secular society is redolent with anxieties of all sorts: its personal sins of abuse, of radical self-interest, of materialism, and of greed not only destroy individuals and families alike but overflow into our natural environment to despoil it; its technological advances pose nightmarish possibilities. People are hassled, anxious, guilty, lonely— tortured by their personal vices, their isolation from others, their impending deaths, and by the stark meaninglessness of their existence.

For all of this they need a supportive community, a community to rescue them from themselves, their talents, their weaknesses, their life—the church not as contracted community but the church as *Ark*, the church where finitude, fate, sin, and death are articulated, confessed, and resolved through grace. (There is every indication that the growth since 1970 of the religious communities of other, especially Asian, religions, is based precisely on this supportive, rescuing, and healing function of the community.) Proclamation here may provide such a gospel;

but only a rescuing community can embody this gospel in repentance, confession, and absolution. The secular world as a fallen world—and that it surely is—calls for a religious community of grace, devoted to rescue, just as the secular world as a wonderful creation of intelligence, moral responsibility, political liberation, and technological skill calls for a liberal religious community devoted to accommodation to the world's creativity. How to balance these two polar requirements is a trick practiced with accomplishment only in the Kingdom! I suspect that the mainline denominations have not yet quite found the secret of this paradoxical requirement, though a host of creative and courageous ministers have surely given it a try.

I have intimated that possibly the mainline churches not only have remained too religious for an evolving secular world—as many earlier commentators have insisted—but also have been too accommodating, too secular, to meet the new religious needs of a distraught modern society. This "guess"—hazarded long since by Tillich—seems bolstered by the concurrent growth of conservative, even fundamentalist, congregations during the recent two decades, precisely as the liberal churches declined. Every statistic points in this direction, even if the prominence of conservative evangelicalism in the public, political, legal, and media arenas did not already proclaim it.[15] Conservative churches have steadily grown in numbers as mainline congregations have declined; their laity are noticeably younger than the now aging congregations of the latter; their contributions are mounting as those of the others recede; and it is they who are present in the political scene and on the media stages whereas the mainline churches there now remain invisible and weakened.

The ups and downs of Protestant conservatism are not our present subject. Its current astounding growth, however, shows that modern culture is by no means as inhospitable to religion as was once thought. In fact it suggests that modern culture breeds religious enthusiasm as fully as apparently it calls for it. To be sure, these groups accommodate to American culture in their own ways: they are nationalistic, commercial, almost frantically materialistic and capitalistic, implicitly racist and exclusivist, and completely at home (as the mainline is not) in the media, in Wal-Mart and Disneyland, and in the eye-shadow culture that is also America. Whether these flag-waving groups accommodate more than do the dissident liberals is a debatable question; each one views itself as representing Christ *against* culture (and possibly transforming culture), and each sees the other as representing the Christ *of* culture.[16] These groups, however, leave no doubt that they *do not* accommodate their religion to certain clearly visible pressures of modernity. On the contrary their religion remains fundamentalist; and they emphasize and boast of their belief in absolute inerrancy, in a view of creation clearly at variance with science, in miracles, in the Blood Atonement, in the coming apocalypse, and so on—all of which represent the epitome of the antimodern. Moreover, they do not accommodate their stated ethical standards to the new ethic of the sixties (or before). Vigorously and explicitly antialcohol, antidrugs, anti-sexual-permissiveness, anticontraception, and antiabortion, they parade before us as representatives of "old-time morals" as well as of "old-time religion."

Theories about the factors causing or even aiding a large spiritual movement are always risky; they reveal as much of the worldview of the proposer as they mirror history's real causes. Still, it seems safe to suggest that a religious resurgence, even of fundamentalism, has religious as well as secular causes.

Our culture is full of anxiety; its admired creative powers in science, industry, and medicine are redolent with ambiguity, with possibilities of destruction as well as of benefits; our lives subliminally are surrounded by possibilities that are full of dread—even if we do not articulate them all. Moreover, the last decades have witnessed many fundamental changes in the social world that support or threaten us. Again, not all are articulated, but all are felt. The loss of Western and now even of American dominance of the globe, a dominance that the nineteenth and the early twentieth centuries quite took for granted and that most Americans still feel to be "normal"; the vast shifts in personal and sexual mores; the abuses of alcohol and drugs; the disarray of family life; the insecurity of almost every place after dark—these are not new to history, but they are new to these generations of Americans. An ordered, moral, "American" world, a world where we knew what was right, but even more, because of our own secure, dominant place, a world that was *established* and firm, has been lost almost overnight. An equally firm and definite "God of the law" might set this right; and correspondingly a saving, redemptive God might set us right. The need for an ordered world, and more, for "a way out," in a time of vast change and anxiety is very great indeed.

For this need, a definite creed about God and creation, about God's moral law, about sin and atoning salvation can become not only relevant but essential—especially its *definiteness* and its rock-hard firmness in a shifting world. If, moreover, it be the "world" that is so badly slipping, accommodation to that world has little existential or religious value. The world—its standards of credibility or of tolerance or its up-to-dateness—is now recognized as the problem, and a religion from beyond that world as the answer.

This, I suggest, helps us to understand the resurgence of fundamentalism in the latter half of the twentieth century. The self-understanding of a liberal, moral, reasonable, and autonomous community, secure in a reasonable and controllable history, is too vividly counterfactual to our time to be deeply credible, except with the upper bourgeois classes in that liberal, modern world. The mainline denominations "bet on" that world. As its products and in part its leaders, they could hardly do anything else. But its insufficiency in a time of troubles, a religious more than a moral insufficiency, is now evident. Here we can in part make sense of our paradox: the liberal churches that accommodated their gospel, their ethics, their mores, and their liturgies to the culture have not flourished as that culture became more and more secular. (Here the secularist will say: Of course not. Religion is about to go out of business entirely.) On the other hand, the religious groups that have refused accommodation to the culture, and have in fact defied it at certain key and public points, are growing: in numbers, in public recognition and support, in economic and especially in political influence. Paradoxically, as modern society becomes more and more scientific, technological, and industrial, it is they, not the "moderns," that now claim to represent mainstream America.

What the secularist does not see, nor perhaps even the liberal, is the radical ambiguity of that culture's life, its deep levels of anxiety and of anomie, its hidden layers of guilt, and its fear of death. To this radical ambiguity and anxiety conservatives offered a religious option visibly different from the culture and thus capable of promising the latter's rescue. To me only this understanding of a culture whose creativity (its rationality, moral ideals, tolerance, devotion to freedom) continually lures liberals to accommodate their religion to modernity, and yet whose deep faults cry out for a noncultural religious response, can make sense of the paradox of a declining liberalism and a resurgent fundamentalism. The mainline churches apparently offered nothing different enough from the culture either to stem the slippage to the secular or to answer the religious problems generated out of the secular culture. If this be so, we can now see for the first time what a difficult task faces those whose destiny lies with both of these communities, the liberal churches and the wider culture of modernity.

The Presence of the Holy

My thesis in the first half was threefold: (1) among the "external" causes of the decline of mainline Protestantism in the second half of the century were the loss of Protestant dominance in the economic, social, and political realms and the onset of a new pluralistic cultural situation; (2) an additional factor was the apparent lack of a religious and moral center, something both important and different to offer to the culture *from* this religious center as well as an accommodation *of* this religious center to the culture; (3) a consequence was mainline Protestantism's apparent failure to deal with the deepening spiritual problems of modern existence, problems revealed to be important by the sudden rise of conservative/fundamentalist religion. But how do we usefully talk about, locate, and nurture a *religious center* in our congregations? These congregations were charged to be creative and living *participants* in modern culture; they could hardly choose any other course than the "liberal." And yet here I am suggesting, nay demanding, that they be *different*, offering something deeper than, other than, the culture. Is this whole enterprise, then, hopeless?

The issue could hardly be more elusive and apparently intractable. Any number of approaches suggest themselves and then dissolve in our hands. The one I count on is historical: it begins with an inquiry into the "types" of *religious centers* that have characterized historical Christian congregations; it then seeks to assess our present situation and our possibilities for the future. Such an inquiry is, as I noted, "historical ecclesiology."

Three quite distinctive interpretations of the church as a religious entity, as the locus or center of the "holy," can be identified.[17] The first type finds the holy center of the ecclesia, and so of each congregation as an embodiment of that ecclesia, in the *sacramental presence* of the divine spirit, a presence guaranteed to the ecclesia insofar as the latter is in valid (apostolic) succession with the earliest church established by Jesus the Christ. Hence the ultimate importance for this type of a valid succession of bishops back to the beginning. Nevertheless, the center is the real presence of divine grace through the sacraments: baptism, confirmation, eucharist, marriage, ordination, penance, and absolution—each one veritably communicating healing grace insofar as each recipient participates "obediently" in these sacramental acts. The traditional Catholic churches (Orthodox, Roman, and to some extent Anglo-Catholic) also, to be sure, preserve, bear, and teach sacred dogma, authoritative teachings guaranteed to be valid by the promised presence of the Spirit; and they formulate and pronounce authoritative religious and moral (canon) laws. Both doctrine and law are, of course, quite necessary for the church and for the Christian lives led within the ambience of the church. But the central gift of grace and the locus of the holy—what makes the church a saving institution—are the presence in it of the sacraments, especially the eucharist where Christ's body and blood are present. The other central sacraments provide the necessary bases for this guaranteed presence: laying on of hands and ordination by which a valid episcopacy and priesthood are maintained; baptism, confirmation, and marriage by which continuing legitimate memberships are determined; and penance (and absolution) by which a lay population, prone to continuing sin, is rendered holy enough again to participate throughout their life and in their dying in the sacraments. One notes that none of this (especially eucharist, ordination, baptism, or penance) is submitted to criticism, testing, or reformulation by the "world." On the contrary, whatever rationality in doctrine or casuistry in morals may be part of historic Catholicism, this center remains (at least by the present pope) untouched by the relativity of popular revision and also by the shifting winds of modernity. Hence, furthermore, the primary locus of the holy in the Catholic congregation is the *altar* on which the body and blood of Christ are placed and before which the priest kneels as suppliant and as mediator. The questions for modern Catholicism, therefore, are (1) how can this sacramental center be preserved in a less hierarchical structure, a more lay-determined community, and (2) how can this center remain vital in a "revised" ecclesia that recognizes historical change and hence change in all the church's structures and expressions, including its forms of ultimate authority, its liturgy and liturgical sacramental rites, its exclusive rules of participation, and its surrounding ecclesiastical dogmas?

The second major historical form of the church centers itself not so much on the sacraments and so on legitimate apostolic or episcopal succession as on the purity of the Word that is proclaimed in the church. This is the form, of course, of the two great Reformation churches: Lutheran and Calvinistic, and their descendants. For them the church is the Church, the true church, if and when the Word of God—the apostolic gospel (and the law)—is truly preached (and heard) in the congrega-tion. Both add, "where the sacraments are truly administered"; but the key point is the presence of the Word, since for them no sacraments are "true" unless received in true faith, which is dependent on the pres-ence of the Word. Since the Word of God as gospel and law is present and available only in the Holy Scriptures, these become the concrete locus in the church of all ultimate authority, doctrine, and morals; the episcopal succession has vanished as the locus of concrete authority and been replaced by the authoritative interpreters of the Scriptures, the theologians and the preachers. Both Reformation churches were conscious of the necessity of good works, of obedience to the law of Christ, if the congregation was to be fully Christian. Luther felt this would follow inevitably if the true Word, both gospel and law, were purely preached; Calvin was less optimistic and insisted the church must stress, as well as the Word, the Law as a "guide" in the Christian life. The community must itself become obediently "holy" and must obediently harken to the Word—but in the end, even for him, the church's status, like that of the believer, depends on the mercy en-shrined in the Word rather than the perfection achieved through works. It is, then, the Word that is holy in the church, symbolized by the raised, dominating pulpit on which an open Bible rests. A major ques-tion for these churches in our day is how a holy gospel and holy law can be mediated *as holy* in the light of all the radical changes in funda-mental presuppositions—scientific, metaphysical, theological, politi-cal, and moral, and perhaps especially historical—that characterize any modern congregation's understanding of Christian truth and Christian obligation.

The final distinctive form of the church is what church historian Ernst Troeltsch called "sect-type"; historical examples were the so-called Spiritualist "left-wing" groups in the Reformation, some of the more radical Independent congregations in seventeenth-century England, Sep-aratist groups on the Continent (Anabaptist, Hutterite, Amish), Quak-ers in seventeenth-century England, and in recent times the (early) Mormons, Jehovah's Witnesses, and many other perfectionist and thus separatist groups. Troeltsch defines these in terms of their ethics, as possessing a "drive to perfection of life"; to me the center is rather the inward and empowering presence of the Spirit, directly experienced and so "known" on the one hand and empowering into a visibly new and sanctified common life on the other hand. Holiness here is neither priestly and sacramental nor doctrinal; and it certainly does not for the sectarian lie in ordination or in theological academic credentials. Rather it is *inward*, experiential, and moral, and thus it can appear quite without the benefit of ordination, of education, of gender, of class, or of race, and it appears only in human lives, never in material elements (wine and bread) nor in so-called holy doctrines. These groups are therefore originally egalitarian, democratic, classless, nonsexist, interracial, and frequently directly concerned with social liberation. Although they were not ascetic (they had families, and they plied crafts and trades), they abhorred violence, police power and courts, and any excess of personal property. They also shunned all visible personal vices and worldly display. Unlike the other two forms, which located the holy in a particular aspect of the church's life, here, because the locus of the holy resided in the experience, the conduct, and the lifestyle of the congregation itself, their common life was radically disciplined, frequently separatist, and dominated from morning to night by religion and its rules. To these groups, therefore, the modern lifestyle has posed the greatest threat. Most mainline Protestants, deeply immersed in that lifestyle, have been largely unaware that the basis of the "holy" in older forms of their own denominational tradition was represented by this same sort of separation, and hence that a major element of holiness in mainline churches has quite dissolved in the toxicity of modern life.

I have described each of these types not with the notion of suggesting any as an answer to our present predicament but rather for two more indirect purposes. First, it is clear when one looks at these distinct historical types, and then at any of the modern denominations (even the post–Vatican II Roman Catholics), that none of the latter represents anything approaching the "pure" form of a historic type. Rather each seems a combination of traits from these historic types, a strange admixture, if not in many cases a confusion, of elements drawn from each. Second, such is the character of that admixture, of that new synthesis which is the denomination as we know it, that our directing query—what is the locus of the holy?—becomes almost impossible to answer. The holy in *any* discernible form seems almost to have slipped away in the night; and what is more, almost no one seems to have noticed its departure or to ask where it has gone.[18] If that be so, we are now perhaps in a position to understand how it is precisely "a religious center" that more than anything else might be lacking in the mainline denominations.

The first point is clear enough: none of the mainline denominations represents an untransformed continuity of any of these three types, although in most cases the rhetoric of the churches about themselves would suggest just such a continuity. Most of them stem from either Reformation or sectarian backgrounds; thus they are on the whole non-sacramental and nonsacerdotal, and therefore woefully weak in liturgical weight or beauty. If there is to be a presence in the common life of these churches, one would expect it to be realized through either the hearing of the Word or the empowering and transforming presence of the Spirit. However, as churches thoroughly participating in the cultural, the intellectual, and the scientific life of modernity, their "doctrines" have been perforce "revised," liberalized to fit modern views of time, nature, history, society, and psychology, not to mention the relativism and historicism of our period. This is not a *fault* of these liberal churches; it is their destiny in modern culture.

There is, however, a price to pay: neither the biblical words and biblical sermons of these congregations nor the teachings present in the churches represent in and of themselves a holy revelation to the congregation, as they once did. Each of these is of necessity presented as being too historically and too personally relative, a "perspective" on the faith. Moreover such has been the general lack of interest in the theological content of the Word that few in typical Protestant churches know more than a minimum about either the content of the Bible or the theological tradition of their church.[19] Correspondingly, as members in good standing of chambers of commerce, professional associations, academic faculties, not to mention country clubs or their middle-class equivalents, the members of these congregations are more determined in their lifestyles by twentieth-century liberal or conventional standards and mores than they are by any relation to biblical law. There is little, except church attendance, that differentiates qualitatively the lifestyle of the members of these congregations from the liberal, responsible, and respectable, that is, moral, members of secular society. Their veneration of the Word may be inspired by the Reformation (as in Presbyterianism and Lutheranism), but their confessions are liberal and permissive; their respect for Christian standards of behavior may hark back to the sectarian heritage (as with Congregationalists, Baptists, and Disciples), but their actual "Christian" standards are now the liberal standards of the enlightened world. The denomination represents the sect type *in* Christendom (non-hierarchical, nonliturgical, nonsacramental),[20] yet, accepting the world and reflecting therefore its presuppositions and mores, it is liberal in doctrine and liberal in morals—a community church in its own spiritual substance and hence unable to rescue the community when the community's life is itself in disarray.

These elements of accommodation are, to be sure, essential aspects of these churches as modern liberal congregations, in tune in thought as in lifestyle with the culture in which they are participants. It is their destiny to live in the culture, to be a part of it in mind and in action, in their thoughts and their ideals alike. Nevertheless, it is also their destiny as churches to express there a genuine, recreative, transformative, and healing Christian stance, to be a *Christian* congregation in the world. Surely such a possibility is not confined to the historic types of the church. Nevertheless, it is arresting to note that at the points where preceding Christian congregations have received and experienced the presence of grace in their common life—and in these cases Word and Spirit especially—these churches seem to be lacking, to have ceased to represent the holy in their own tradition as thoroughly as they have more consciously *not* represented the holy in other traditions, for example, sacrament and liturgy. Hence we are left with our three queries: (1) where is the locus of the holy in the mainline congregations? (2) does their ambiguity at this point have anything to do with their present apparent weaknesses? and (3) what, if anything, might they do to improve this situation?

I might add that this problem of how to accommodate and yet how to remain creatively and redemptively "religious" is, analogically, the problem that Jewish congregations have faced since Moses Mendelssohn and that Catholics have faced in one way since Vatican I and in another way since Vatican II. The only difference is that these two (as relative outsiders) *knew* they faced this problem of "accommodate and *therefore* die," while the Protestants, under the delusion that they had invented modernity and so could safely ride that tiger, did not know it!

Issues in the Current Congregations

There is no way to discuss in this concluding section all the possible loci of the holy in the congregation: sacrament, liturgy, proclamation, congregational prayer and witness, lifestyle, and practices of spirituality or piety. I shall instead reflect on three areas central to historical Protestantism and, it seems, full of ambiguity in our day.

The first is the problem of the Word of God in the congregation, surely for Protestants the original and for most still the primary locus of whatever is holy in the church: "The church is where the gospel is preached and heard." What can this mean in our day? First, when both Reformers defined the church as the place where the Word is preached, they intended by "Word" a very strict theological definition, namely the "apostolic faith," a very definite theology directly expressed in the confessions of their respective churches. They did not mean "any" theology current in their day, Catholic, sectarian, or spiritualist; or, in the options of our day, liberal Catholic, neoorthodox, process, liberal Protestant, modernist, New Age, liberationist, feminist, naturalistic, and so on. Today in mainline congregations no *one* theology can claim, or would seek to claim, to represent the Word; on the contrary, any particular theological position is recognized as at best "a perspective" on the gospel and not *the* gospel. And all these perspectives reveal themselves to critical modern hearers as, for example, white, male, American, conservative, leftist, and so on. Thus as with the text of Scripture itself, the holy and authoritative Word (whatever it might turn out to be) is separated from the human (and therefore relative) words of proclamation; the latter remain perspectival, debatable, even controversial—tolerated or seconded; in any case, of little ex officio authority. This is not to deny that preaching can touch the vital nerve of a congregation, and often it does. But when that occurs, it is more an example of an act of the Spirit than of the proclaimed Word itself. Inescapably a contemporary liberal church moves at its best in the direction of a spiritual community rather than a community of the Word. At worst, granted this difficulty with the Word, preaching can tend to represent the peculiar wisdom or insight of the pastor, elements of expertise from the wider culture, or a bland and inoffensive plea for goodness of heart—blessings to be sure, but far distant from what the Reformers had in mind.

As is well known, this problem repeats itself with the issue of biblical proclamation. In historic Protestantism the confessional theology of the church was assumed to be *the meaning* of the Scriptures, *the gospel* of Jesus Christ. Now both pastor and congregation—insofar as the congregation is concerned with these matters—recognize innumerable theological voices in the Scriptures, and even more among professional interpreters of the Scriptures. Like the Word, biblical preaching is now a principle exemplified in a wide variety of viewpoints. The authority generated in the absolute claim "This is what God has revealed in his Scriptures" is now gone. There is much of grace in this development, of course: loss of dogmatism, of exclusivism, of intolerance, openness to much that is new, and above all a concentration on love rather than on purity of faith (doctrine). But again, there is a price to pay: the holy manifests itself here in a possible *inward* spiritual response to what is said rather than in what *objectively* is said.

Protestantism has always been based on *assent*. To be sure, *trust* represents the major ingredient of the crucial word *faith;* but personal assent is also necessary. "I hold to be true what I believe in faith" is a historic part of all of Protestantism, and the emphasis has been on the *I* who holds this to be true. Asserting something to which no conscious inward assent is given, and to which possibly a conscious inward *dissent* is made, is regarded as inappropriate, in earlier times as quite lacking in real faith, in our times as in fact neurotic or politically craven. One may disagree with any particular expressions of the gospel, certainly; but faith requires assent to some articulation of it, the inner assurance of the truth of what is believed. One consequence of all this is that Protestantism cannot avoid the issue, even the requirement, of credibility: what is said or claimed must be credible to all its participating adherents. Liberal Protestantism has followed this road to its end; its genius has been its courageous quest for credibility, for assent from active participants in modern culture, including changes in the latter. But in the modern age, this quest has set a most difficult requirement for proclamation and teaching.

Modern civilization is replete with a variety of accepted and authoritative "truths," that is, apparently valid knowledge covering an immense range of subjects: natural science, social science, psychology, history, economic and political theories, and so on. To be credible, any proposition about reality, human nature, history, society, culture, obligations, and future hopes must be in some general accord with this vast array of cultural wisdom; and as this wisdom changes, the proposition too must change. This is a taxing burden for each responsible preacher (not to mention the theologians). Even more it raises a problem in principle: if something is credible to modern secular wisdom, can it also be in some significant way *different* from that wisdom, different enough to rescue us from the latter's errors? Interestingly, conservative and fundamentalist congregations say something *incredible* to modern wisdom and yet gain the assent of their congregations. We are baffled by this, especially if the congregations participate fully in modern commercial and media existence. But credibility can radically shift its requirements if enough security, support and rescue come along with what might formerly have seemed incredible; one will pay the price of incredibility readily enough if enough of ultimate concern is at stake.

All the issues of modern theology—in its swings from credibility to revelation and back again, from radicality to conventionality and back again—are illumined by this problem. The most common answer is to serve up something that is *bland;* credible but inoffensive, thoroughly in line with the general requirements of modern culture, helpful perhaps in some general way or perhaps psychologically, but surely not the holy Word of God that might bring grace out of sin, freedom out of fate, or life out of death. Of course, as Tillich said long ago, the Word can be spruced up and made apparently vital by idolatry, by making an ultimate concern out of nationalistic, class, racial, or ideological interests.

One lesson is clear. In order to escape the slow demise represented by blandness or by the scourge of idolatry, and to generate a credible message that is at the same time a saving message, at least a modicum of theological reflection is necessary. The church as a center only for operations and groups, as an active community of good works inside and outside the congregation, is surely useful; but it cannot be the church of the Word unless some *congregational* and *pastoral* reflection is given to the status and presence of that Word in our time. How is the Word to be understood in modern culture, in relation to its own sources in Scripture and tradition, and in relation to all the other "secular" words—creative and idolatrous—heard in the wider community? A liberal church is devoted to credibility and so must accommodate to all these voices; its destiny and vocation alike require assent in relation to all the facets of modern culture. But lest it have no spiritual substance at all, it must also have somewhere a real Word. If the presence of the Spirit is to come in relation to proclamation and teaching, in relation to faith and assent, theological reflection is required on the part of both speakers and listeners, reflection directed to uncovering what the Word might be for us today. Theology won't save the congregations; but a totally nontheological congregation will be fated not only not to hear anything saving but also to become either bland or idolatrous.

This drive toward conscious assent (the essence of a liberal congregation), this telos toward theology, must include the pastor; but it cannot stop there. It must represent a *congregational* commitment and a *congregational* act, realized not only in intelligent listening but even more in common study and discussion, study of both Scripture and tradition. Such commitment is a part, a large part for historic and now for liberal Protestantism, of what is entailed in the "priesthood of all believers."

Ambiguity also appears in another locus of the holy in the Protestant tradition, namely holiness of lifestyle, of moral action. The characterization of the church as the Holy People of God almost defines the sectarian tradition and has been of extreme importance in the history of Protestant denominations in America, most of which in various ways stem from sectarian groups. In almost all mainline churches it is assumed that a congregation is "Christian" if and only if it is in its actual life in some sense holy.[21] The basic ethical question for the modern Protestant church in culture is, therefore, "What *sort* of life or behavior does this requirement of holiness entail?"

To the sects this requirement meant, among other things, denial of violence and even of self-defense, refusal of wealth and of status, and the promise never to use secular courts. But having joined wholeheartedly in "membership" in the world, few denominational Protestants ever entertain these radical options. (Members of formerly sectarian Protestant groups now make up the *majority* of the Protestant military chaplaincy, so thoroughly have they joined the world.) To this tradition holiness has meant personal holiness: "clean living," eschewing the recognized vices—drinking, smoking, gambling, dancing, theater, and of course sex outside of marriage. Again, although these requirements held firm in evangelical and in some liberal churches into the early twentieth century, as those groups have moved increasingly into the managerial and the suburban communities, first in the North and now in the South, the lay people in the churches have slowly relinquished these rules and accepted the more relaxed standards of bourgeois America (moderate drinking, moderate sex, moderate vices). This was surely the case with the "Protestant Establishment" of 1900–1960, and it has slowly become the case since in the South and the Southwest.

Only the minister and his or her spouse are now expected to obey these traditional rules; in other words, almost alone (like Cyprian's bishop), as a kind of scapegoat, they are destined to preserve the holiness of the congregation.[22] This move toward relative worldliness, even for the preacher-priest, has seemed eminently sensible to the economic, intellectual, and professional elite of modern societies, educated in colleges and universities in the middle of the twentieth century. An antivice ethic appeared to them in danger of self-righteousness, triviality, and irrelevance in the face of society's massive injustices, sins, and even more massive forms of suffering. Elite Christian ethics shifted radically, therefore, from interest in questions of personal holiness to concern for justice; love working its way into justice is much more important, all have agreed, than any rules of personal holiness. But the question lingers: if the churches are at best similar to the reasonable, self-disciplined, and morally concerned "world"; to, say, moral and responsible *humanists* (or liberal Jews?), what is the distinctive lifestyle of the Christian people of God?[23] And if they have *none*, where, for God's sake, is the holy in the Church, or, the more fundamental question, why have the Church at all?

The very creative answer of the liberal tradition in Protestantism has been that the church in the world or, better "the sect in the world," becomes the *reformist* church, the church devoted to the transformation of the world's structures toward justice and its relations toward love, "Christ not against but transforming the world." This new interpretation of the requirements of Christian life began, I suspect, in the reformist and antislavery movements of the nineteenth century, was first formulated in the liberal social gospel, was perpetuated and even strengthened (surprisingly) on a quite different theological basis in most of neoorthodoxy, and is now very evident in liberationist theologies of all sorts. Three generations of liberal church members, not to mention three generations of clergy and theologians, have supported and enacted this creative answer, with significant results in important movements against nationalism, prejudice, persecution, and cruelty and toward peace, social justice, racial and gender equality, and now ecology. It may be that this is *one* important source of the new social ethic of the 1990s. The churches have not by any means done all this alone; Jewish groups have done more, and now Catholic groups are very active. Nor are any of these issues by any standard resolved. But much has been done. Certainly a "prophetic stance" toward the worldly world has become, one hopes, a permanent aspect of the holiness of the mainline churches, an aspect they share with some evangelicals but not at all with the new fundamentalisms. This too—along with credibility—is their *destiny* as churches accommodating to the world they actually inhabit. It is a noble destiny, possibly only enactable if one is consciously a minority voice and therefore unafraid to sound an unpopular note. This is one real *asset* in the new status of minority; a self-conscious majority will always be ambivalent about this essentially critical role.

Two problems have, I believe, manifested themselves, at least insofar as this drive toward radical reform has come (as it has in some liberationist theologies) almost exclusively to define the church as church, as holy. First, this has become actually more a redefinition of the holiness of the *clergy* than a definition of the people as a whole. Social action, we have suggested, has replaced an older antivice ethic; but it has done so in the later stages of the development of denominationalism when a "perfectionist ethic" has come to qualify only the minister and his or her few followers rather than the entire congregation as equals. For actually this has been, let us admit, more a matter of pronouncements, of actions of clerics and of church leaders, and of theological proclamations, than of concerted congregational action. By no means have all the laity (themselves often among the economically privileged) agreed that the church is a community of radical reform, that it favors the oppressed, that its essence is its continual identification with those who suffer. More than the differences in theology and in interpretation of Scripture, this ethical difference, this different moral view of the task of the church, has created a gulf between pulpit and pew, leadership and laity, that has characterized mainline denominations for half a century and has vastly increased since 1960: in sexual morals, in race relations, in the Vietnam War issue, in family issues, in ecology, in economic and political reforms for the poor. The modern Protestant church, as a church type, a church inclusive of many in the world who are not politically, economically, and socially liberal or radical, must not be defined in terms of a modern "counsel of perfection," validly Christian as the latter may be. Even as a minority, it must be a church for followers as well as a church for leaders, a church for repentant, graced sinners—and so inclusive of liberationists and of those who are not so.

The other problem with this definition of the church's task, of its holiness, is that to the surprise of many liberals and most neoorthodox, our population finds itself burdened, maimed, and even in many cases destroyed by what can only be called "the vices." These are neither, as we thought, unimportant, nor are they easily brought under creative control. Nor are they very far behind "systemic injustice" in causing suffering; in fact the two forms of evil, institutional and structural, individual and personal, go hand in hand. Alcohol and drugs seem to threaten people of every class; abuse, physical and sexual, is rampant; and greed seems the approved national sin ("What is wrong with greed?" "You can have it all!"). As a result our families as well as our personal lives are in dangerous disarray, even where injustices having to do with race, class, gender, or sexual preference do not arise; and they are devastating where these injustices do arise. Sin and fatedness appear, in other words, both in social-systemic and in personal forms. The evangelical tradition and the liberal tradition each had one wing of this problem firmly grasped, but not the other. Even to serve creatively their now dwindling constituents, mainline Protestants must rethink the matter and the scope of their ethical task.

We return to the theme of the importance in Protestantism for congregational, that is *communal*, participation in the moral locus of the holy. And this congregational participation is central (as it was in theology) to both facets of the moral as here discussed. If the congregation is to fulfill its role as aid and abettor toward justice and liberation in its community, it cannot be only the minister—or the association of church leaders—who charts the ethical course, proclaims the moral obligations, and represents justice in the wider community. Although this has been more or less the case with mainline Protestants in the last decades, this pattern represents a non-Protestant clericalism; it also represents, in the end, political and so moral futility. Without the laity, the church's voice has in Protestantism little authority; correspondingly, it is not heard, much less heeded.[24] Most important, congregational discussion includes other professional and vocational voices, other gender perspectives, than that of the minister alone.

Ethical discussion of major communal issues (poverty, violence, abortion, disarmament, racial agendas, discrimination, peace) may well begin with clerical discussion, possibly in sermon, possibly in separate groups or classes (though in many congregations, even this does not happen). But the discussion cannot end there: the laity as Christian citizens are also called to reflect on these things, and to reflect on them in the context of the congregation, where the authorities of Scripture and tradition are easily available, if not so easily applied. But that application is the task—in ethics as in theology—of the *congregation* (not the pastor); at best the pastor is the leader of the congregation's reflection.

As we have reminded ourselves, sin resides not only outside the congregation, calling for the latter's liberationist efforts. Sin also plagues, warps, and destroys the lives of those in the congregation itself. No community is free of drugs, of alcoholism, of violence, of shattered unity; fathers, mothers, sons, and daughters alike confront addictions, be they to drink, drugs, or sex, which destroy relations and with them possibility and hope. And if sin is not enough, the weaknesses of finitude are also there: sickness, debilitating if not lethal, haunts every home, and no one, even in our age, escapes death—and if they do for a time, they face the possible horror of advanced old age. Fate, sin, and death are with us all, in the intimacy of the family as in the crises and systemic structures of society. Liberationist efforts, like those of the social gospel, rightly see the latter—and direct the church toward those social manifestations of finitude and sin. Without minimizing the importance of that concern, however, we must recognize that these manifestations of fate, sin, and death in personal life are just as real, just as devastating, and somewhat more universal because they stalk the homes of the rich and powerful as doggedly as they do those of the poor. These too are therefore relevant to the life of the congregation; as much as injustice itself, these personal crises represent religious issues that present the congregation with a fundamental vocation.

Here the congregation is not so much the community dedicated to the prophetic criticism and the transformation of culture, as in the liberal and neoorthodox visions, as it is the *rescuing* community, the supporting community: the community embodying judgment, acceptance, and mercy, and ultimately the bonds of love on the one hand and the presence of eternal grace on the other. This is the church as *Ark*, an image from the patristic period where the consciousness of sickness (corruption, decay, mortality) and separation from eternity dominated Christian experiencing and so Christian liturgy and theology alike. Sickness and death have been put off, ignored, often forgotten in our time, but they return; and sin as vice is ever with us. This rescuing role of the congregation is as relevant today as it ever has been. For most bourgeois congregations, I hazard, modern medical care, psychoanalysis, and the minister as counselor have seemed to suffice to fill this abyss. Experience, however, shows they cannot. Few addictions, cases of adultery, or examples of abuse are brought to the congregation in confession as they were in the early church; at best they surface in the secrecy and solitude of the minister's office. There are innumerable reasons for this silence with regard to the sins within the congregation itself, some of them good. But the result of this silence is that the church ceases to be the community in which the serious religious issues of life are dealt with. Along with the clericalism of Word (theology) and of moral action (liberationist efforts), a clericalism of grace seems to have afflicted our communities: the counseling minister deals with these problems alone, when what is needed is a community of rescue, a supportive people, a community to subsist in while the storm rages.

I do not know, but I suspect that here evangelical and fundamentalist communities more nearly represent communities of mutual confession, repentance, and grace—and so of religious support—in this sense than do the mannered intellectual and moral and therefore relatively "respectable" communities of the mainline denominations. In any case, this is an issue of no small moment for the congregation: here is the place where the existential reality of healing law and of rescuing gospel may first appear, and where the scourges of sickness and death may first be turned into instruments of grace.

Finally, I wish to broach the subject of *spirituality* in the congregation, or, to use the older Protestant word, *piety*. These are words beginning to be heard again in clerical and church circles whenever the deeper ills of congregational life are discussed; and it is interesting and instructive how quickly serious mention of these (by a theologian) evokes first surprise, and then immediate and ever quickening interest, as if here a real key to our problems had been uncovered. It is helpful to recall how peripheral these words were and for how very long. My father told me that President H. C. McGiffert of Union Theological Seminary came to seminary chapel at 11:30 every Sunday "so as to avoid all that liturgy stuff," and how he followed Immanuel Kant, who referred to all non-moral components of religion as "superstitions."[25] To be sure, liturgy and sacrament are not spirituality or piety; but in strange ways they are close, and these bizarre tales show us how far from these matters of feeling and experiencing, of public worship and private piety, much of liberalism really was—despite its Schleiermacherian origins. Liberalism concentrated on the credibility of Christianity amid the modern scientific and historic consciousness and on the moral works of responsible citizens in modern society. Perhaps unconsciously it assumed the self-sufficient and autonomous person of humanistic liberalism, and then asked about the relevance and possibility of religious belief and the moral call to creative action. If, by the twentieth century, the soul seemed to need healing, it was probably sent to the analyst.

The neoorthodox were hardly better. They were as much against mysticism as they were against natural theology. And although they did center their accounts of religion on *existence*, a deeply inward category, rather than on belief and action, this category had reference to the inward anxieties of contingency, loss of identity, meaninglessness, and guilt (and the religious answers thereto) rather than reference to the problems of nurturing, by deliberate practices of some sort, the inward life of piety, the experiencing of self in relation to the divine. Hence spirituality in the neoorthodox period appeared as at best a contrapuntal motif—also "serious" religiously but a quite different genre—to the new biblical kerygma and the new realistic theology, a motif witnessed to and borne by mystical Quakers like Douglas Steere and Presbyterians like John Oliver Nelson. Just as significant were the powerful "anti-works" currents of these neo-Reformation theologies. At best one might wait for signs of grace; or one could encourage faith by concentration on its opposite, *angst*; and possibly one might protest in the streets in moral obedience—or sin boldly with Luther! One certainly did *not* subject one's self to a regimen of spiritual works, a spiritual discipline, regular acts of piety; all this sounded Catholic and *felt* like an imitation of one's evangelical grandfather, neither of which was relevant or acceptable, if not because of one's neo-Reformation theology, then surely because of one's elitist repudiation of the naiveté of evangelical piety. In any case most of us, rationalist liberals and neo-orthodox alike, attended spiritual retreats as if we were in some foreign land, attracted by the allure of bizarre customs, impressed and even awed by experiences of communal silence, but quite unable to integrate these exotic practices into our paradoxical theologies and our active social concerns. The neo-orthodox emphasized existence rather than theory, but the existence we knew was more a *theory* about existence, and the encounter we treasured a *theory* about encounters. In Hastings Hall at Union Seminary few of us knew how to have an experience of existence or an experienced encounter with the divine. It took me several decades to realize this.

One should not allow a single personal experience, however typical, to be the evidence for a general theory, though it can certainly prove suggestive. Nevertheless, looking back over many sorts of experiences, I believe these reminiscences point me on the right track. Let us therefore try another such experience. My father was a committed American Baptist liberal. He preached directly neither liberal theology nor biblical criticism; but the theological world he lived in was built on the theologies of Hermann and Harnack; his sermons used the Bible as a modern liberal historical critic would, and they breathed a passion, communicated through images and analogies from ordinary experience, for tolerance, justice, human rights, and democracy. Like his friend Harry Emerson Fosdick, he was about as liberal theologically and religiously as you could get. Nevertheless he spent an hour each day on his knees at prayer, another hour reading the Bible, and each morning we had family prayers for twenty minutes. Every Sunday evening he taught Bible at the church, and on Wednesdays led the regular prayer meeting. Fosdick could recite incredibly long passages from the Bible—page after page, psalm after psalm. These were authentic "liberals," but they continued, perhaps almost without a question, the habits of piety, of spiritual nurture, that their evangelical fathers had also taken for granted. None called these "works"; certainly no one identified them with the spiritual steps of contemplation in mystical religions. But they were nevertheless practices of spiritual nurture, disciplines devoted to a continuing health of soul, like the exercises, the jogging, and the swimming that our generation has found to be essential to any health of body.

My point is that all these evangelical practices declined in the 1930s and then vanished without a trace in our World War II generation—the generation that emphasized existence but never learned how to pray. Most of us read the Scriptures only for the purposes of theological inquiry, of preaching, or possibly to settle a point in ethics. This is, I suspect, true not only for large numbers of laity (who assume that the minister is religious in this sense) but also for many clergy. I recall in a Nashville men's class after hearing repeatedly about "the power of prayer"—to these folks prayer of some sort, or at least "belief in prayer," almost made the church the church—I asked who in the class prayed. No one raised his hand. When, having admitted my own difficulties at this point, I turned to ask the minister, he had gone into the kitchen to begin the coffee. My experience is that laity are apt to leave piety and religious discipline, as they do Scripture, theology, and difficult ethics, up to the minister. In turn the minister, as a professional, is almost always asking how to bring about an "atmosphere of prayer," a "spirit of prayer," a "worshipful atmosphere" into the congregation. Few *themselves* participate, either externally or internally; few share in either the acts of spirituality or the experiences of spirituality. Whatever else is going on in the churches in theological understanding or in ethical ultimate concern and action, in most not much is done to nurture piety in the soul or to accustom us to receiving experiences of the sacred.

Once I became convinced of this vacuum at the heart of mainline congregations, I looked with new eyes on the curricula in our schools of divinity. Somewhat as courses on polity or church structure has replaced ecclesiology courses, so spirituality—the nurture of piety, or maturity of soul—was the element noticeably absent from almost all curricula I encountered. There was study of Scripture, of church history, of theology, and of ethics; there were courses in preaching, church management, and the education of children; there was strong emphasis on counseling and pastoral care as well as on social liberation. But there was little reflection or guidance on spirituality, on how the piety of the minister and of the congregation, either individually or together, might be encouraged. Only in historical courses on mysticism, Puritanism, and pietism did these issues arise—and in most (not all) Catholic seminaries, spirituality had been captured by the conservative forces seeking to undermine Vatican II. Things are rapidly improving in seminary after seminary, as I have recently found.

Another example: at a Buddhist-Christian conference in Berkeley in

1988, I was asked to present a paper on Christian ethics, to provide a complement or contrast with a similar paper on Buddhist ethics by a Theravada monk. I was fascinated by the sharp difference between our two efforts: almost all of my discussion dealt with the influence of religion on ethics: how religious faith might empower, guide, criticize, and purify ethical action in the world. I exemplified in a way a modern version of Augustine's "faith finding its perfection in love," or of Luther's "faith is the doer, love the deed." The monk's treatise reversed all this: all the ethical acts he referred to (the "steps on the way") preceded and made possible the religious: the slow discipline of the self and its desires, ascetic practices, meditative techniques of all sorts, acts of charity and confession, and so on. For him ethics made possible religion because it trained and nurtured the soul; how else, he asked, can we possibly move from our earthly, secular, dried-out selves to any selves worthy of Nirvana? I decided we needed each other, quite possibly I more than he! How strange that, however theologically *un-Barthian* we may be, we seem to think religion or grace will just hit us where we are with no preparation! How strange that with all our liberal talk of autonomy, initiative, and the importance of "doing," we never applied this to devotional acts, to works of piety, to the preparatory nurturing of the soul. Conservative and fundamentalist groups have stressed and even required such practices; their growth surely is partly a result.

What are we to do to begin to recapture what has been lost? For without piety, without spiritual discipline, and especially without any experience of the holy, the congregation will hardly find new life. This may be too personal a reaction, but I do not think a return to the acts of the evangelical past is feasible, at least for congregations that recognize their own destiny to be liberal in our general sense. In our present pluralistic world, however, such practices are fortunately not the only ones available; and many of the forms of meditation circulating in Zen, in Vedanta, and in Sikh communities represent perhaps more appropriate places to begin than do those religious habits of the Protestant 1880s and 1890s. Such modes of meditation (yoga exercises, breathing exercises, mantras, zazen, and so on) do not only create inner integrity and strength, an experience of infinity and eternal transcendence. They also are productive of community, of a sense of oneness in and through a common spiritual presence—an Energy that is neither simply bodily nor simply spiritual, but, being divine, participates in both. These are strange thoughts for Western dualists (and for an

American Baptist *or* a theologian) but possibly thoughts that can help us refind the holy we have all but lost.

NOTES

1. Incidentally, this same formula defines for Tillich both the incarnation and the fullness of revelation, namely "unbroken unity with the divine ground" and "self-criticism leading to self-sacrifice." The essay is found in Paul Tillich, *The Protestant Era* (Chicago: University of Chicago Press, 1948).

2. Langdon Gilkey, *How the Church Can Minister to the World Without Losing Itself* (New York: Harper and Row, 1964).

3. Ernst Troeltsch, *The Social Teachings of the Christian Churches* (New York: Macmillan, 1949), vols. 1 and 2, but esp. 1:328–82.

4. Mainline denominations are identified by Wade Clark Roof and William McKinney and by William Hutchison, and others as the "seven major Protestant denominations: Episcopalian, Presbyterian, Methodist, Congregationalist, American Baptist, Disciples and (later) United Lutheran." See Roof and McKinney, *American Mainline Religion* (New Brunswick: Rutgers University Press, 1987), esp. pp. 20ff; William Hutchison, ed., *Between the Times* (Cambridge: Cambridge University Press, 1989), esp. the introduction.

5. Hutchison, *Between the Times*, chaps. 1 and 2.

6. Ibid., pp. 3–6.

7. I refer to the increasingly evident "secular option" in intellectual and academic circles, in middle-class life generally, and especially to the almost total removal of religion from "worldly affairs" downtown and its lodgement only in the growing suburbs outside the work world, that is, the apparent growth in the United States as in Europe of a nascent "secular culture." This growth of the powerful "secular option" has been evident enough for over a hundred years in regions inhabited by the Protestant elite here referred to, especially in urban America, among the intelligentsia, and in academia. An interesting discovery of mine in the last decade or so has been that apparently the scope and power of this option were until recently quite unknown or unrecognized outside these "regions." Hence has the appearance in our day of "secular humanism" come as a shock to much of rural, small-town, and lower-middle-class America; and hence also the bizarre view that it represents a "conspiracy" of Darwinism or communism recently allowed onto the national scene.

8. See especially Hutchison, *Between the Times*, chap. 3, and Roof and McKinney, *American Mainline Religion*, pp. 15–39, and esp. chaps. 3 and 5; for the relevant statistics, see Hutchison, chaps. 10 and 11.

9. These two recessions are, of course, interrelated. Western technological, industrial, political, and cultural dominance over the remaining so-called backward sections of the world largely defines the idea of progress so common from the 1880s through the 1920s and 1930s; correspondingly the dominance of Prot-

estantism, especially liberal and congregational Protestantism, over other forms of religion—from Hinduism, Buddhism, and Islam to priestly Catholicism—was regarded by liberals as the religious and moral correlate to the first form of progress. Thus Ernest DeWitt Burton (president of the University of Chicago) could say in 1923 that, because of progress, the liberal, congregational form of Protestant Christianity would become the predominant form of world religion in the future. A worse prediction could hardly be imagined.

10. As one small example, when in the early 1920s my father was the minister of Hyde Park Baptist Church, many of the heads of departments of that once-Baptist university sat in the pews of that church, as did the presidents of the University of Chicago until 1933. Now such a relation between university and Protestantism, let alone a particular denomination such as the Baptist, seems inconceivable. The University of Chicago is not only "secular" but vividly pluralistic; few heads of departments are, I warrant, even Protestant. Correspondingly the congregation itself is largely evangelical, much less in touch with either the leadership or the geist of the university. Entering classes in the university in 1928 through 1936—when my father began his deanship of the chapel—were predominantly Protestant and, as at most Protestant universities, most students therefore participated in clearly Protestant religious groups such as the Chapel Council, did extra work at Hull House in the stockyards, and joined in Sunday evening discussions of the sermons heard that day in the chapel. We are now separated from this era of the "liberal establishment" almost as thoroughly as from its Victorian and Edwardian predecessors.

11. See esp. Roof and McKinney, *American Mainline Religion*, chaps. 1–3, 5 (esp. p. 150).

12. Ibid., chap. 2.

13. One cause of this remark is that while the neo-orthodox generation (1940–65) was certainly theologically less secular, their lifestyle was palpably more so, inclusive of smoking, drinking, card playing, and most of the other vices, in ways their liberal fathers never allowed themselves.

14. See Roof and McKinney, *American Mainline Religion*, chap. 5.

15. Ibid. See also James Davison Hunter, *Evangelicalism: The Coming Generation* (Chicago: University of Chicago Press, 1987). Hunter's book is very informed (theologically as well as sociologically) and perceptive, but the limits of his inquiry confine his survey to the most upwardly mobile and most "liberal" wings of American conservatism, wings long distrusted by the right-wing and fundamentalist movements.

16. I refer here, of course, to the typologies defined and illustrated in H. Richard Niebuhr's memorable *Christ and Culture* (New York: Harper and Row, 1951).

17. The inspiration for this analysis is Ernst Troeltsch's *Social Teachings*, vols. 1 and 2, esp. 2:328–82. We will not include the earliest church, the church of the first century, because the scholarship and teachings of each of the three types, not surprisingly, view that original set of congregations as having embodied and established their own type!

18. These two points represent the burden of my argument in *How the Church Can Minister to the World Without Losing Itself;* fuller vindication is therefore to be found in that volume.

19. Victor Obenhaus, *Church and Faith in Mid-America* (Philadelphia: Westminster Press, 1963), pp. 72ff, 152–57.

20. Gilkey, *How the Church*, chap. 1, especially pp. 18–20.

21. In fact, such has been the power of this tradition in evangelical and liberal Protestantism since the eighteenth century that the words *holy* and *holiness* have come to be defined almost exclusively in moral terms, namely as "a holy life." The holy as the numinous, for example, as sacred power, as therefore terrible, awesome, and so on, is regarded by most American Protestants, following Kant, as a primitive and therefore unchristian interpretation of holiness. For Kant's age, and for a host of Protestants after his time, all this was extramoral (and extracredible); in fact these aspects of religion were termed *superstitions.* The task of true liberalism, of "religious enlightenment," was therefore to expunge from religion all that was neither rational nor moral—all except issues of belief and of moral action. This stream in nineteenth-century liberalism became, it seems to me, quite dominant, and nearly expunged the "mystical" experiential strain represented by Schleiermacher; here was one point where Ritschlian liberals and neo-orthodox fully agreed. See Kant, *Religion within the Limits of Pure Reason* (New York: Harper Torchbooks, 1960), p. 158.

22. For examples of the "two-level ethic" (one for the laity, the other for the preacher) in moderate to conservative Protestant circles, see pp. 38–39 in Gilkey, *How the Church.*

23. I once phrased to myself this difference as "the furrowed brow on the face of the Christian liberal (read neo-orthodox), one who knows that, granted he or she must do right, that is, act for justice, also knows the ambiguity of all that he or she is able to do."

24. This "rule" seems to be falsified by the example of Roman Catholicism, where episcopal pronouncements (on nuclear war and on the economic system) have had both a stunning and a creative effect on a wider American discussion of these issues. There is, however, a residual clerical authority in Catholicism, where the episcopal voice is the voice of the church. How long this will last is an interesting question. But the rule surely applies to Protestantism, where the same positions long made by the National Council of Churches have just as long been quite unheard and unheeded.

25. See n. 21 above.

FOUR

Public and Private:
Congregation as Meeting Place

MARTIN E. MARTY

The Modern Situation: Dividing Private from Public

SO STRATEGICALLY LOCATED are congregations that most controversies about the social character of religious life must come to focus on them sooner or later. Sooner, not later, is the case with debates over the ways "public" relates to "private" in religion during the second half of the twentieth century. The individualist believer may insist, with the unofficial culture at large, that "religion is a private affair." The sociologist of religion may also discover a trend toward "privatism" in modern spiritual life. Even many congregants think of the congregation as a refuge from the public sphere. All of them do so against the background of a rich debate over public and private in history and religion.[1]

Unfortunately, the historiography of the congregation (as opposed to the histories of individual congregations) is anything but abundant. A contemporary sixteen-volume work, *The Encyclopedia of Religion*, has no index references to "congregation," "congregations," or "congregating," or to any of their synonyms. Of course, there is therefore no reference to "the historiography of congregating," the topic to which this chapter devotes itself.[2]

Prophetic and theological analyses of local religious gatherings, on the other hand, have ancient and honored roots. Thus the prophet Amos voiced Yahweh's rejection of "solemn assemblies" that had gone wrong. In the New Testament, the Apocalypse's critique of "the seven churches in the province of Asia," in early Christianity carried on the tradition.[3]

Social-scientific and historical inquiry of a more formal character, however, is of rare and recent vintage. The writing of histories which treat individual congregations is the great exception to this observation.[4] Even sociologists who focus on religious assemblies frequently complain of the meager attention scholars have paid in the recent past to the co-ordinated history of local assemblies of believers.[5]

The Framework of Contemporary Inquiries

Out of a broad range of possibilities, we are to concentrate here on only one dimension of congregational existence in the modern period and in America: the division between private and public spheres as they affect such organizations. Three phases of scholarly work provide the framework, some would say the paradigms, for writing today. This framework is made up of exemplars, which can be defined as "the specific, concrete puzzle-solutions which, employed as models or examples, can replace rules as a basis for the solution of the remaining puzzles of normal [in this case, social] science."[6]

No thinker has done more to contribute to the forming of this framework in America than Peter Berger. Since we shall be focusing on him at some length, it is proper to let him set the terms for approaching the modern distinction between public and private spheres. Berger observed, as do most social theorists, that in modern times there has been an increasing pluralism and thus, in certain ways, a secularizing, with this result:

> Institutionally, the most visible consequence . . . has been the *privatization of religion*. The dichotomization of social life into public and private spheres has offered a "solution" to the religious problem of modern society. While religion has had to "evacuate" one area after another in the public sphere, it has successfully maintained itself as an expression of private meaning.
>
> . . . The transparency of the private world makes the opacity of the public one tolerable. A limited number of highly significant relationships, most of them chosen voluntarily by the individual, provide the emotional resources for coping with the multi-relational reality "outside." Even religion has become largely privatized, with its plausibility structure shifting from society as a whole to much smaller groups of confirmatory individuals.[7]

Three phases of scholarly interest since mid-century are of interest here. The first of these focuses on exemplars or models which derive from the critiques of congregational life in mid-century America. At that time sociologists of religion began to concentrate on the mass of congregations formed in the burgeoning postwar suburbs. Almost without exception, as we shall see, these analysts located congregations in the private sphere alone, and then judged them for being self-enclosed in that sphere. The public realm was then the approved one.

The second set of models that contributes to the present framework emerged in the 1970s. At that time some critics of the public order began to see congregations more positively, even marking them as valuable if threatened survivals, using a breakthrough concept of "mediating structures." This meant that they were located between the private and the public spheres and found their functions in this zone of commuting.

The third cluster of exemplars, typified by the attention paid local assemblies in this University of Chicago–based Congregational History Project and the corollary Notre Dame Study of Catholic Parish Life, moves the program a step further. Contributors to these studies have begun to notice that congregations do more than merely mediate between spheres. They function instead in realms beyond the concept of mediation. Scholars find congregations serving as places or events where some sorts of public activity actually occur. For instance, the title of part 1, volume 1, of the Notre Dame study is "From Sanctuary to Involvement: A History of the Catholic Parish in the Northeast." The accent on involvement, with all it implies for publicness, also characterizes the accounts by authors of five additional parts of the two Notre Dame volumes.[8]

The Congregation as Private Colony and Public Irrelevance

To make any sense of these three phases, we have to become conscious of the fact, already implied, that scholars do work with frameworks, and that these are made up of exemplars, paradigms, and models. This is not the place to elaborate on that reality.[9] But it is important to illustrate the ways such frameworks influence analyses and critiques. A chosen example, the study of congregations in the mid-century suburban setting, is especially appropriate. It concentrates on that secular environment of the congregations which received most postwar attention. The publications of that period have influenced the vision of congregational existence offered by most social scientists ever since.

Scott Donaldson, in his accounting of the "Onslaught Against the Suburbs," goes so far as to speak of the "myth" that colored the research and writing.[10] His *The Suburban Myth* necessarily gave much attention to the fate of but one major religious invention on the postwar scene: the modern, suburban, residentially-based congregation. Donaldson and the critics he studied observed that congregations were often "the first major organizations to be set up" in new communities. They were designed to serve as active centers for "social activity, group identification, family counseling, and spiritual security." These local synagogues and churches, it was charged, soon denied their larger mission and instead merely took on the form of spiritual "comfort stations" marketed so that they could serve personal and individual needs.

In the works of almost all the authors, Donaldson alleged, there was a consistent view that "no breath of the real world penetrates [or was allowed to] disturb the vacuum of suburban religious life." Typically among these writers was Gibson Winter, who saw the churchgoers obsessively "seeking privacy" and expressing "a growing insulation," "exclusiveness," and "homogeneity" in their churches. All the critics accused the congregations of promoting the isolation of their members. Private existence came to be seen as the be-all and end-all of spiritual strivings.[11]

Peter Berger, who persistently explored the rationales for the public/private schism, deserves careful attention as the most astute and persistent commentator on the exclusively private character of congregational existence. Berger's book-length contribution to this first phase of study, in which critics concentrated on the privacy, insulation, exclusiveness, and homogeneity of local churches, was the influential *The Noise of Solemn Assemblies: Christian Commitment and the Religious Establishment in America* (1961). In that work he did not content himself with mere observation. He advocated instead the emergence of new forms for religious mission. These might give better attention than could congregations to publicness, exposure, inclusiveness, and heterogeneity—all necessities, thought Berger, if such communities of believers were to fulfill their mission in modern society.

"One important facet" of the problem meeting such emergent new forms, Berger wrote, was "obviously the relationship of these new forms, whatever they may be, to the old forms now institutionalized in our religious life [as in] local congregations, and so on." He noted that "in the minds of most people," and it was evident in his as well, "the problem comes to a focus (and rightly so) in the consideration of the local congregation," the institution to which most believers related directly. For most of the laity, Berger repeated, the form that "means anything to them personally is their own local congregation." He noted the existence of a considerable body of literature which promoted the "revitalization" of these congregations. But this literature, unfortunately, he thought, was "characterized by an essential conservatism concerning the institutional forms of religion." Thus it begged "some important questions."

Berger focused then on my own first book, *The New Shape of American Religion* (1959), which, he recalled, charged that "too often the critics of contemporary religion join[ed] in massive assault on congregation[s]." Their authors had appeared to me to be "new iconoclasts, [who] would shatter the forms that centuries have developed and that the good sense of [believers] has brought to maturity." Berger was particularly critical of one italicized sentence in *The New Shape of American Religion*. It read: "And I for one believe that *we already possess the institutions we need to undertake the religious task set before America today.*"

Berger treated such a counsel of "moderation and common sense," as being partly attractive but in the end "intellectually dangerous." In dictionary usage, to "undertake" is "to decide or agree to do; to set about; begin." Berger instead took the verb to mean that through such institutions American believers could "fulfil . . . the mission." Quite properly, on those terms of understanding, he found the proposal to be based in a faulty a priori. It represented a "morphological fundamentalism."

Berger went on to criticize another contemporary, George Webber, who had spoken of the congregation as a divine colony in the world. Berger discerned in that and similar analyses and prescriptions the characteristic "anti-empirical animus of neo-orthodoxy." That animus made "ecclesiology," of which the congregation was the prime example, "an escape from social reality," from publicness. Berger judged that the empirical reality was quite different than Webber described it. Far from being even potentially a divine colony, the congregation suffered from economic pressures which confined it within the private and thus self-serving realm. When thus situated, such congregations had to succumb to the force of local opinion. In response to such pressure, members had to spend their funds on their own buildings, in order to promote "success," which was the prime American value. Meanwhile, bureaucratic pressures from denominations also conspired to force congregations to concentrate energies on the promotion of private and local achievement and self-aggrandizement. The minister, the focus of all these pressures to produce success, had to summon all his industry in order to satisfy the interests of the privacy-minded constituency in the "valley of dead bones" which, in Berger's eye, the local congregation had to be.

"The sharp edge" of religious engagement with the modern world,

Berger concluded, was therefore "not likely to be in the parish." A sympathetic critic, he thought, might make "some hopeful concessions about the potentialities of the local congregation in the task of personal conversion." Everything else, however, including the public and social tasks of people with a religious mission, demanded new "supraparochial" settings such as "laymen's institutes, the industrial missions" and other gatherings of believers "outside the walls." Each alert local congregation, Berger urged, would henceforth have to "abandon its favorite prima-donna illusions about its capacities to make an impact upon the community."

Berger admitted that he found himself voicing a paradoxical conclusion. He claimed that he was pessimistic about the mission of congregations but was too conservative to wish them simply to be destroyed and abolished. His way out? Speaking of the institution of the congregation, he went on: "The clue to the paradox, of course, is our contention that the most urgent tasks before us can be dealt with outside the institution and, at least in certain cases, with little reference to it."

Where did that dismissal leave the local congregation? Since Berger was concentrating on the Christian congregation, his language reflected its practices. The congregation could "be left to what it has always done and perhaps will always do in the future—liturgy, preaching, the administration of the sacraments, and the like. But, *essential tasks of the Christian mission in our society can then be undertaken (radically, if need be) outside the local congregation*" (emphasis mine). Berger said that he wanted to be fair to "the aged and the sick and the emotionally crippled" members of the congregations, who deserved the ministry of personal and private solace that went on apart from the larger public and social missions. "So it is quite possible to concede that for some Christians the local congregation may continue to be the primary locale for the expression of their faith."[12]

This relegation of the local congregation to the private sphere left Berger describing an institution whose history would be of interest chiefly to pathologists and antiquarians but would inspire little curiosity among later historians. At that time no cohort of social history specialists of the sort who later would write books with titles like *A History of Private Life* had yet emerged.[13] Whoever would express scholarly interest in the public or social spheres of religious life would have to turn elsewhere, to the story of denominations, ecumenical agencies, "supraparochial activities," and almost anything else "outside the walls."

Often unexamined in the writings of that period was the assumption locked into such generalizations. Why give preference to the public? Why value it so? In some periods, it would seem, scholars and critics have shown preference to the public and at others to the private sphere. Around 1960 the public was consistently being favored, often unaccompanied by much of a rationale. Behind these acts of preference lie two grand early modern archetypes. For the first, the privileging of the public, Robert Nisbet, with good warrant, suspected a Rousseauian and Benthamite presupposition. Thus "for Rousseau the state is a political community that succeeds all other forms of community; the relation between it and the individual must be as close and direct as possible." Jeremy Bentham took this theory and turned it into an apparatus for modern administration. Both philosophers, said Nisbet, shared evident "distaste for the smaller patriotisms," including the church. In their lineage, he went on, "it is no wonder, then, that we see everywhere in the West how the ethos of the *public* and its supposed superiority in moral terms to the *private*, the individual, and the traditionally social and economic came to prominence."[14]

The Congregation as Mediating Structure between Private and Public Spheres

The American scene changed suddenly during the 1960s and the turn it took called for the projection of new exemplars or models as part of the framework for historical inquiry. If Peter Berger wrote the miniature *summa* for the first phase, he also wrote the pioneering proposal for the second, and deserves continuing attention. There were several reasons for establishing new priorities and assigning new premiums, and he grasped these well.

As one part of the turn, it was evident by then that the hoped-for supraparochial "outside the walls" religious institutions or "emergent new structures" had failed to emerge. At least they did not develop in sufficient numbers or with enough staying power for them to assume the tasks that local congregations at their best regularly undertook. As these nascent alternatives failed, it became necessary for those who cared about the religious mission to take a second look at congregations and their potential. Meanwhile, in their secular surroundings there were also changes. The liberal theological critics, on whom Scott Donaldson had concentrated, increasingly lost interest in religious institutions and changed their focus, or they simply disappeared into the secular milieu.

Meanwhile conservative critics, among whom Berger now positioned himself, also faced a new agenda. In this phase, the problem of the culture had less to do with the irrelevance of the private sector than with the encroachments of the overwhelming public sector, especially as these took the forms of bureaucracy and the state. Henceforth there was to be less criticism of religious people when they went about "seeking privacy" in contexts of "growing isolation," "exclusiveness," and "homogeneity." Indeed, said these critics, precisely the zone where personal, private, individual, and smaller-group communal institutions flourished was the one that needed protection.

Without dropping his critique of "privatization," Peter Berger now led in developing and pointing to the concept of "mediating structures." Donald L. Redfoot summarized the background of this new interest:

> Berger's political analysis may . . . be viewed as a search for structures that meet the needs for objective legitimacy and subjective plausibility as alternatives to totalitarianism. He locates an alternative in the division between public and private spheres, an alternative [Max] Weber overlooked because of his macro-historical focus. This division represents an implicit deal in the "cognitive bargaining" of modernity that has served individuals rather well. In exchange for the rationalization of the public sphere with its attendant alienations is a vast amount of goods and services that only modernity can supply. Moreover, the surrender of the ability to engage in "individually differentiated behavior" in the public sphere is compensated by time off when individuals have considerable control over their lives to pursue activities which are meaningful to them. This deal works, says Berger, because of the pivotal role played by "mediating structures" such as families, neighborhoods, churches [=local congregations], and voluntary associations. These institutions mediated between megastructures and the individual, providing plausibility structures for the lives of individuals, on the one hand, and moral sustenance, on the other hand, to megastructures which would otherwise be experienced as hostile, alien forces without legitimacy.[15]

Following this political argument, Berger maintained that modernity set forth forces which have threatened these mediating structures. When people have no barriers between themselves and the state, they are tempted to drift into support of totalitarian political structures. For Berger and his intellectual kin, "the attractiveness of totalitarianism—whether instituted under left-wing or right-wing banners—is that it overcomes the dichotomy of private and public existence by imposing on life one comprehensive order of meaning."[16] In Berger's view, liberal intellectuals were on the other hand promoting "the equality of all life styles" in law and polity and thus were exaggerating individual liberation. In so doing they were undermining family, neighborhood, congregations and other mediating structures. These intellectuals consistently demanded freedom *from* such structures.

The second set of alleged underminers were members of what Berger called a "new class." They derived their livelihood from the acts of producing and distributing symbolic knowledge. In the course of such work they acquired inordinate power and a distorted angle of vision. He charged that they supported governmental expansion in the delivery of many kinds of services that structures such as congregations had provided. Such expansion benefited these members of the new class and thus rendered mediating structures irrelevant.

The third set of people who merited criticism for undercutting such structures were reactionaries who saw modernity itself as a total threat. Berger, positioning himself in the center, considered that these antimodern, antilibertarian "neotraditionalists" were at home on both the political right and left. Whereas the accused who belonged in the first two groups tended to dissolve the private into the public sphere, this third group would resist the public and be engrossed only in the private.

As Redfoot observed, when Berger moved from sociological description to moral advocacy, he supported the strengthening of mediating structures. This meant promoting a strategy which called for "capturing the middle ground" in order to promote human freedom. In partnership with Richard John Neuhaus, Berger advocated a search for such freedom within the plurality of "pluralistic" mediating structures like congregations. "Liberation is not escape from particularity but discovery of the particularity that fits."[17]

In this advocacy of the congregation as one of the prime mediating structures, Berger helped provide a charter for extending scholarly inquiry directed to local religious institutions. Such a move would give encouragement to endeavors like this Congregational History Project. "Religious institutions form by far the largest network of voluntary associations in American history," and thus merited study. "Yet," came his complaint, "for reasons both ideological and historical, their role is frequently belittled or totally overlooked in discussions of social policy."

The joint authors of this argument published in 1977 focused on the two spheres that had long preoccupied Berger and a generation of sociologists, political thinkers, and theologians: "The view that the public sphere is synonymous with the government of the formal polity of the society has been especially effective in excluding religion from considerations of public policy." The various privileged theories of secularization also biased intellectuals against the idea of finding power in religious institutions. More relevant in the present context: Berger and Neuhaus charged that there was current a second assumption, "that religion deals purely with the private sphere and is therefore irrelevant to public policy." That assumption "must also be challenged." True, many specifically religious activities had been largely privatized, but that fact did not make them irrelevant to public policy. To illustrate this point, Berger and Neuhaus quickly moved beyond concern for congregations as such and discussed political issues.[18]

This second phase of discussion concerning the relations of private to public would not by itself do justice to all the concerns evident in projects such as the Chicago and Notre Dame congregational studies. A major reason for this can be seen if one pays attention to a limitation implicit in Berger's definition of mediating structures. He described them as "those institutions standing between the individual in his private life and the large institutions of public life." These institutions resulted from the oft-repeated observation that "modernization brings about an historically unprecedented dichotomy between public and private life." On one hand is the *megastructure,* while on the other is "that modern phenomenon called private life." Now "for the individual in modern society, life is an ongoing migration between these two spheres, public and private." Life is seen as "hard" in the megastructures and "soft" in private life; it is unsatisfactory in the former and unreliable in the latter. The result of the migrating would be a need for a perpetual "balancing act," were it not for mediating structures which alleviate each facet of the double crisis of modern society.[19]

For all its contribution to a new charter for congregational studies, however, limitations are apparent when one uses this framework for contemporary inquiry. Faithful to empirical reality as it may still be from one point of view, it must be noted that these descriptions and prescriptions are more closely wedded to political interests than to inquiries concerning the nature of congregations on their own terms. The intent had been to promote three propositions: "Mediating structures are essential for a democratic society. Public policy should protect and foster mediating structures. Wherever possible, public policy should utilize mediating structures for the realization of social purposes."[20] It is clear

that "society," "public policy," and "social purposes" were the dominating interests. Such an approach inspires curiosity about "mediating
structures" chiefly for the service of these political interests, because
congregation-like structures are to be seen "standing between" two
other realities.

American revivalists used to speak of people standing in a temporal
situation of "betweenity."[21] Mediating structures, when viewed chiefly
in the context of social and political criticism, suffer relatively from their
location in a spacial "in betweenity." In that circumstance they still
would inspire less curiosity than would the two spheres they connect.
Historians writing about congregations solely in such terms would not
satisfy what anthropologists call the "agents' description," the views
held by congregants themselves. The narratives in the Congregational
History Project find their authors addressing congregations not because
they are "standing" between other spheres to serve the purposes of
those spheres. Instead, they appear to be dynamic agencies which on
their own terms also have their own purposes, be these personal, sociological, theological, spiritual, or whatever. Very few of the priests and
congregations about whom the Notre Dame historians wrote expressed
much interest in seeing themselves in functions of mediating, though
they were often effectively doing so. Very few of the religious leaders or
laity who appear in the first volume of *American Congregations* evidence
much interest, explicitly or implicitly, in finding themselves keeping
megastructures off at some mediated distance, or serving the private
sphere for social and political purposes.

For comparative light on the subject, a picture comes to mind from
the oral tradition of the late theologian Joseph Sittler. He remarked on
how religious leaders of mediating structures *as* mediating structures—
though he did not use that term—would in that posture have to see
themselves acting out roles much like those of parking attendants in
multistory urban garages. Inept drivers characteristically come to the
entrance, yielding their autos and keys, to return hours later at the exit
to retrieve them. Meanwhile, the attendants take over as the experts,
indeed, as virtuosos at the art of parking, wizards at backing, demons at
racing, shamans of shoehorning automobiles between pillars and posts,
and rhetoricians of skill in arguing that it was not *they* who dented the
customers' autos. But Sittler also pictured these artists of parking peer-
ing down, now and then, from the upper stories, moved by envy for
the people in the traffic who, with less expertise and often no sense of

destination, were actually *getting* somewhere. Congregants are not content to see their gatherings exist chiefly as connectors.

The Congregation: The Meeting Where Public Religious Life Begins

The participants in congregational life and the historians who study them, their participations, and their social forms, have begun to see ways in which they have an integrity of their own. Without abandoning the legitimate and often urgent implicit criticisms of congregations for their devotion to the private sphere, they position themselves somewhat differently than did the earlier social scientists who spoke of "mediating structures." In recent decades, some things have happened in social-scientific analysis and in the experience of religious people to call forth still another phase of inquiry, as exemplified in the present study. We can isolate at least three new circumstances.

First, the private sphere has become ever more private, also in religious matters. The critics of suburban and other prospering religious institutions after mid-century found their adherents too preoccupied with the self-enclosed and self-seeking group. But then, at least groups of some sort were still normative. The question back then had to do with the integrity of what went on "within the walls," and thus in the privacy of the congregations on one hand or, on the other, "outside the walls," in supraparochial but still communal and social expressions of religion.

In recent decades most observers and critics have seen the religious impulses, energies, and expressions of millions go off into utterly private realms of experience. Peter Berger's own sometime intellectual partner, Thomas Luckmann, had provided the most profound theoretical probe of this trend in late modern industrial societies in his *The Invisible Religion*.[22] Berger himself often joined in the analyses of religious forms which often became entirely eclectic, individualized, "privatized." Louis Dupré rendered this social trend personal, and in doing so explained the moments when involvement with a group was attractive to seekers:

> "The religious person embraces [in that circumstance] only those doctrines which cast light upon his inner awareness, joins only those groups to which he or she feels moved from within, and performs only those acts which express his self-transcendence." The external and institutional elements of religion seem to have been reduced to an instrumental role. . . . The center of gravity had to shift from the objective institution to the subjective individual.[23]

Privatization in such cases had proceeded so far that the very idea of affiliation with a religious institution, especially a congregation, was itself a kind of exceptional (Berger would once have said "vocational") act, a mutation, a surprise, a phenomenon that needed to be explained and could no longer be taken for granted. On one occasion, writing on a Minnesota survey, I proposed such colloquial terms as "do-it-yourself religiosity" and "pick-and-choose" religion to describe the privatized set of choices in which congregational participation now seemed to be arbitrary, accidental, and chosen.[24]

Critical observations of pure privatism reached a kind of classical status when Robert N. Bellah and his colleagues came across one Sheila Larson. She described her private faith as "Sheilaism," a faith not expressed through religious institutions at all but through "just my own little voice." Bellah and his colleagues, musing on Sheilaism, made a historical comparison when they asked how "the tight linkage of religion and public life that characterized the early New England 'standing order'," one that survived through the eighteenth century, had finally come to this present state. Now, in privatization theory and the practice of millions, institutional religion of even the basic congregational sort had become "segmented and privatized." The authors traced a long development which need not occupy us here, but one which illustrates why in recent decades the congregation has come to be seen less as the "colony" or refuge for private faith and instead is *itself* an expression of a kind of public commitment.[25]

To summarize the implications of this first observation: political interests motivated some scholars to see how to ward off the oppressive and encroaching reach of the public "megastructures." It was then natural to look for congregations of faith to serve as "mediating structures" and to be content with where they "stand" in their "betweenity." But when religious and social interests motivate such scholars to see what had once been publics now "cocooning"—to use one word in vogue in the years of this study—and withdrawing into virtual solipsism in their religious pursuits, the congregation appeared to be less a mediator between spheres and more as itself an important first expression of a public commitment, albeit of a particular sort. (All public commitments are of particular sorts.)

Now, second: *For public religious expression, supraparochial organizations in the course of time saw their own strategic potential and practical activity reduced.* We have already mentioned that after mid-century, "emergent new structures for mission" largely failed to emerge or survive. In their

145

absence the existing congregations appeared to demonstrate compara-
tively more potential than did the utopian alternatives which had the
advantage of being ideal but were not available in any numbers for realistic appraisal. (This is not to say that those who favor religious institutions should not hope for such structures still to emerge; it is only to
note that observers are now more realistic about the congregational
base, resource, and connection needed consistently for these alternatives to develop and to be sustained alongside them.)

If the "supraparochial" structures did not emerge in intimate congregation-like forms, the larger *denominational* and *ecumenical* institutions also later in the century experienced some dwindling of their
power and promise. At the time of the earlier, mid-century critiques of
suburban and other "exclusive, insulated" local institutions, it had appeared to many social scientists and religious strategists that supra-
parochialism could also find vital expression in these connecting and
sometimes hierarchical agencies. Almost all of these major institutions
survived: near the century's end there were not now fewer denominations than before. Ecumenical organizations remained on the scene. But
any number of factors reduced their place. First among these factors
were massive reactions against the bureaucratization of religion. Add to
these the rejections of or acts of creative foot-dragging in the face of
assertions of power from leadership that was in remote and presumably out-of-touch circumstances. "Rome," "Constantinople," "Geneva,"
"Canterbury," "Jerusalem" and the like may have symbolic importance,
but in most cases they no longer commanded reflexive obedience. Their
leaders were unable effectively to persuade local congregations simply
to comply with their directives.

Along with this spirit of rejection or mistrust, there was a second
obvious factor: economics in American synagogue and church life mili-
tates against the channeling of locally gathered funds to remote larger
institutions when the local needs cannot be met. Or, if that observation
by itself sounds too institutionally self-serving, one might also note that
congregations often find their mission and express their stewardship
through instrumentalities of their own choosing, whether they direct
these to the immediate environment or to national or international ven-
ues far away.

Sociologist Robert Wuthnow has written with impressive documen-
tation and at considerable length about "The Declining Significance of
Denominationalism." Denominations had been the primary alternative

to local congregational life, and had a somewhat more public character, according to presumptions.[26]

Wuthnow helped set the stage for the newer research agenda when he described "The Growth of Special Purpose Groups," again at chapter length. These groups were indeed "supraparochial" expressions of America's long-term ability to invent voluntary associations to achieve particular purposes. They also satisfied their billing as having public implications, since most of them were and are designed to alter the circumstances and thinking of people beyond the private circle: through mission, education, reform, or legislation. These organizations are in many ways the result of the "pick and choose" impulse just as are the congregational choices people make. Many involve only responses to mailings, receipt of periodicals, and participation through listening to radio or watching television.[27] That these forms of supraparochial "parachurch" institutions meet the criteria of offering a public engagement is obvious. The fact also has historiographical implications. Participation in these, however, is more a challenge to denominations than to congregations, Wuthnow observed.[28]

Wuthnow pointed to some elements of this form of supraparochial or extracongregational religion that have a bearing on our mainly historiographical subject. How are these agencies "public"? Wuthnow wrote: "Almost by definition, these groups appeal to narrower segments of the population" than do denominations or congregations, which are themselves "publics" of sorts. Yet, "as far as the society as a whole is concerned, these organizations may be the ones that increasingly define the public role of American religion." That is why historians have paid them so much attention, from the rise of voluntary associations two centuries ago into the recent past. Political historians turn to them as social historians do to congregations.

At the same time, Wuthnow saw that these special-purpose groups themselves have in many instances "added further layers of bureaucracy to the already highly bureaucratized structure of American religion" and thus relate in a way to the "megastructural" world that Berger criticized when he looked to congregations for mediation. And, Wuthnow went on, "to the extent that these groups have distinct, specialized identities and distinct constituencies, they drive a potential wedge between the two emphases that have been precariously welded together in most denominational bodies and local churches." They are concrete and programmatic, and often leave only "traditional teaching and preaching functions to the churches," thus widening the gap between these religious institutions and public life.[29]

What is evident in the historiography of American religion is that a somewhat different set of interests and even techniques comes into play when historians study the supraparochial and paradenominational forms than when they concentrate on local congregations or historic denominations. The modes of involvement by participants tend to differ, depending upon the structure of the agency, and these differences demand attention. Sociologist William Stephenson provided one handle on this phenomenon when he offered a distinction between agencies that are developed by "convergent selectivity" and those that operate by "social control." Most of the access to the "special-purpose groups" is of the "convergent selectivity" sort. That is, clients, constituents, consumers, or caucus members "converge" on a project or an appeal by twisting a radio or television dial, buying a book, or sending in financial contributions—but not necessarily by ever meeting each other or forming even a miniature "public" of their own:

> The principle of social control is made manifest in our inner beliefs and values. It gives us our religious belief, our political faith, our status and place in life. Depending upon the region in which we live, each of us follows the same customs, worships the same God, and has the same basic way of life. These are all subject to social control. The principle of convergent selectivity is very different. It concerns new or non-customary modes of behavior, our fads and fancies, which allow us opportunities to exist for ourselves, to please ourselves, free to a degree from social control. It is here [thus] that mass communication is important, and, as will be shown, in a fundamental way.[30]

A third reason for fresh interest in forms like the congregation as public expressions results from *a growing awareness that there are many kinds of publics.* The critics of religious congregations after mid-century, in the nature of the case, were usually academic intellectuals who were poised to deal with "mega-" and "macro-" structures and expressions. To them the public was located in these structures. This meant that whatever in a congregation was not designed to address the mass society or the largest and most diverse aggregates of people seemed to them to be relatively trivial. Congregations suffered by comparison to what occurred on the larger stage.

The notion of the "public," however, had not always been conceived on such a grand scale. Sociologist Stephenson turned historian for a moment to recall the roots of the public concept in ancient Greece. "Publics, traditionally, have concerned issues, controversies, faiths, and ideologies. People were supposed to get together to discuss courses of action for their mutual well-being, to share ideas, and to make concessions, so that after due consideration they might act collectively." This kind of gathering occurred precisely in congregations, now seen *as* publics of their own. They are not merely mediating structures which acquire their status from the undifferentiated megastructural world to which they carry reports of private life and against which they shield private persons. Stephenson did not agree with the idea that the "mass," which is differently conceived than the "public," exists only to be manipulated. The reality of mass society can offer citizens a certain element of freedom, as expressed in acts of convergent selectivity. Still, there is something more impersonal about the products of these acts than there is in the miniature publics which make up the zones of social control.[31]

As for the concepts of the public which surrounded the critique of congregational life after mid-century, these developed in a world marked by the prevalence of centripetal symbols and trends. One thinks of the United Nations, United World Federalism, World Council of Churches, or National Council of Churches. Metaphors such as "global village," "spaceship earth," and the *oikoumene* came to be in vogue. For better or for worse, publics more recently have come to be thought of as aggregates of aggregates. New nationalisms, each of them made up of smaller publics of their own, complicate the life of the United Nations. Tribalism, with its frequently expressed religious cast, marks the existence of many groups smaller than nations, each group contending for its place. Denominations, however they had weakened, retained more staying power than ecumenical organizations. In the United States the public is also obviously not made up simply of an almost undifferentiated two-party political mass. Instead, for the past quarter-century America has seen and heard increasingly assertive claims by complex movements: women's, black, homosexual, Native American, Hispanic, Left and Right, and more—with each of them, in turn, constituted by smaller aggregates. Each individually represents more subpublics and together they make up what might be thought of as a megapublic moved in part by megastructures.

One hopes that it is not a mere Aristotelian bias about the public and political order but rather an observation of historical trends that leads to this recent concern with what we might call "communal publics" which make up a larger public. For Aristotle, "a *polis* by its nature is some sort of aggregation. If it becomes more of a unit, it will first become a household instead of a *polis*, and then an individual instead of a household."[32]

Congregations as aggregates and part of an aggregation are themselves publics and parts of a larger public. Members by taking part in them venture out of privacy into a zone of interactions. These ventures may not impress the political scientist or social critic who defines "public" in extremely heterogeneous terms. If one begins from an Everest called "the public sphere," the congregations will look like the plains. If, however, one begins on the plains of "the private sphere," activities in congregations will often look at least like substantial foothills. The framework for inquiry depends upon where one begins, with what perspective and interest. Authors of contemporary congregational studies, looking back at the world of Sheilaism and invisible religion, of privatization and spiritual solipsism, discover and report on the many ways in which adherents, when they become part of dynamic congregations, venture not just into a mediating structure standing between other structures but into what is to them a public.

The New Congregational Studies and the Concept of "Meeting"

The new congregational studies do not simply replace the old; they build upon the earlier stages, which remain as sedimental deposits capable of being stirred up. Certainly anyone bringing neoorthodox ecclesiologies, Jeffersonian myths, the mantle and credentials of prophecy, or a bias that favors megastructures, will find everything that is said about and against the privacy of localized, exclusivist, insulated congregational life appropriate. Whoever has the humanistic burden of protecting private persons and the political calling to ward off bureaucracy and totalitarian governmental interests, will give an accounting of congregations that stresses their role among the other mediating structures.

In the new phase of studies which is evidenced in *American Congregations*, however, there is need for the development of a concept to place alongside that of "mediating" to represent the lived experience of members. One candidate for this supplementation is "meeting." Historians of the congregation in culture find it to be the place where people experience a meeting between private and public. But, as is less the case with a mediating structure, it has a form which possesses its own intrinsic worth and integrity and which deserves scholarly concentration of a sort this form of assembly had not previously received.

One modern philosophical developer of the concept of meeting was Martin Buber. In 1921 in *The Great Maggid and His Followers* Buber began to build upon his concept of "I and Thou" and to stress the encounter with otherness, the Other, an other. For him human meeting was analogous to the primal meeting of God as Other with people. But Buber came down to earth and reminded readers: "our world is in truth the world of man." In his theological terms, meeting meant a working out of the otherness, the freedom of creation through which God enters into the fate of the world in order to find a partner for mutual knowing and mutual love. Such a freedom is by analogy also at the heart of publics, religiously conceived.

Buber posed the concept of meeting over against mere *Erlebnis*, experience, since in modern times *Erlebnis* had come to mean "that life is subjectivized, that out of a great continuum, out of a great continuity, space-time continuity in which we stand, in which we are inserted, in which we take part, life is transformed into a fetching forth of things for the use and task of our subjectivity." Then "religion is made into one of these precious moments, so to speak." This kind of isolated *Erlebnis*, said Buber, was a fiction, a concentration on "inwardness," a phenomenon which prospers best inside privatism. Buber also posed life-as-meeting over against the "political" imposition of values. This posture meant a stress on education as "opening up," "unfolding," which is to be experienced in the encounter with an Other and with others. Therefore, "Every real happening of the spirit is meeting (*Begegnung*)."[33]

It would be foolish to suggest that the members of congregations or the historians who write about them are or should be in any technical sense "Buberians." Nor need such scholars be Jewish, Judeo-Christian, biblically informed, existentialist, or theist to participate in and chronicle the concept of congregational life as meeting with Otherness and with others who represent elements of a public. Such meeting as Buber describes in the "human world" occurs each week in Unitarian-Universalist assemblies, presumably in gatherings of non-theistic Buddhists, and in other gatherings which do not draw specifically on the traditions which informed thinkers like that one Jewish philosopher.

It would also be an embarrassment to most historians if we pictured them approaching their task with an express intent to work out a philosophy of meeting. The test of these suggestions and claims about the congregation as place of meeting between the private and the public spheres is in the actual accounts, the descriptions of what happens in such gatherings. While these religious assemblies protect personal sides of life within private spheres, evidences abound that to the participants, the agents, the adherents, congregational life also represents the beginning of meeting. This encounter begins with the possibility of meeting one's own family in exceptional, other than ordinary, contexts. Further, in congregation one meets with friends and neighbors; with the stranger; in other words, with representatives of the beginnings of "the public" and representations of public experiences.

The Longer Historical Context

The postmodern concept of the congregation as meeting has premodern roots in America. The notion of congregating as an act which initiates actual participation in a public has an honored lineage that goes back to colonial America. In New England the Puritans worshiped in a place significantly called the "meetinghouse." Theirs was a time when the sacred and secular spheres were less differentiated than they became later. Footnote number one in *Meetinghouse and Church in Early New England* found the author, Edmund W. Sinnott, reminding readers that "some old New England church buildings are still sometimes called meetinghouses, and going to church is 'going to meeting.'" He pointed out that technically the meetinghouse was a structure used for both secular and religious purposes, while the church was primarily a house of worship, but that the two linguistic usages overlapped. "Here people met for every purpose and hence it came to be called, in all directness, the 'meetinghouse.' It was an edifice neither sacred nor purely secular, but appropriate for any honorable service." While it served as a house of prayer and while it might be open for private devotion, the meetinghouse actually was the physical representation of and setting for the congregation as a public or part of a public.[34]

It does not take much imagination or empathy to picture most modern congregants also thinking of their congregation as being ordinarily associated with a building. They may regard "going to meeting" to be a folksy archaism, but they do know that their community lists churches and synagogues as "public buildings" and that they enter a public when they attend.

In the middle of the Middle Colonies the Quaker pioneers called their equivalent of a denominational jurisdiction a Meeting, as in Yearly Meeting. In their gatherings for discipline they spoke of the "sense of the meeting." Their places for reflection and testimony were Meeting Houses, as recalled in the book title by Frederick B. Tolles, *Meeting House and Counting House.*[35]

When telling the story of predominantly Anglican establishmentarian Virginia, historian Rhys Isaac led off a chapter on the subject: "Churches were the important center for community assembly, dispersed at the most frequent intervals in the countryside." Evidencing the presence of a public, a body of worshipers with diversity, was the fact that "concerns for the world, brought to the church door as a matter of course, were not so readily abandoned in order to cross its threshold into the more hallowed time and space set apart for worship." Isaac quoted a contemporary account by Philip Vickers Fithian: "It is not the Custom for Gentlemen to go into Church til Service is beginning, when they enter in a Body." There was pride of rank, and "the architectural plan maximized the visibility to the assembled community of a numerous emulative gentry." Clearly, publicness was in the mind of the designers and the patrons of the buildings.[36]

At book-length Dell Upton also stressed the public dimensions of the place of meeting under categories of "power" and "hospitality," aptly titling his book *Holy Things and Profane: Anglican Parish Churches in Colonial Virginia.* Private and public spheres met, as did the worshipers who inhabited both, in such meetings in such places.[37]

While some of the historians of congregations reach back to such colonial beginnings, most of them deal with more recently founded institutions. This means that by the time of the beginnings of such congregational stories a legal line of distinction had been drawn between the civil authorities and religion ("the separation of church and state"). With this action came greater division into denominations than before, and much more differentiation and specialization between "holy things and profane" and among whatever it was that "holy things" themself signified. Each such movement meant a potential which further jeopardized the publicness of congregations, as represented in a process or set of events which we cannot here review. Yet whether one listens to Alexis de Tocqueville in 1835, to Robert and Helen Lynd who gave a close-up view of the congregations of "Middletown" in 1927 and 1937, or to a team of sociologists who visited there in the 1970s, the testimony seems consistent. Theodore Caplow and his team summarized it in the typical case of Middletown: 35 denominations were represented in this middle-sized midwestern city, Muncie, Indiana.

> For the most part, they hold common views about private and public morality, supporting, in the private sphere, monogamous marriage, family solidarity, the Ten Commandments, private charity, self-control, self-improvement, dutifulness, and patience under suffering and, in the public sphere, patriotism, the authority of the law, democracy, and human rights. [Of course:] They are less unanimous in their opinion on those specific issues in which the separation between religion and politics has been breached, either by the rise of social activism within the denominations or by the expansion of government activity into the domain formerly reserved to religion.[38]

Caplow and colleagues did use the term "privatization" to refer to characteristic activities of Muncie's churches, but went on to say that there had been little change with respect to this phenomenon since anyone first took the measure of that city ninety years earlier. Insofar as there is a predictably narrow focus in the sermonic life, the authors could say of Muncie religion: "Privatized it may be, but since it has followed the same style for nearly 90 years, we must hesitate before ascribing the character of this religion to any recent developments in the larger society." They made this judgment after having done some content analysis of the congregational sermons, which may be less representative than the rituals and activities. The religion of recent sermons, we hear, is "diffuse, hopeful, absorbed in personal experience and moral self-improvement within the narrow sphere of family and local church." It is in the world of the church bulletin and the intercessory prayer, in the meeting of member with member and stranger, where the public encounters are more likely to occur.[39]

Whatever else happened in America's "Middletowns" in intervening decades, it suffices for us to recall that the critics of congregation life by the late 1950s had seen such trends toward privatization becoming virtually complete. In their eyes, "holy things" were now simply private, "profane" things were public, while "sacred" and "secular" were sundered and congregations tended to make the choice of serving holy and sacred spheres chiefly in private life. The congregations as "God's colonies" and conclaves, we recall, were said to have become homogeneous, exclusive, insulated. What someone in France—variously said to have been Talleyrand, Royer-Collard, or Stendhal—called the "wall of private life," had putatively fallen around the boundaries of the congregation. It is with the legacy of such congregations, and with the social scientific study and criticism, that the present Congregational History Project contends.

Behind and then Beyond the Wall of Private Life

It is not difficult to see why especially around mid-century and again today one could and can treat the congregation as living behind the "wall of private life." This dimension of its existence demands notice in every telling. Thus, a definition of a sectarian congregation would have to include the notion of assemblies setting high and rigid boundaries, of their making every effort to screen out a world in which pluralism and relativism abound. Many congregations which describe themselves as Orthodox, whether Jewish, Eastern Christian, Protestant, or whatever, thus make it part of their effective mission to keep their members from public meeting and encounter.

To illustrate: in a book written in 1970 I watched one wing of Protestantism which developed in the nineteenth century while resisting modernity and modernism. It concentrated on soul-winning and other-worldliness and became by choice "Private," as opposed to "Public," Protestantism.[40] It can be assumed that the congregations in such a wing worked to keep public dimensions at some distance and to keep the private element pure "inside the walls." David O. Moberg has spoken of this event of their turning to specialize in the private realm as "The Great Reversal" in evangelicalism.[41] Congregations within that movement of reversal intended to turn their back on public life just as Amish, Jehovah's Witnesses, and "come-outer" fundamentalisms and orthodoxies long have done, even though evangelical theology historically had not led to such withdrawal.

For a sample of such enclosure: Alan Peshkin has described a fundamentalist Protestant congregation with its huge parochial school "inside the walls" as a "total institution." He cited Erving Goffman's essay "On the Characteristics of Total Institutions" to show how "encompassing tendencies" set out to create a private world within a public world for their adherents. Some such institutions display "locked doors, high walls, barbed wire" to provide a "barrier to social intercourse with the outside."

Of course, prisons, mental institutions, convents and cloisters express such intentions. But, says Peshkin, congregations like the one he studied also are such total institutions dedicated to privacy. The key New Testament passage quoted by members to him as a participant-observer was 2 Corinthians 6:17: "Wherefore come out from among them, and be ye separate, saith the Lord, and touch not the unclean thing." Members are there prevented from participating in "outside" organizations whose publics might even accidentally sow seeds of doubt. The congregants may vote and take part in public life as individual citizens, but only with great wariness and under considerable scrutiny by leaders and peers.[42]

Such total institutions designed to protect the congregants in privacy apart from the public have prospered during the past three decades. Yet it is precisely the growing opposite theological tendency which has been more notable in congregational, denominational, and supraparochial organizations of religion in these same decades. The news made by fundamentalism, evangelicalism, pentecostalism, conservative Catholicism, and orthodox Judaism, all of which were historically private and stay-at-home types, has been concentrated in their choice to reverse their Great Reversals and to reenter the public sphere. While mass media, with their appeal to "convergent selectivity" played their part in organizing clienteles, the faithful and enduring constituency of the new agencies is in the local congregations. These reach out to and are reached by political leaders. The old private/public distinction no longer is so appropriate even among the heirs of those who earlier invented institutions on the "private" side of that line. A fundamentalist First Baptist Church in Dallas may seem to be a refuge from the public world, but its broad programs also turn it into an effective public and its clear intentions are also to mobilize members to participate in general public life. Mediating may be an implicit part of the mission; bolder meeting and intervening is explicitly encouraged and nurtured.[43]

The Choice to Go Public with Congregations

The choice to go public in the case of once-private conservatisms finds its counterpart in almost all the other religious sectors of American society, and each of these is organized in no small measure in and through the congregations. Roman Catholicism, the largest cohort, is highly visible on the public scene because of the bishops' pastoral letters issued in the 1980s. These teach and advocate public and political positions among Catholics. Anti-abortion movements make Catholic headlines.

But while these are "denominational" or "supraparochial" endeavors, they gain whatever power they have not from the "convergent selectivity" of mass audiences but by drawing upon the "social control" nurtured in congregations.

For another example, the one-third of Americans who "prefer" moderate or liberal Protestantism are veterans at living with public encounter and exposure. While their congregations guard private spirituality and personal endeavor, they have also been the most habitually dedicated to public involvement of any of the religious cohorts. Black Protestant congregations also serve as they always have as the public meeting place for African Americans. Television images every election year show how urgent it is for candidates who wish to be mayors of metropolises to draw upon the aspirations and proclivities of such congregation members.

A sweep of the spectrum further substantiates our thesis. The intervention of the Latter-day Saints in public life, for instance, has been characteristic through the history of what to outsiders looked like a sect. The local embodiments of Mormonism are the key to the church's entire political venture. American Judaism relies on synagogues for much of the spiritual energy that stands behind public Jewish commitments for the support of Israel or for participation in support of causes which "supraparochial" or "denominational" Judaism has long promoted. All these mentioned cohorts have joined the one in six Americans who "prefer" conservative Protestantism, most of whom have no longer preferred to remain "within the walls" of private life.[44]

The move into the public sphere has not been made without ambiguity or conflict. A large literature demonstrates the reluctance of congregation members to be spoken for or even to agree with positions of denominational or ecumenical leadership. It also shows disagreements by members with the stands their leaders often voice. As long ago as 1969 Jeffrey K. Hadden was reporting on surveys which amounted to *The Gathering Storm in the Churches*. The storm existed, Hadden showed, because of a widening gap in respect to public affairs between clergy and lay people. The clergy, as occupational gatekeepers to the larger society, were clearly more ready than the laity to see their congregations as publics or participants in the public order. Response to controversial statements on civil rights, nuclear warfare, social programs, and the like demonstrated this. Hadden presented seventy-two tables, most of which confirmed his generalizations about the gap. But that gap did not mean that the laity did not have public concerns or did not express them in congregational forums. They simply did not often agree with the substantive political positions of their own local clergy and denominational leadership.[45]

Similarly by focusing on the political activism and pronouncements of the clergy in congregations, Harold E. Quinley could show that *The Prophetic Clergy* were often out of step with the bulk of their laity. He found evidences that liberal laity were naturally more kindly disposed to the liberal views of their pastors. But he could also confirm the existence of a gap, of an out-of-step relation between clergy and laity. Here again, however, it is misleading to collapse all that the term "public" implies into the formally political encounters to which Quinley's surveys pointed. Ask members of a typical congregation if they want their denomination or pastor to support specific candidates or specific pieces of legislation, especially in their name, and they will normally say they do not want this. Observe them, however, participating in all that public life involves, whether in town meeting or marketplace, gallery or concert hall, charitable life or acts of mercy, and they will declare themselves favorably disposed to congregational involvement.[46]

Indeed, it may be to protect the public concerns found in the meetings implied by congregational life that so many congregants fear the expressly political species of that life. Were congregations and their pastors simply homogeneous, exclusive, and living "behind the walls" of private life, there would be few reasons for them to be uneasy with political expression. We have to distinguish, as they instinctively do, between "public" and "political." The *Oxford English Dictionary* is helpful. It does not provide clear definitions but it draws one line of distinction. In thirty definitions and elaborations of the term "public," not once does the dictionary use or need the word "political" as an explanatory factor.

Ministerial and lay leadership are normally concerned lest their congregations become full of political dissensions, subject to schism, or distracted from other ministries precisely because they *are* miniature publics, and thus they evidence internal pluralism. That is, the minister may hold one set of convictions and the laity another; the lay people in a single congregation will likely represent more than one political party. However much congregational life based on class, ethnic, racial, or residential segmentation and segregation may be a fact which tends toward promoting homogenization, there is always the fear that a significant minority will feel or will be unrepresented by specific political claims made on behalf of the whole.

What contemporary Church Growth Movement people call "The Homogeneous Unit Principle" is present in much congregational life, where like often finds like in those matters of class, ethnicity, race, and the accident of residence. But homogeneous is as homogeneous does. Ministers who prepare sermons addressed to whole congregations or who minister to members in crisis regularly report on the bewildering variety of interests and factions which make up their assemblies. They set out to protect and enhance the congregation as a meeting place or as an event for expression of elements representing both public and private spheres, not as a political battlefield.

Historians of American religion find evidence that in many cases the most effective public-minded clergy throughout American history were not social analysts approaching congregations from a distance. They were actively involved exemplars in the leadership of congregations. In the centuries of Protestantism, these exemplars were, for example, Jonathan Edwards, Horace Bushnell, Walter Rauschenbusch, Reinhold Niebuhr, and Martin Luther King, Jr., all of whom drew strength and vision from years in local congregational life. In Catholicism, because of hierarchical and episcopal organization, it has been easier for leadership to come from the hierarchy, the seminary, or the publishing world. But on local levels, public life is usually monitored also by the priestly and lay leadership, who are only selectively responsive to extraparochial demands. In Judaism the rabbi in congregational roles has had power rarely matched by Jewish seminary professors or isolated intellectuals. In black churches clerical leadership of local congregations has dominated; the pastors know where the power is, and without their cooperation the African-American religious public is almost unreachable.

Acquiring Eyes for Seeing the Public Roles

How acquire the eyes to see congregations as publics again? Edmund Husserl, a founder of the phenomenological school in philosophy, suggested that one must acquire a kind of disciplined naiveté to perceive the essence of what confronts one. Observers are then wanderers in "the trackless wilds of a new continent" where they undertake "bits of virgin cultivation." [47] Husserl's disciple Maurice Natanson elaborated:

It is not a question of sharpening some special sense, of looking in some extraordinary corner of the mind, or of locating the philosopher's stone. What is called for, above all, is that each one of us examine his style of being in the world at the level of ordinary, common-sense life, so that the philosophical character of that level of experience be clarified. . . . What, then, is it that the character of common-sense life is going to reveal which will make being in reality understandable? The direct answer is curious: the mark of common-sense life, the very essence of its style of being, is its failure to make itself an object for its own inspection. . . . That common-sense life has a style, has an essential structure, is an insight that necessarily transcends the understanding of common-sense men. . . . Yet it is exactly that absolute awareness of the style of our being in common-sense life which must be made an object for inspection if the datum of being in reality is to be gotten. And this is the most difficult of all tasks, largely because what it is that is required of us is exactly the problem. There is a built-in mechanism of protection in the stream of daily life which guards against this awareness; philosophy is an effort to crack this barrier.[48]

It is such an approach which the new generation of writers on congregational history employs when it approaches the "common-sense" life of the modern congregation. The historians come upon buildings thought of as "meetinghouses," a first signal that participants there move physically beyond the cocoons of pure privacy. The observers then find congregants "going to meeting," there to encounter the Other, and others, the mix of familiar cohorts and strangers.

Upon arrival, the congregant is handed a Worship Bulletin, an overlooked art form for those who want to assess the spheres of congregational life. Some of the activities listed there address the private interests of the religious: there may be announcements of times when the sanctuary is open for private meditation, for example. The schedule may include reference to education in the techniques of such meditation. Yet the common-sense eye sees that most of the activities are not mediations toward the public world but actual meetings with it. The congregational committees as often as not lead members to activities "outside the walls": blood-donor appeals, ecumenical gatherings, tutoring among people of different social classes, invitations to lobby, calls for ministry to AIDS victims, addresses to the homeless, to strangers, all parts of an intrusive public. There may be announcements of sessions designed to minimize conflict within the congregation and to work for reconciliations.

All these are more common-sense signals that public exposure is part of the design and makeup of the congregation. Worship itself, usually called "Public Worship" and announced on bulletin boards saying "Public Invited," for all its routine character at least contains vestiges or promises of the possibility that the Other and diverse others are to be met. A sermon quite likely makes public if not political reference to world events, now interpreted through a particular theological prism. What Christians call "intercessory prayer" is a public remembrance of the members, the neighbors, the otherwise overlooked, and the enemy.

Richard Fenn has made particularly acute observations about the public devotional dimensions which usually get accounted for only on the purely private side of congregational life. He concentrates on ritual, which is a "means of bridging the gap between discourses," private and public. The rites "simply make public the purposes and meanings of individuals in a variety of words, gestures, and deeds on a wide variety of topics; take any list of intercessions, for example, and one will find the topics on which individuals are thus publicly expressing themselves for the benefit of those who are not then and there present." Fenn says that is precisely the point of intercessory prayers that introduce some occasions of public life into the apparently private sphere.[49]

Contrast this picture with the observation of Gibson Winter, written in the first phase of debate over private and public dimensions in postwar congregational life:

> We are attempting to understand the process by which the mission of the church became circumscribed by the private interests of middle-class enclaves. One crucial reason for this circumscription of the ministry was the identification of the forms of church, parish, and congregation, with familial and residential interests which have become more and more restricted to the problems of personal inwardness and emotional balance during the past century. This process has led to a restriction of the context of religious life to the most private matters.
>
> In this sense, "public worship," as common liturgy in which the richness of the Word and Sacrament intersect with the common life of a people, has disappeared. We simply do not enjoy the experience of public worship, for the intersection of concerns in the religious context does not reflect public matters.[50]

Either the situation, or the eye of the beholder, has changed. No doubt something of both are factors, but it is legitimate to speak of an overall trend among observers. This would indicate that congregations in the recent past have been coming to recognize that they are custodians of languages which do not always otherwise get voiced in political or public transactions. A secular society and its academic delineators are likely to want to restrict discourse over urgent matters—medical ethics or whatever—to the norms of secular rationality.

Law professor Kent Greenawalt is not alone in reminding the public that congregations speak "publicly accessible" languages. These are most deeply rooted in what congregations are designed to cultivate: reasoning based on tradition, memory, community, joint action, "the heart," intuition, hope, and affection.[51]

Members of such congregations, eager to protect the legitimate zones of privacy as these occur in confession, counsel, and personal devotion or ministry in times of crisis, where confidentiality is all-important, will not be ready to see that they are irrelevant inside "the walls of privacy." Nor will they be content only to mediate between two autonomous realms on whose existence they depend for whatever integrity they have. Congregations are durable and have become ever more interesting to social historians because they have an integrity of their own, however ambivalent their postures and ambiguous their intentions and achievements may be. The accounts in the first volume of *American Congregations* are efforts to treat these religious and social forms in some of their ambivalences and ambiguities. Along the way, they show why over three hundred thousand congregations survive in the United States and why their number grows daily, on a scene where they become components in the public world. Just as they are publics themselves.

NOTES

1. An excellent update, with a helpful bibliography on the literature, is Clarke E. Cochran, *Religion in Public and Private Life* (New York: Routledge, 1990); see especially "The Institutions of Private Life," pp. 69–72. The book has almost no references to congregations, local churches, or parishes.

2. Mircea Eliade, ed., *The Encyclopedia of Religion* (New York: Macmillan, 1987), vols. 1–16.

3. Amos 5:21–24; The Revelation of John 1:4–3:22.

4. See James P. Wind, *Places of Worship: Exploring Their History* (Nashville: American Association for State and Local History, 1990).

5. For a context, see the call for "a history of religious practices" by sociologist Gabriel Le Bras, quoted in Henri Desroche, "Domaines et méthodes de la sociologie religieuse dans l'oeuvre de Gabriel Le Bras," in *Revue d'histoire et philosophie religieuse*, no. 2 (Strasbourg, 1954).

6. See David A. Hollinger, "T. S. Kuhn's Theory of Science and Its Implications for History," in Gary Gutting, ed., *Paradigms and Revolutions: Appraisals and Applications of Thomas Kuhn's Philosophy of Science* (University of Notre Dame Press: Notre Dame and London, 1980), p. 219.

7. Peter L. Berger, Brigette Berger, Hansfried Kellner, *The Homeless Mind: Modernization and Consciousness* (New York: Random House, 1973), pp. 80, 186.

8. Jay P. Dolan, ed., *The American Catholic Parish: A History from 1850 to the Present*, 2 vols. (Mahwah, New York: Paulist Press, 1987), 1:7–116.

9. For example, in the theological sphere which relates to religious congregations, see Hans Küng and David Tracy, eds., trans. Margaret Koehl, *Paradigm Change in Theology: A Symposium for the Future* (New York: Crossroad, 1989), esp. pp. 7–10.

10. Scott Donaldson, *The Suburban Myth* (New York: Columbia University Press, 1969), chap. 1, "The Onslaught Against the Suburbs."

11. Ibid., "Churches and Comfortable Religion," pp. 126–46, especially 136, 137–39. Among writings to which Donaldson refers are Stanley Rowland, Jr., "Suburbia Buys Religion," *Nation* 183, no. 4 (July 28, 1956): 78; Andrew M. Greeley, *The Church and the Suburbs* (New York: Sheed and Ward, 1959); Gibson Winter, *The Suburban Captivity of the Churches: An Analysis of Protestant Responsibility in the Expanding Metropolis* (Garden City: Doubleday, 1961). Donaldson credited Albert J. Gordon for his *Jews in Suburbia* (Boston: Beacon, 1959) as being a "balanced view. . . . at once regretting what he regards as the standardization and conformity . . . and yet acknowledging the preservation of basic values" (p. 260).

12. Peter L. Berger, *The Noise of Solemn Assemblies: Christian Commitment and the Religious Establishment in America* (Garden City: Doubleday, 1961), chap. 10, "The Problem of New Forms," pp. 157–71. Berger made reference to Tom Allan, *The Face of My Parish* (New York: Harper, 1953); Abbé Michonneau, *Revolution in a City Parish* (Westminster: Newman Press, 1949); Ernest Southcott, *The Parish Comes Alive* (New York: Morehouse-Gorham, 1956); Martin E. Marty, *The New Shape of American Religion* (New York: Harper, 1959); George Webber, *God's Colony in Man's World* (New York: Abingdon Press, 1960). In some instances I have translated Berger's comment on "Christian" to "believer" or "congregant" where it was relevant to the mission of Jewish or other congregations and where the Christian mission did not need to be the direct focus as it was for Berger, writing a theological critique. At other times, where it was appropriate or necessary, I preserved his "Christian mission" terminology.

13. See the four volumes edited by Philippe Ariès and Georges Duby, trans. Arthur Goldhammer, *A History of Private Life*, including, for the access to modern times, vol. 4, Michelle Perrot, ed., *A History of Private Life: From the Fires of Revolution to the Great War* (Cambridge: Harvard University Press, 1990).

14. Robert Nisbet, *The Making of Modern Society* (New York: New York University Press, 1986), pp. 136–38.

15. Donald L. Redfoot, "The Problem of Freedom," in James Davison Hunter and Stephen C. Ainlay, eds., *Making Sense of Modern Times: Peter L. Berger and*

the Vision of Interpretive Sociology (New York: Routledge and Kegan Paul, 1986), pp. 106–7.

16. Peter L. Berger and Richard John Neuhaus, *To Empower People: The Role of Mediating Structures in Public Policy* (Washington, D.C.: American Enterprise Institute for Public Policy Research, 1977), p. 3. In this and other work on mediating structures Neuhaus became a full partner of Berger and more consistently pursued the theological and ecclesiological dimensions proper to his calling along with the political interests he shared with sociologist and culture critic Berger.

17. The quotation at the end of the paragraph is from ibid., p. 43; see also Redfoot, "Problem of Freedom," pp. 107–10 for a description of the camps which threaten these structures.

18. See Berger and Neuhaus, *To Empower People,* pp. 26–33, for a discussion of "The Church" as a complex of mediating structures.

19. Ibid., pp. 2–3.

20. Ibid., p. 6.

21. Charles G. Finney, for example, as quoted by William G. McLoughlin, *Modern Revivalism: Charles Grandison Finney to Billy Graham* (New York: Ronald Press, 1959), p. 26.

22. Thomas Luckmann, *The Invisible Religion* (New York: Macmillan, 1967).

23. Louis Dupré, "Spiritual Life in a Secular Age," *Daedalus* 111:1 (Winter 1982): 24; Dupré also quoted his own *Transcendent Selfhood* (New York: Seabury Press, 1976), pp. 29–30, and cited Peter Berger, *The Heretical Imperative* (Garden City: Doubleday, 1979), pp. 32ff.

24. Joan D. Chittister, O.S.B., and Martin E. Marty, *Faith and Ferment: An Interdisciplinary Study of Christian Beliefs and Practices* (Minneapolis: Augsburg Publishing House, and Collegeville, Minnesota: The Liturgical Press, 1983), pp. 218–29.

25. Robert N. Bellah, Richard Madsen, William M. Sullivan, Ann Swidler, and Steven M. Tipton, *Habits of the Heart: Individualism and Commitment in American Life* (Berkeley: University of California Press, 1985), pp. 221–23.

26. For an elaboration of these generalizations, often drawn from his chapter subtitles, see Robert Wuthnow, *The Restructuring of American Religion: Society and Faith Since World War II* (Princeton: Princeton University Press, 1988), chap. 5, "The Declining Significance of Denominationalism," pp. 71–99.

27. Ibid., pp. 100–131.

28. Ibid., "The Public's Involvement," pp. 118–21. These figures resulted from a 1984 Gallup Organization poll.

29. Ibid., pp. 121–31.

30. William Stephenson, *The Play Theory of Mass Communication* (Chicago: University of Chicago Press, 1966), p. 2; Stephenson develops this distinction throughout an analysis and critique of mass media and various "publics."

31. Ibid., 34.

32. Quoted by Bernard Crick, *In Defence of Politics* (Baltimore: Penguin Books, 1964), p. 161.

33. For the sake of brevity I have relied on condensations and citations as they appear in Maurice Friedman, *Martin Buber's Life and Work: The Early Years, 1878–1923* (New York: E. P. Dutton, 1981), pp. 119–21, 320–21, 278–81, 299.

34. Edmund W. Sinnott, *Meetinghouse and Church in Early New England* (New York: McGraw-Hill, 1963), pp. 5–6.

35. Frederick B. Tolles, *Meeting House and Counting House: The Quaker Merchants of Colonial Philadelphia, 1682–1783* (Chapel Hill: University of North Carolina Press, 1948), pp. 7–8.

36. Rhys Isaac, *The Transformation of Virginia, 1740–1790* (Chapel Hill: University of North Carolina Press, 1982), pp. 58, 61.

37. Dell Upton, *Holy Things and Profane: Anglican Parish Churches in Colonial Virginia* (Cambridge: MIT Press, 1986).

38. Theodore Caplow, Howard M. Bahr, Bruce A. Chadwick, Dwight W. Hoover, Laurence A. Martin, Joseph B. Tamney, Margaret Holmes Williamson, *All Faithful People: Change and Continuity in Middletown's Religion* (Minneapolis: University of Minnesota Press, 1983), pp. 7–8. For background, see Robert S. and Helen Merrell Lynd, *Middletown: A Study in American Culture* (New York: Harcourt, Brace, 1929); *Middletown in Transition: A Study in Cultural Conflicts* (New York: Harcourt, Brace, 1937; Alexis de Tocqueville, *Democracy in America* (Garden City: Doubleday, 1969; originally published in 1835).

39. Caplow et al., *All Faithful People*, pp. 105–6.

40. Martin E. Marty, *Righteous Empire: The Protestant Experience in America* (New York: Dial, 1970), p. 179.

41. David O. Moberg, *The Great Reversal: Evangelism and Social Concern* (Philadelphia: J. B. Lippincott, 1977), esp. chap. 2, "The Great Reversal," pp. 28–45.

42. Alan Peshkin, *God's Choice: The Total World of a Fundamentalist Christian School* (Chicago: University of Chicago Press, 1986), pp. 257–58; see also Erving Goffman, *Asylums: Essays on the Social Situation of Mental Patients and Other Inmates* (Garden City: Doubleday, 1961).

43. The literature on this return to the public is enormous; see, among others, David G. Bromley and Anson Shupe, *New Christian Politics* (Macon, Georgia: Mercer University Press, 1984).

44. For this picturing of a spectrum of American religious preferences I have drawn on Wade Clark Roof and William McKinney, *American Mainline Religion: Its Changing Shape and Future* (New Brunswick: Rutgers University Press, 1987); see especially the graph on p. 82.

45. Jeffrey K. Hadden, *The Gathering Storm in the Churches* (Garden City: Doubleday, 1969).

46. Harold E. Quinley, *The Prophetic Clergy: Social Activism Among Protestant Ministers* (New York: John Wiley, 1974).

47. Edmund Husserl, *Ideas: General Introduction to Pure Phenomenology* (New York: Macmillan, 1931), p. 23.

48. Maurice Natanson, "Existential Categories in Contemporary Literature," in *Literature, Philosophy and the Social Sciences* (The Hague: Nijhoff, 1962), p. 120.

49. Richard Fenn, *The Dream of the Perfect Act: An Inquiry into the Fate of Religion in a Secular World* (New York: Tavistock, 1987), p. 102.

50. Winter, *The Suburban Captivity of the Churches*, pp. 133–34.

51. Kent Greenawalt, *Religious Convictions and Political Choice* (New York: Oxford University Press, 1988), esp. pp. 57–71, 109–10, 149–52, 208–11.

PART TWO

CONGREGATIONS AND TRADITIONS

FIVE

Congregations and the Bearing of Traditions

DOROTHY C. BASS

IN 1877 OR SO, in a fictitious settlement created by the Norwegian-American novelist Ole Rölvaag, a few immigrant families glimpsed "the glory of the Lord" in the founding of a new congregation. They had been building new lives on the Great Plains for some six years, planting crops, raising children, and devising a rudimentary civil life. All the while, they had suffered from the loss of familiar places and practices, and they had also stored up their share of the common hurts and regrets of humankind. And then a minister arrives, summoning them to worship that very afternoon. His vestments, though threadbare, are those of "a real Norwegian minister in ruff and robe!" Next to an ordinary table set up as an altar in a sod house, he baptizes the children born in the New World, as their Old World parents sing the baptismal hymn by heart.[1]

In the scene Rölvaag paints, old ways mingle with new ones; Norway, as well as Christ, is made present to the worshipers. An unmistakable particularity marks this gathering, and an unmistakable particularity will mark the congregation it initiates. "One woman had it in mind that they would of course start a ladies' aid," the novelist reports as he tours the daydreams of the assembly, "and that would be great fun, with meetings and cakes and coffee and sewing and all the rest." Others think of "fine new clothes for the confirmation," or of where to put the cemetery, or of whether they will be chosen for certain leadership positions. Though thousands of miles from Norway, these people know what a congregation should look like, if it is to be theirs.[2]

And yet this gathering is not only a conservative event, in which old forms are enacted in a new place. It also points towards a future in which some genuinely new and expansive elements are incorporated into this community's shared religious life. For instance, the years without clergy have already fostered the lay initiative that will characterize

American Lutheranism more than Norwegian. More profoundly, this people's journey to the Great Plains has permitted them to understand portions of their biblical heritage that were previously obscure to them. The pastor's plain eloquence links the story of this particular people to the Exodus story of the people of Israel; he recounts their recent hardships in ancient terms, and he sets before them the Deuteronomic choice between blessing and curse. In so doing, he adds an element to their European theological heritage, one with much significance both for their appropriation of the great stories of their faith and for their participation in the nation of immigrants to which they now belong.[3]

The settlers' yearning to be nurtured in the faith of their parents, and their delight when the occasion arrives, has been echoed in many other locations on the American religious scene. Over a hundred Greek-Americans wept for joy the first time the Divine Liturgy was celebrated in Baltimore, in 1906. More recently, Gujarati Indians meeting in one another's homes in suburban Chicago were happy enough in their regular feasting and fellowship, but their greatest excitement took place when holy men came from India to visit them. Yet it was not only the reception of religious substance from the Old World that was at stake in these instances, for the subtle, often unconscious renewal and transformation of that which was received was occurring at the same time. For the first time in their lives, the Greek Orthodox lay leaders collected an offering at the service, so that they could pay the clergymen they had invited to Baltimore to conduct the Divine Liturgy. And the Hindus changed the dates of major religious festivals so that they would fall on weekends, to accommodate American work schedules. Neither change was an insignificant one, within the heritage of these groups.[4]

In these cases and many others, congregations have stood at the crossroads of conservation and change in American religion, facing back to a cherished inheritance and forward through the contexts of the congregants' contemporary lives. And at this crossroads, a characteristic tension prevails. At first glance, it is a tension between Norway and South Dakota, Greece and Baltimore, or Gujarat and Chicago. In a larger sense, however, the tension is also one between each of these places and the transcendent claims of religions. This tension inheres in each congregation's dual nature as a local, culturally enmeshed entity and as the member, nonetheless, of a great transnational tradition.

Part of the genius of congregations lies in their ability to express the particularity of a people; the very idea of a church causes a pioneer woman to think of a certain kind of cake. Another indispensable part of their genius, however, is to link people to something that extends over the centuries and across the nations. When that happens, a pioneer woman can liken herself to the biblical figure Miriam. And she is not the only one who gains when that connection is made. For the story of the Exodus and the historic faith tradition to which it belongs have thereby become alive and meaningful in a new social and cultural context, and thus extended, renewed, and made available to the future. Congregations impart to individuals and families a place in a tradition, to be sure, but at the same time congregations form and impart life to the tradition itself.

How is it that great religious traditions, which in the consensus of large segments of humankind encompass and sanctify much of our wisdom and experience as a race, are borne into the future by such small and culturally restricted (some would say tedious and claustrophobic) institutions as the majority of American congregations appear to be? This mystery is at the heart of this essay. I wish to propose that the work of the philosopher Alasdair MacIntyre can provide substantial help in thinking our way through some of the questions that are raised by this mystery. Although not developed with congregations in mind, MacIntyre's concepts offer a framework for analyzing how traditions are transmitted, sustained, and constantly reformed, from which students of the congregation have a great deal to learn.

In *After Virtue*, MacIntyre develops a concept of tradition that seeks to account for both the past's claim upon the present and the present's availability for change. Personal identity and meaningful human action are shaped by and rely upon the traditions we bear as participants in history, he insists. He explicitly rejects, however, the "concept of a tradition [that] has been put by conservative political theorists." Far from being sheerly defensive against conflict and change, a tradition is "partially constituted by an argument."[5]

At the heart of a tradition is a pursuit, not a final attainment. Every tradition pursues certain "goods," which give to that tradition "its particular point and purpose." These goods are the excellences which the bearers of the tradition honor and in which they seek to participate; for Christians, for example, they would include reconciliation and eternal life. Such goods are internal to traditions, ends in themselves, fully comprehended only from a vantage point within the tradition. Yet a tradition's internal goods characteristically possess a richness that always prevents their full and final definition; Christians are not of one accord, for example, about what arrangements within their communities best express the meaning of divine and human reconciliation. When a tradition is "living," in MacIntyre's terms, its members are engaged in a vibrant, embodied "argument," stretching across time and space, about what the fullest participation in its particular goods would entail. Traditions that are living, therefore, provide individuals and communities not only with an inheritance but also with the critical and inventive resources that enable them to transcend the prior limitations of the tradition itself.[6] In these terms, the sod-hut worship service, the initiatives of Greek-American laymen, and the rearrangement of a ritual schedule are not departures from traditions but rather signs that they are living, signs that may even disclose new aspects of the goods that their traditions have been pursuing for centuries.

Another of MacIntyre's definitive claims—and one of particular interest to students of the congregation—is that traditions must be "socially embodied."[7] Living traditions, he argues, are embodied in the social world in two related ways: through *practices* and the *institutions* where practices are sustained. Individuals can learn and participate in traditions only in the company of others; they do so by entering into the practices and institutions through which particular social groups, versed in specific activities and gathered into specific organizations, bear traditions through time.[8]

Practices embody traditions in distinctive forms of "socially established cooperative human activity." An activity that qualifies as a "practice" is complex, coherent, and governed by its own internal standards of excellence, which must at first be learned from others but which later provide access to the goods the practice bears. Take, for example, the game of chess. An adult, MacIntyre proposes, might lure a child to learn chess by promising a monetary reward for her progress in the game. As long as the child plays primarily to win the reward, however, she is only skating on the surface of the practice, pursuing goods "external" to it (money) and having little reason not to cheat. But when she catches on and seeks to achieve excellence in chess herself—when she understands "those standards of excellence which are appropriate to, and partially definitive of" chess—then she has discovered the internal goods that constitute this practice; were she to cheat, she would be cheating herself most of all. She soon recognizes that excellence in chess is not something to be finally grasped but something to be pursued as long as life (or interest in chess) lasts. Moreover, in the course of pursuing excellence in chess, she finds that her "human powers to achieve excellence [in the practice], and human conceptions of the goods involved, are systematically extended."[9] Thus she becomes a practitioner of chess and a member of the international company that sustains that practice.

The student of the congregation may appropriately substitute "praying" or "studying holy scriptures" for "playing chess" in this example. The practical theologian Craig Dykstra has led the way in extending the analytical range of MacIntyre's concepts in this direction. Dykstra argues that the Christian life may be understood as participation in a set of practices that includes prayer, service, mission, study, and other activities. These practices and the institutions that sustain them represent the social embodiment of the Christian tradition. As Christians pursue excellence in these practices, they discover that both their powers to achieve excellence and their conception of the ends and goods involved in these practices are systematically extended. Moreover, Dykstra concludes, through this participation Christians pursue and take part in the good that is at the internal center of the Christian tradition itself: the redemptive practice of God in the world.[10]

Another helpful aspect of MacIntyre's conception of tradition is his claim that living traditions must be "historically extended," incorporating "the pursuit of goods" through whole generations, and "sometimes through many generations." Further, he asserts that one can hardly pursue the goods of a tradition and engage in its practices if one does not know their origins and place in the lives of past generations. Practices, as we participate in them, are "characteristically embedded in and made intelligible in" the larger and longer histories out of which they have grown. We learn practices and recognize their excellent pursuit not only from our own teachers but also from the longer history of the practice, and comprehending the past of a practice permits its historical extension into the future as well.[11] This is clear enough with regard to portrait painting, a favorite example of MacIntyre's. It is even more clear with regard to the practices of religious groups, which often honor exemplary historic practitioners with stories, statues, paintings, and relics that frame the experiences of the devout. In Western Christianity, for example, the images of saints and martyrs appear in many places of worship, while in Swaminarayan Hinduism the veneration of a line of swamis makes members aware of the history of the community's practices and of those "who extended the reach of the practice to its present point."[12]

Congregations, as institutions where practices are transmitted, are in these terms the bearers of traditions, providing both practices and individual lives with their "necessary historical context."[13] As institutions, they continue the quest for the full meaning, in their time and place, of the traditions they bear. They also provide settings within which individuals can search for their own good, as it is shaped by the traditions that constitute their own distinctive resources for personal identity. In other words, congregations, as tradition bearers, are arenas within which individual and collective identity can be discovered, in all the local particularity that enables people to experience a deep sense of belonging. At the same time, they are also places where the conflict that characterizes living traditions takes place, and where the larger tradition's challenges to restricted local forms of individual and group identity are encountered.

In the following pages, we shall bring MacIntyre's conception of a living tradition as a "historically extended, socially embodied argument" to an analysis of American congregations and their bearing of the great religious traditions to which they belong. This bearing of tradition has two dimensions, each integrally related to the other. Congregations impart to individuals and families a place in a tradition, and conversely, those same individuals and families, through congregations, give back to a tradition its own being and vitality, constituting and reconstituting it through time. In the dynamic relation between these two dimensions we can discern a general narrative of how congregations bear tradition, which will serve as the framework for the remainder of this essay. In the beginning, people who have been touched by a living tradition deliberately seek their own continued nurture in that tradition, the nurture of their children, and the nurture of others, by founding congregations. Once in operation, congregations induct individuals and families into a tradition by engaging in and teaching the practices that are intrinsic to that tradition, and also by providing connections to the historically extended tradition beyond its own parochialism. By doing these things, congregations enable great traditions to find expression in ever new historical settings, and thereby to be both perpetuated and changed.

People who have been touched by a living tradition deliberately seek their own continued nurture in that tradition, the nurture of their children, and the nurture of others, by founding congregations.

Every congregation possesses a story of its origin, and in many cases the mythic quality that the congregation's storytellers invest in the tale years later may not be disproportionate to the drama of the actual event. For to start a congregation is a strong statement of commitment, and no small job. A remarkable degree of passion for the tradition at stake is indispensable. This is not to deny that ethnic, class, racial, and other factors often play a part in bringing congregations into being; but even when they do, congregational founders are not after the formation of a social club, which can usually be accomplished more easily by other readily available means. They are trying to make possible the vital living of their religious lives in a new place.

For those who have been touched by a living religious tradition, the challenge of continuing to share in that life in the absence of its social embodiment as a congregation can appear daunting. Joseph Jonas, the "founding father" of the Cincinnati Jewish community, was urged by Philadelphia Jews not to settle in Ohio. "In the wilds of America, and entirely amongst gentiles, you will forget your religion and your God," they warned him. Jonas "solemnly promised . . . never to forget his religion nor forsake his God." This meant worshiping alone for two years, until more settlers arrived. At that point, Cincinnati Jews began to gather for holiday services; then they bought land for a cemetery; and then, in 1824, they organized a congregation, K. K. Bene Israel.[14]

Common themes mark the founding stories of many congrega-tions.[15] For those allied with the dominant regional culture—the New England Congregationalist, midwestern Presbyterian, Utah Mormon, and Southern Baptist congregations—the story is one of plantation, of setting a congregation on a newly developing landscape. For those who began later and possessed a culture and religion at odds with the domi-nant Anglo-Protestantism of the United States, the stories emphasize a desire to pass distinctive ethno-religious heritages on to the next genera-tion; here the Orthodox, Hindu, Muslim, Jewish, and Roman Catholic congregations come to mind.

In spite of common themes, however, different congregations em-body different traditions, and the distinctiveness of each tradition is one of the factors that make each founding unique. In every case, the for-mative power of the particular goods of the living tradition involved plays an important role in shaping the motives and forms of the found-ers. At Mt. Hebron Baptist Church in Leeds, Alabama, for example, the free church tradition made community of spirit among members a cen-tral purpose of the founders in 1819. Their "Abstract of Principles" de-clared that those who had been touched by God's grace should "embrace his covenant, acknowledge his government, profess his name and unite in the faith and fellowship of the gospel." The mutual bonds shared within this fellowship should cause members "to endeavor to keep the unity of the spirit in the bonds of peace," to meet together at "all convenient seasons," "to sympathize with each other and to pray with and for each other," and to contribute a portion of their substance to providing worship and helping members in need.[16] As this congregation's historian, Wayne Flynt, concludes, what the founders envisioned was "a sacred community." Flynt aptly ties this vision to the white democratic ethos of the Alabama frontier and to the personal need of frontier settlers for supportive social life. It should also be noted, however, that the longer tradition that lay behind this founding—the tradition of the free or believers' church—had been emphasizing this aspect of religious life for generations. The practice of congregational self-government, embraced in another of Mt. Hebron's founding documents, "Rules of Decorum," was also particularly well-developed within this tradition.

To some, the communal orientation of the Mt. Hebron Baptist Church may seem commonplace. Yet community, in the sense of "a special feeling of closeness," as one member of this congregation put it, is seldom as theologically and spiritually privileged in other traditions as it is in the free church, though it may well be present somewhere in the life of every congregation. Other living traditions privilege other claims. At Bene Israel, the founding members were most concerned to set in place the institutions necessary to leading an observant Jewish life; among their early acts were to arrange for ritual slaughter, the baking of Passover matzah, the honoring of sacred times, and the proper burial of the dead.[17] In other traditions, other urgencies shaped the foundings— the celebration of the Divine Liturgy, the baptism of the young—each of them self-evident to those who belonged there.

Some congregations begin by breaking away from others. When this happens, the cause is often conflict over the interpretation of the particular goods whose pursuit led to the founding of the parent congregation in the first place. In MacIntyre's terms, such splinterings would represent a continuation of the argument about the goods of a tradition that partly constitutes the tradition itself. Disagreement about the strictness of Jewish observance, for example, led several more conservative groups to break away from Bene Israel over the years, the first as early as 1840. And a cadre of ardent evangelicals departed Mt. Hebron for a new congregation in the 1870s.[18] Ironically, the schismatics' quest for a purer church indirectly affirmed the "sacred community" tradition of Mt. Hebron, by extending the long argument in the believers' church tradition about the distinguishing marks of a true church.

Sometimes the multiplication of one congregation into several is a happier process, deliberately initiated by the parent congregation for the sake of extending the faith into new contexts. Some of the older Christian congregations studied in this project have solid procreative records—Center Church in New Haven founded mission congregations in poorer neighborhoods during the nineteenth century, as did Chicago's Fourth Presbyterian—while the youngest, Calvary Chapel, has hundreds of offspring around the country. Among the non-Christian groups, sending financial contributions to aid the early efforts and building funds of sibling congregations in other parts of the country has been common.[19]

Another of the congregations in our study has played this important missionary role in the support and founding of other congregations, and in its denomination as a whole. The Bethel African Methodist Episcopal Church in Baltimore had its own origins in a now obscure narrative of exodus and schism. The exclusion of African-Americans from full participation in white Methodist structures was one factor in creating the group that would become the seed of a new congregation, and a controversy over leadership within an older black congregation was another. And schism continued to plague this congregation through the generations—the result, according to its historian, Lawrence Mamiya, of "the competition for power and control" that is common in black churches, which have been "the sole institutional area owned and controlled by the people themselves." As Mamiya continues, however, "schisms constituted only one part of the story in the creation of new churches." The missionary motivation of Methodism, Bethel's own sense of stewardship for the black community as a whole, and growth beyond the capacity of its building led Bethel to support the founding of twenty other Baltimore-area A.M.E. congregations between 1827 and 1982. In most of these cases, Bethel appointed "missionaries" to create a church in a poor neighborhood, with financial assistance and additional members also flowing from the mother congregation.[20] This maternal activity extended Bethel's tradition into new situations. Just as important, it also sustained and reinvigorated Bethel's own participation in the living tradition of mission-oriented, socially concerned, freedom-seeking African-American Methodists.

In many ways, traditions can be like the air that is breathed, so taken for granted as not to be noticed. When congregations are founded, however, commitment to a particular tradition is highlighted, and its most urgent practices gain priority. Founders must reflect upon what matters. Later, often, some members will reenact a founding, breaking away to continue the argument that shapes the tradition. In other congregations, later members will seek to extend their congregation's tradition in a different way, by sharing it with a younger institution. In every instance, the pursuit of the goods that the tradition bears is for at least a while not taken for granted but explicitly claimed.

Once in operation, congregations induct individuals and families into a tradition by engaging in and teaching the practices that are intrinsic to that tradition.

In every congregation, deliberate efforts to transmit tradition are evident. In American congregations, these often take shape in forms associated with schooling, which dominates the American educational imagination. Sunday schools, Bible classes, Hebrew schools, Catholic parochial schools, and a Swaminarayan Hindu correspondence course in which exams are graded in India provide good examples. These activities seek to teach tradition in a sustained and deliberate way. MacIntyre's insistence that living traditions are socially embodied suggests that the classroom transmission of ideas and texts can play only a limited part in congregations' bearing of traditions, however. Instead, it is the group of practices intrinsic to that tradition—the "coherent and complex forms of socially established cooperative human activity through which goods internal to that form of activity are realized"—that need to be learned.[21]

Craig Dykstra, working within the Reformed Christian tradition, has explored the implications of MacIntyre's concepts for education in Christian faith. Likening MacIntyre's "practices" to John Calvin's "external means by which God invites us into the society of Christ and holds us therein," Dykstra argues that the Christian community "carries on its life through certain 'practices' that are constitutive of the shape of its life together in the world." When a community is participating in the practices of Christianity, "an environment is created in which people come to know the presence of God and experience new being in the world. . . . By active participation in practices that are central to the historical life of the community of faith, we place ourselves in the kind of situation in which God accomplishes the work of grace." Among these practices Dykstra includes worship, telling the Christian story, interpreting the Scriptures and the history of the church, praying, confessing and forgiving, carrying out acts of justice and mercy, suffering with and for others, resisting destructive powers and patterns, and providing hospitality and care, even to strangers and enemies. When people seek excellence in these practices, there becomes available what MacIntyre would call the "internal goods" that Christian tradition pursues, and what Dykstra calls "the presence of God and the experience of new life." These practices constitute the church and "place people in touch with God's redemptive activity," and it is by participating in them that "people come to faith and grow in faith."[22]

The complex of practices that socially embody the Christian tradition, as here described in the Reformed version, differs from that of other traditions, of course, but Dykstra's extension of MacIntyre's work suggests an approach that can be carried to the study of other traditions as well. Swaminarayan Hinduism, for example, emerged in India in 1802 as a new religious community committed to the reform of Hindu religious practices, and a succession of swamis has overseen the community's devotion and discipline ever since. As Swaminarayans have moved to the United States, congregations have become the places in which this oversight, now international in scope, is made effective. Within this religious movement, the division of the men into "world renouncers" and "householders" is embodied in the different practices of the two groups; each man gains his identity from his own participation in the practices appropriate to his status, but the community as a whole is identified by the fact that both sets of practices are in place. Householders and their families feast at weekly gatherings, marking their sharing of food with rituals; the ascetic class eats little, mixing food with water to mask the food's flavor. For householders, daily prayers and rituals, as well as the observance of lifelong vows of moral discipline, embody the pursuit of the good of this tradition, the divine presence; for the congregation's resident priest, the entire day is spent in historic practices of temple service that make possible that pursuit for the whole community.[23] If the Gujarati who now live in the suburbs of Chicago were to stop participating in the practices of Swaminarayan Hinduism—if they were to discontinue their home devotions, their prescribed schedule of temple worship, their ritual feasts, and their observance of their vows—they would no longer be Swaminarayan. Similarly, if their children do not learn to participate in these practices, this tradition will be weakened, if it survives at all in this new location. In MacIntyre's terms their tradition, lacking social embodiment, would no longer be "living" in Illinois.

This is not to say that practices may not be adapted and amplified, while still authentically extending the tradition in the new location. In fact, the quest for the full meaning of the goods internal to a tradition often results in the extension of the reach of its practices. When congregations, in their local particularity, extend historical practices in ways that are uniquely their own, they can enable a great tradition to possess a life in a place where previously it had none. When Chuck Smith baptized hundreds of hippies in the Pacific surf in the early 1970s, he let them participate in a historic practice in a way distinctly suited to their immediate situation; this also proved to be an identity-forming practice for his congregation, Calvary Chapel. Moreover, through this one practice Smith invited these young people, who came to be known as Jesus freaks, into a larger set of related practices.[24] In a different adaptation of a practice, Latin American base Christian communities have made the historic practice of Scripture study available to their own membership and location. In doing so, they have extended the reach of the practice itself and added something to the living tradition that is Christianity.

MacIntyre's insistence that social embodiment is essential to the bearing of living traditions challenges the common notion that traditions are principally borne by texts. Yet the observable fact that texts are prominent and influential in congregations should not be overlooked. A practice-oriented view of how congregations bear traditions would suggest that, instead of viewing texts as an independent force in congregational life, we should look for the ways in which congregants practice the presence of the text. In a Southern Baptist Bible class or a Talmud study circle, for example, we can observe participation in a practice, a socially coherent activity that has pursued an excellence internal to itself across the generations. In these instances and others, congregational life stirs the desire to learn the texts, sustains the motivation to teach them, and creates the context in which the goods to which the texts testify may be pursued. The text attests to the history of the other practices that constitute the life of the congregation, and the practice of being in the presence of the text is supported by a cluster of related practices.[25]

The Christian educator Marianne Sawicki has argued persuasively that texts and practices mutually rely upon one another, and that both require the life of a community. Within Christian tradition, she writes, the transmission of faith includes three elements: texts, worship, and a way of life. These "three media" of verbal teaching, expressive liturgy, and healing lifestyle are inseparable. "The word 'reconciliation,' along with its stories and theology, says the same truth that is acted out in feetwashing and that is also demonstrated in a lifestyle wherein the trusting intimacy of friendship can be built gradually. The word 'sabbath,' along with its stories and theological discussions, says the same truth that we express by assembling for prayer together on Sunday and that we also express in a lifestyle that lavishes the gift of time on one another."[26]

MacIntyre and Dykstra might call all three of Sawicki's media "practices," as all are socially learned and embodied, and Dykstra would join Sawicki in the affirmation, from within Christian tradition, that one practice is strengthened by the presence of other related practices.[27] The most striking aspect of Dykstra's and Sawicki's explications of the practices, however, does not reside in their efforts to define and describe, helpful as those are. Most striking—and most important—are their theological accounts of how the practices bind practitioners to the transcendent realities they affirm, as tradition's bearers rather than simply tradition's observers. This is what it means, from a perspective within Christian tradition, to pursue the internal goods of that tradition: through the practices, reconciliation and participation in God's work of redemption in the world become real. When this is so, the transmission of practices through institutions entails not only the replication of historical forms of social activity, nor even the bearing of living traditions in MacIntyre's sense. Instead, what is taking place is the realization of transcendence in the midst of an unmistakably historical process.

Congregations also induct individuals and families into a tradition by providing connections to that which is beyond each congregation's own parochialism.

Living traditions and the practices and institutions that bear them help to form the identity of the individuals who participate in them, in MacIntyre's view. The history of congregations shows that founders have sensed this dynamic, for many have been explicit in their hopes of providing an identity-forming place for their children. This has often been most notable in the case of immigrant congregations, in which first-generation founders have sought to preserve the cultures and languages of home within the sacred world of the congregation. In other North American congregations, among groups as different as sectarian Anabaptists and African-American Pentecostals, concern for the formation of identity within the congregation in opposition to the pressures of the dominant culture is also evident.[28] These efforts at identity-formation tend to create congregations that are internally homogeneous.

In many ways, the view of tradition that we have been exploring would seem to drive towards congregational homogeneity and enclosure, as immersion in the practices of a living tradition differentiates each group from those outside its boundaries. MacIntyre's approach, however, insists that the bearing of tradition is not an enterprise that shelters its participants from conflict and otherness. Instead, to participate in a tradition is to participate in an argument about the very goods the tradition pursues. Moreover, since living traditions are historically extended, they necessarily include elements that are distant, and therefore unsettling, to any local social embodiment. Any congregation that is pursuing the practice of reflection on its tradition in an excellent way will encounter some elements that disturb its own localism and particularity. The great religious traditions of the world are historically extended not only in time but also in space, finding different, and sometimes conflicting, embodiments in different continents, different cultures, or different neighborhoods. As much as congregations can bestow identity, they can also be places where the conflict that characterizes living traditions takes place, and where the larger tradition's challenges to narrow versions of identity are encountered.

A Presbyterian congregation studied by a team of scholars in the mid-1980s provides an example of how congregations, though indispensably tied to their local settings, can become places where the unsettling claims of the longer and wider tradition challenge parochialism. Located on the main street of a medium-sized town in Ohio, this mostly Republican congregation seemed to the scholarly team to epitomize comfort within the limited world of the white middle class. These were all-American people living in an all-American town, whose high school football star was featured on the Wheaties box cover at the time of the study. Since the founding of the congregation in 1831, just four years after the building of the canal upon which the town's early life depended, its leaders had been pillars not only of the church but also of society, as prominent members of the local establishment.[29]

The history of this congregation discloses much more than smug midwestern parochialism, however. The Church of the Covenant attracted the attention of the scholarly team because it had taken an action that seemed out of keeping with its local culture of middle-class Republicanism. It had offered sanctuary to a group of refugees, fleeing war in El Salvador, who were defined by the United States government as illegal aliens. The study team wanted to know how this ostensibly conservative congregation had chosen to act in opposition to civil law. Implicitly, they were also asking the basic question under consideration in this essay: how is it that a great religious tradition (which in the scholars' view would support the sanctuary movement) can be borne into the future by such a small and culturally restricted institution as this congregation?

What became evident during the study was that the congregation acted in a surprising way because its members attained access to parts of its tradition that were distant in time and space from its own location—in MacIntyre's terms, to the historical extendedness of Christian tradition. In their own account, congregants reported that their reading of the Bible was crucial to their decision. In the view of the scholars, these laypersons had very limited access to the relevant range of biblical texts, but those were powerful, as were several other forms of connection to the extended tradition. Like other congregations in the sanctuary movement, this one studied the history of the practice of sanctuary, expanding their view of the Christian past to include information about sanctuary in ancient Israel, medieval Europe, and the pre–Civil War antislavery movement in Ohio. Dietrich Bonhoeffer's writings, which were introduced by one graduate-student member, were very influential. The fact that the congregation is associated with the wider church also contributed. It was a speaker at a regular leadership retreat who introduced the idea of sanctuary, after himself encountering it through his work in Habitat for Humanity, which provides a network among people with a common concern. The Church of the Covenant became part of a similar network among sanctuary congregations maintained by the Chicago Task Force on Central America, and Presbyterian denominational officials also contributed information and advice. Most influential of all, perhaps, was this congregation's response to the strangers who advocated sanctuary (including Roman Catholic nuns who had served in Central America) and the strangers who needed sanctuary—the refugees themselves.[30]

All of these factors, which drew the congregation beyond its local resources as a face-to-face community, contributed to the decision to offer sanctuary. Yet the tradition did not offer a univocal response to the ethical question the congregation faced. Argument about the nature of the goods the tradition pursues—in this case, the Reformed Christian tradition's pursuit of social justice—was heated at times, and many members disagreed, on the ground of tradition, with the action that was taken. Some similar congregations answered the sanctuary question differently.

Congregations, thoroughly immersed in their local settings though they are, are places where people deliberately expose themselves to that which is strange to those settings. At the least, the strangeness inheres in the ancient texts that are honored in almost all American congregations; sometimes it also appears in personal form, as when Ohio Republicans help a handful of Central American refugees at considerable risk and expense to themselves, or when young professionals at Fourth Presbyterian Church volunteer to tutor children in one of the Chicago Housing Authority's toughest projects.[31] Local cultures alone, without the historical extendedness of the traditions these congregations bear, would not sustain these encounters with the stranger. Moreover, in receiving the mandates of the longer tradition and widening the circle of their practice, these congregations historically extend the tradition itself, adding unfamiliar combinations of people and practices to its embodiment in that place.

Some congregations are more aware than others of their participation in traditions that extend far beyond their own time and place. Mt. Hebron Baptist Church, for example, probably thinks less about the national and international contexts of its life than does St. Boniface Roman Catholic Church in Chicago, where powerful ecclesiastic structures and strong ethnic identifications with Europe and Latin America shape the practice and self-image of the congregation. Other means by which congregations have historically been tied to extended traditions are also differently manifested in these two settings; Mt. Hebron has chosen its own ministers from a pool of men untouched by seminary education while St. Boniface has been assigned leaders shaped first by ecclesiastical educational institutions, and Mt. Hebron has stood aloof from its denomination in a way that a Catholic congregation cannot. In some ethnically identified congregations, ties to the home country—Lebanon for the members of our Canadian Muslim congregation, Greece for the Baltimore Orthodox, India for the Swaminarayans—dominate the historical consciousness and persistent relationships of the members.[32] In primitivist or restorationist congregations, in contrast, an image of early Christianity seeks to displace other forms of connection to longer and wider communities of meaning and relationship. Through all of these diverse forms of attachment to distant times and places, congregations expose people to that which is strange to the ordinary American cities and towns where they live.

Because the great religious traditions are extended through centuries of time and continents of space, they encompass a variety of practices and arguments that may not be in use in any given local setting at a particular time. Yet this variety is available as a resource for present and future practice.[33] Practices can emerge, fade, and reappear; at Bethel Church, for instance, musical reminders of the African past have been welcomed at some stages in the congregation's history and suppressed at others.[34] Practices can also be adopted from contemporary but geographically distant coreligionists. The sanctuary movement in the northern United States, for example, was powerfully influenced by pioneering sanctuary congregations in the Southwest. This movement has also introduced methods of Bible study developed in Latin America to more affluent North Americans. Even though the whole range of practices that make up a living tradition are not ever fully enacted in any specific place, they are available within the extended past and present of the tradition.

By their doing of these things, congregations enable great traditions to find expression in ever new historical forms, and thereby to be both perpetuated and changed.

Tradition, though associated with the past, also has a future; it continues "a not-yet-completed narrative."[35] For MacIntyre, the openness of a tradition's future is evident in the unresolvable argument that constitutes it (what exactly *is* redemption? is it what is happening in this case or not?) and in the quest it engenders in its bearers to learn both about themselves and about the fullness of the tradition, including what more and else it may yet become. The question of what any tradition means is part of that tradition itself, and as long as the tradition lives the question remains in dispute. Congregations, even without knowing it, are immersed in this argument. They do not simply inherit tradition; they contribute to it. A living congregation does not leave a living tradition unaffected.

Lawrence Mamiya's history of Bethel Church shows how one congregation conducted a coherent argument about the goods of its tradition, the African-American Christian tradition. Freedom has always been an ultimate value within this congregation, Mamiya writes, but "its multiple meanings have changed in different historical circumstances: for 250 years freedom meant freedom from bondage; during Reconstruction it meant the right to vote and in the twentieth century it carried the connotations of political, economic, and social equality." Turning the corner into each new understanding of freedom has involved argument, and sometimes schism. Before and after the Civil War, for example, freedom from bondage and the pursuit of civil equity engendered a black middle-class ethos, which militated against the spontaneous and enthusiastic worship of black folk culture. The result was a conflict between two styles that became an arena of identity-definition for this community. This conflict finally enriched the African-American religious tradition with a greater institutional diversity, as Holiness and Pentecostal groups sprang up around the turn of the century. In recent years, the neo-Pentecostal revival within the African Methodist Episcopal Church has reintroduced this formerly suppressed strand into relatively staid congregations such as Bethel, which has experienced amazing growth as a result. Accompanying this expansion of the congregation's spiritual tradition has been an expansion of its social ministry; within this context, "freedom" has acquired the new meaning of freedom from drug abuse, and the urgency of ministry to the urban poor has led to greater acceptance of lay ministry and women's ordained ministry. As a living tradition has embraced its future, the institutional weight and organizational experience of Bethel Church has been marshaled, through an influx of spiritual vigor nurtured through the previous decades in other congregations, to extend the African-American religious tradition into new forms of outreach to the poorest of Baltimore's poor.[36]

In countless instances, apparently minor happenstances in a congregation's story can lead to amplifications of its tradition. At Calvary Chapel in Southern California, for example, a chance meeting with a hippie introduced pastor Chuck Smith to a previously overlooked remnant of the unwashed; before long, their media-covered washing was transforming Calvary Chapel itself. Later, as Smith's flock of increasingly affluent baby-boomers stabilized, the charismatic outbursts that had earlier marked the congregation's worship were moved to the sidelines.[37] In the specificity of Calvary Chapel, in other words, the Pentecostal tradition was augmented and reshaped. Moreover, these changes helped to move Pentecostalism itself closer to the major currents of American religious expression, thereby strengthening its profile and impact, and extended it historically by attracting persons whom Pentecostalism would otherwise not have touched. The not-yet-completed narrative of the American evangelical tradition gained a new chapter.

Changes introduced under the pressures of local circumstances can open a chapter that adds new plots to the larger whole of a living religious tradition. The expansion of women's role in the Jewish and Christian traditions has often come about in this way. Mt. Hebron gave women leadership responsibilities in the 1930s largely because no men were available to assume them. Annunciation Cathedral in Baltimore abandoned the ancient Greek Orthodox division of men and women into separate, pewless worship areas when the building it acquired, formerly a Congregationalist structure, turned out to have not only pews but pews undivided by a center aisle. Men and women henceforth sat together. A similar seating change had taken place a few decades earlier, when K. K. Bene Israel began to seat husbands and wives together rather than separately.[38]

In the aggregate, it is such congregational events that constitute a living tradition's socially embodied embrace of its future. Whether religious traditions generally and necessarily require congregations for their sustenance may be open to debate, but within the North American context of religious voluntarism it is evident that congregations have provided ancient transnational traditions with indispensable means of extension into new historical settings. In some cases, this gain may have been accomplished at some cost; the historians of K. K. Bene Israel, for example, seem to regret that the American Reform Judaism that developed in Cincinnati has vitiated the family-centered heritage of Judaism, becoming dependent upon the synagogue rather than the home for its practice.[39] In other cases, it is difficult to imagine how a tradition could have survived at all without its embodiment in congregational form. Earle Waugh's history of a Muslim community in the Canadian North, for instance, suggests that only "North American congregational culture," which places an institution of education and worship at the center of a religious community's life, permitted the establishment of Muslim group identity in the New World. Unlike the Muslim world, where the structures of religious life are not congregationally shaped, America forced Muslims to band together voluntarily for the education of their young and the maintenance of the requisite observances of their faith. Waugh hints that the Canadians' successful practice of congregational life may even add a new dimension to Islam itself, by disclosing how the universality it claims can extend far beyond the Muslim world.[40] If this hunch is correct, a small gathering of Lebanese-Canadians will have contributed to the process by which a great religious tradition embraces its future on a shrinking planet, its uncompleted narrative enriched by the inclusion of adherents who face north when they bow to pray, because for them the shortest way to Mecca passes over the North Pole.

In this and a myriad of other small, unpredictable ways, traditions are sustained and advanced in their very being by congregations, as surely as congregations are brought into being by persons nurtured in traditions. Even so, and in spite of increased scholarly interest in the meaning and transmission of traditions in recent years, most prominent interpreters have overlooked the important role played by congregations.[41] A few have even explicitly belittled their importance, locating the significant religious action in other realms altogether.[42] In doing so, they seem to have implied that great religious traditions are above the need for specific social embodiment, or at least above the limitations of most congregations. Our analysis would suggest that this cannot be so, not if these traditions are living. Those who care about a living tradition, whether as its students or as its bearers, must meet it, embodied, in the lowly institutions that carry it into the future.

In addition, our analysis suggests that congregations cannot be understood without attention to the traditions they bear. Even though congregations have attracted considerable scholarly interest in recent years, the clusters of practices that constitute the lives of congregations remain largely unexamined. We shall understand congregations better as we learn to hear in their speech and recognize in their activities the ongoing arguments in which they participate. And we shall understand congregations better as we learn to discern their pursuit of the goods inherent in the traditions they bear, as part of a transgenerational and transnational quest to discover what more and what else they may yet mean.

Finally, our analysis suggests that congregations' bearing of traditions is particularly crucial within the American context of religious voluntarism and diversity. Not only do congregations rely upon traditions, but traditions rely upon them. This claim, if persuasive to contemporary religious leaders, calls the other institutions that bear traditions in common with congregations, such as theological schools and governing bodies, to heighten their attention to congregations. It also calls the local leaders of congregations to place at the center of their efforts the deepening of their members' ability to participate in the practices that embody their tradition. And in a time when many believers see themselves only as the receivers (and sometimes even as the victims) of tradition, this claim constitutes a call to members to see their tradition as something that is not alien but theirs, something to be argued with and within, something whose meaning is not yet fully understood, something that can live only as they themselves, in all their particularity, bear it into a future that is still in the making.

NOTES

1. O. E. Rölvaag, *Giants in the Earth* (New York: Harper and Brothers, 1927), p. 370. The chapter on the church is called "The Glory of the Lord."

2. Ibid., p. 375.

3. Ibid., pp. 372–76.

4. See George Papaioannou, "The History of the Greek Orthodox Cathedral of the Annunciation," and Raymond Brady Williams, "Swaminarayan Hindu Temple of Glen Ellyn," both in James P. Wind and James W. Lewis, eds., *American Congregations*, vol. 1: *Portraits of Twelve Religious Communities* (Chicago: University of Chicago Press, 1994).

5. Alasdair MacIntyre, *After Virtue: A Study in Moral Theory*, 2d ed. (Notre Dame: University of Notre Dame Press, 1984), pp. 221–23.

6. Ibid.

7. MacIntyre developed these ideas not in relation to congregations but rather as part of his analysis and corrective of Western moral philosophy. However, the possibility that it is not inappropriate to apply them to the congregation is suggested in the conclusion to *After Virtue*, in which he contends that the development of "local forms of community" is the great need of our time. Ibid., p. 263.

8. Ibid., pp. 221–23.

9. Ibid., pp. 187–88.

10. On the practical theological implications of MacIntyre's concept of practice, see Craig Dykstra, "Reconceiving Practice," in Barbara G. Wheeler and Edward Farley, eds., *Shifting Boundaries: Contextual Approaches to the Structure of Theological Education* (Louisville: Westminster/John Knox Press, 1991). Dykstra develops these insights more fully in "Education in Christian Practice" (manuscript), delivered as the Earl Lectures at Pacific School of Religion, January 22 to 24, 1991. See also *Growing in the Life of Christian Faith* (Louisville: Theology and Worship Ministry Unit, Presbyterian Church [U.S.A.], 1989), a task-force report written by Craig Dykstra.

11. MacIntyre, *After Virtue*, p. 222.

12. Ibid., p. 194.

13. Ibid., p. 223.

14. See Jonathan D. Sarna and Karla Goldman, "From Synagogue-Community to Citadel of Reform: The History of K. K. Bene Israel (Rockdale Temple) in Cincinnati, Ohio," in Wind and Lewis, *Portraits*.

15. The examples used in this paragraph and elsewhere in the chapter are drawn from the congregational histories published in Wind and Lewis, *Portraits*.

16. Wayne Flynt, "'A Special Feeling of Closeness': Mt. Hebron Baptist Church, Leeds, Alabama," in Wind and Lewis, *Portraits*.

17. Sarna and Goldman, "From Synagogue-Community to Citadel of Reform."

18. Ibid., and Flynt, "'A Special Feeling of Closeness'."

19. These congregations are portrayed in historical essays in Wind and Lewis, *Portraits*.

20. Lawrence Mamiya, "A Social History of the Bethel African Methodist

Episcopal Church in Baltimore: The House of God and the Struggle for Freedom," in Wind and Lewis, *Portraits*.

21. MacIntyre, *After Virtue*, p. 187.

22. Craig Dykstra, "Education in Christian Practice," I, 14–16.

23. Williams, "Swaminarayan Hindu Temple of Glen Ellyn."

24. Randall Balmer and Jesse T. Todd, Jr., "Calvary Chapel," in Wind and Lewis, *Portraits*.

25. Samuel C. Heilman, *The People of the Book: Drama, Fellowship, and Religion* (Chicago: University of Chicago Press, 1983), provides a rich portrait of the practice of the presence of the text in Talmud study circles.

26. Marianne Sawicki, "Teaching as a Gift of Peace," *Theology Today*, 47 (January 1991): 386.

27. Marianne Sawicki, "Historical Methods and Religious Education," *Religious Education* 82 (Summer 1987): 384, describes a similar range of activities, including teaching, as "practices" also, though she means the terms in Foucault's, rather than MacIntyre's, sense. Dykstra discusses the way in which the practices mutually support one another in "Education in Christian Practice," II, 6.

28. *Portraits* contains several examples of immigrant congregations that showed this concern: two Roman Catholic, Muslim, Greek Orthodox, Hindu, Jewish. The other examples are described in John A. Hostetler, *Amish Society* (Baltimore: Johns Hopkins University Press, 1963), and idem, *Hutterite Society* (Baltimore: Johns Hopkins University Press, 1974), and Melvin D. Williams, *Community in a Black Pentecostal Church* (Pittsburgh: University of Pittsburgh Press, 1974).

29. Some unfortunate stereotypes of what it means to be "American" inhere in this depiction. But the power of these stereotypes discloses the very local (or even, as I said above, tedious and claustrophobic) character of one side of this congregation's identity. As I will argue below, there is a great deal more than this to that identity. That this congregation deserved to have this "all-American" stereotype attached to it was the judgment of John Hart of NBC News, whose report on his visit to this congregation began thus: "If there is a true-blue America it is here on Federal Street in Centerville, population 30,000, politics conservative, old houses, old values, safe for kids, a church town. And if there is a mainline establishment church here in true-blue America, it is The Church of the Covenant, 133 years old." "Centerville" and "The Church of the Covenant" are pseudonyms assigned by the study team, whose work appears in Nelle G. Slater, ed., *Tensions between Citizenship and Discipleship: A Case Study* (New York: Pilgrim Press, 1989). The Hart quote is in the essay by Dorothy C. Bass, "A Church Town: A History of Presbyterians and Education in Centerville," pp. 27–28. I call this world "limited" in the sense that all local worlds are limited.

30. Slater, *Tensions between Citizenship and Discipleship*, contains a narrative case study of the congregation's decision and several analytical assessments of it by the team of scholars (Dorothy C. Bass, Walter Brueggemann, Bernard J.

Cooke, Don S. Browning, Karen Lebacqz, John A. Coleman, Mary C. Boys, Sara P. Little, and C. Ellis Nelson).

31. Marilee Munger Scroggs, "Making a Difference: Fourth Presbyterian Church of Chicago," in Wind and Lewis, *Portraits.*

32. Each of the congregations mentioned here is described in Wind and Lewis, *Portraits.*

33. Craig Dykstra makes this point in "Education in Christian Practice," III, 8.

34. Mamiya, "A Social History of the Bethel African Methodist Episcopal Church."

35. MacIntyre, *After Virtue*, p. 223.

36. Mamiya, "A Social History of the Bethel African Methodist Episcopal Church.

37. Balmer and Todd, "Calvary Chapel."

38. See Flynt, "'A Special Feeling of Closeness,'" Papaioannou, "A History of the Greek Orthodox Cathedral of the Annunciation," and Sarna and Goldman, "From Synagogue-Community to Citadel of Reform."

39. Sarna and Goldman, "From Synagogue-Community to Citadel of Reform."

40. Earle Waugh, "Reducing the Distance: A Muslim Congregation in the Canadian North," in Wind and Lewis, *Portraits.*

41. For example, Jaroslav Pelikan, *The Vindication of Tradition* (New Haven: Yale University Press, 1984).

42. For example, Peter L. Berger, *The Noise of Solemn Assemblies* (Garden City: Doubleday, 1961), and Gibson Winter, *The Suburban Captivity of the Churches* (New York: Doubleday, 1961).

SIX

Congregational Studies
as Practical Theology

Don S. Browning

A LTHOUGH SCHOLARS are seeing a significant increase in the number of congregational studies, the motivation for this new interest is not immediately clear. Many studies have been either sociological or, as are the essays in the first volume of *American Congregations*, historical. But the interests behind congregational studies are not primarily encyclopedic. It is true that the congregation has been neglected as a social form worthy of academic study and that great gaps exist in our cognitive map of its various manifestations and changes. But the desire to fill in the blanks of our sociological and historical knowledge of congregations does not account fully for the new academic interest in them.

The interests sparking this new research, I maintain, are primarily practical. The crisis that congregations are facing in most Western societies has generated new interest in assessing their value and determining if there are defensible grounds and viable means for their revival. Not only are the motivating interests practical, they are critical. Many contemporary historical and sociological studies of congregations are implicit attempts to assess the validity or usefulness of these institutions.[1] Generally these assessments are indirect; their evaluative judgments are stated softly, as is generally the case in sociological and historical studies. Nuanced normative judgments are advanced in these disciplines, but they are not defended critically. This is understandable, for if they were so defended, historical and sociological studies would be transmuted into something else, possibly ethics or theology. Although some new efforts to develop critical sociological and historical studies take explicit responsibility for grounding the value judgments that inevitably guide historical and sociological work, no practitioners of these critical disciplines have entered the field of congregational studies.[2] If critical sociology or history were to attempt such studies, each might have contributions to make to the ethical and religious assessment of congregations. But, to date, no proposals in critical sociological or historical studies have put forward methods for assessing the distinctively theological and ethical claims of religious communities.

It is not my purpose to criticize either sociological or historical approaches to the study of congregations. I propose instead the creation of a new, fully critical discipline—a critical practical theology—to enter the field of congregational studies. This discipline should make use of the descriptive tools of both sociology and history and also psychology and anthropology, but it also should have tools to assess the theological and ethical dimensions of congregations in relation to their contexts. Hence it should have within it a component of what I call *descriptive theology*.

But it should have a critical component as well. Not only should it advance multidimensional descriptions of congregations, it should have ways to assess critically the practical religious thought and action of congregations. Is such a discipline possible? Can it be given academic credibility? How would it relate to the fields of fundamental, historical, systematic, and moral theology?

In what follows, I both define and argue for the epistemological grounds of a critical practical theology. I show that its epistemological grounds can be established when implications of Gadamer's theory of understanding as dialogue are grasped fully. I then bring this understanding of practical theology into conversation with studies of two congregations—Wiltshire Methodist Church and the Church of the Covenant. Wiltshire is used to illustrate the meaning of descriptive theology, a movement of a critical practical theology. The Church of the Covenant is used to illustrate the movement called strategic practical theology.

Hermeneutics and Practical Reason: Implications for Theology and the Social Sciences

The hermeneutic theories of Heidegger, Gadamer, and Ricoeur have had an enormous influence on contemporary theology.[3] The full implications of their concept of understanding as dialogue and conversation, however, have seldom been recognized by scholars who use hermeneutic theory. More specifically, Gadamer's view of the close relation between hermeneutics as dialogue or conversation and Aristotle's view of *phronesis* (practical reason, practical wisdom) is often overlooked. This close relation is important for my argument because it helps us see how historical reason and practical reason are associated. Gadamer believes that Aristotle's theory of *phronesis* illustrates the true meaning of understanding as conversation. For Gadamer, both *phronesis* and understanding are historically situated inquiries guided from the beginning by interests in practical application: "Application is neither a subsequent nor a merely occasional part of the phenomenon of understanding, but codetermines it as a whole from the beginning."[4] Understanding and interpretation in whatever disciplines they function, says Gadamer, are moral conversations that are shaped throughout by practical concerns about application to current situations. If this is true, light is shed on the recent academic interest in congregational studies.

This formulation replaces the theory-practice view of understanding with a practice-theory-practice model. Human understanding in its basic form is a dialogue or conversation in which practical questions are brought to the object of conversation from the beginning and not just added at the end. Crises in our present theory-laden practices generate questions. These questions are brought to our historically situated dialogues. Out of these dialogues are generated practical hypotheses which may (or may not) prove helpful for the reconstruction of our practices.

Gadamer proposes this model as the key to understanding in both the humanities and the social sciences. Richard Bernstein in *Beyond Objectivism and Relativism* (1983) and Richard Rorty in *Philosophy and the Mirror of Nature* (1979) have developed a synthesis between American philosophical pragmatism and Gadamerian hermeneutics.[5] They help us interpret certain themes in pragmatism from the perspective of Gadamer's concept of understanding as situated dialogue. Both make proposals for understanding the social sciences as basically hermeneutical. Historian of science Thomas Kuhn, without the benefit of Gadamer's theory of hermeneutics, saw the natural sciences also as basically practical and hermeneutical enterprises.[6]

The most striking recent extension of hermeneutic theory has been advanced by Robert Bellah and his colleagues in *Habits of the Heart* (1985).[7] Bellah and his team advance a hermeneutical theory of sociological and historical knowledge. Tradition—what Gadamer calls "effective history"—is given a major role in sociological knowing. According to Gadamer's concept of effective history, all understanding is shaped by the continuing effects of the great cultural and religious texts and monuments that gave birth to a cultural tradition.[8] All members of a culture, including its social scientists, are shaped by its historical tradition; this tradition becomes part of the situated context from which their attempts to understand must necessarily begin. Bellah believes that the social sciences should acknowledge explicitly what this truth means for their work.

> Social science is not a disembodied cognitive enterprise. It is a tradition, or set of traditions, deeply rooted in the philosophical and humanistic (and, to more than a small extent, the religious) history of the West. Social science makes assumptions about the nature of persons, the nature of society, and the relation between persons and society. It also, whether it admits it or not, makes assumptions about the good person and a good society and considers how far these conceptions are embodied in our actual society. Becoming conscious of the cultural roots of these assumptions would remind the social scientist that these assumptions are contestable and the choice of assumptions involves controversies that lie deep in the history of Western thought. Social science as public philosophy would make the philosophical conversation its own.[9]

Not only does this quotation show the importance of tradition for all understanding, whether pursued within the context of history or the social sciences, it suggests a role for religion as well. Tradition has a religious dimension that shapes the cognitive beginnings of the understanding process. In *Habits of the Heart* Bellah and his team use both the scriptural and the republican traditions to analyze and assess contemporary American life. Religious tradition plays a role in their social-scientific description and analysis. If Gadamer and Bellah are correct, the historian too is tradition-saturated and practically motivated in his or her attempts to understand historical records. Bellah is saying that social scientists and historians must not only acknowledge that tradition plays a role in their disciplines but also take responsibility for the critical conversation about the relative adequacy of their tradition-saturated beginning points.

Hermeneutic Social Science and the Movements of a Critical Practical Theology

I illustrate these general points primarily with reference to the social sciences and their relation to a critical practical theology. If tradition shapes the structure of understanding in the social sciences and if religion is a dimension of tradition, then only a thin line separates such hermeneutically conceived social sciences and theology. In addition, if all understanding is motivated by practical concerns from the beginning, this fact has implications for the entire structure of theology. It suggests that theology is *practical theology* at its core. Whatever the differences between practical theology and the hermeneutic social sciences—and some do exist—if we take Bellah seriously, we recognize these differences to be slight. Both hermeneutic social science and practical theology have practical interests. Both are saturated by tradition, which also has a religious dimension. Both, in order to understand the present, must attempt to understand the past. The difference is that practical theology's *primary goal* is to test explicitly the adequacy of its normative religious claims, both their capacity to interpret present situations and their moral and religious truth. If hermeneutic social science were to take critical responsibility for its tradition-laden beginning points, it might indeed cross the boundary into the realm of a critical practical theology.

Practical theology is often associated with the church disciplines of Christian education (catechetics), pastoral care (poimenics), worship (liturgics), and preaching (homiletics). Frequently the social service and missionary activities of the churches are included. Recently the new field of church development also has been classified as a practical theological discipline, especially in Holland.[10] These fields within practical theology have concentrated on the duties of the ordained minister (the clerical paradigm), the church's practical work in building its life (the ecclesial paradigm), or the church's practical life in the world (the public paradigm).[11] This view of practical theology reflects the old Protestant quadrivium which divided the theological disciplines into Bible, church history, systematic theology, and practical theology. Practical theology in this system was caught in a theory-practice epistemology. Bible, church history, and systematic theology produced the theory, and practical theology applied it.

Gadamer's close association of hermeneutics and *phronesis* suggests a very different structure for both theology as a whole and the traditional view of practical theology. If one takes Gadamer seriously, all theology (and all the humanities and the social sciences) becomes practical through and through. All attempts to understand, even within theology, are guided from the beginning by a broad concern with application.

In view of this, an alternative organization of the disciplines of theology seems necessary. I have proposed that theology as a whole be conceived as a fundamental or critical practical theology with four movements: descriptive, historical, systematic, and strategic practical theology. *Strategic practical theology* (sometimes called "fully practical theology") covers what were once known as the traditional disciplines of education, care, preaching, and worship. This proposal, however, breaks down the old theory-practice model. Fundamental practical theology is motivated by practical questions from the beginning. These practical questions are brought to historical theology, are handled more generally and critically in systematic theology, and then bring new insight to the full richness of the concrete situation in strategic practical theology. Strategic practical theology is not the application of theory that has been worked out in historical and systematic theology. It is the culmination of a process that has been practical from the beginning. Furthermore, the new consolidations of practice that occur in strategic practical theology, when tested against experience, soon generate new questions which once again animate the practical hermeneutical circle.

I call this new organization of the theological disciplines a *fundamental practical theology*, and I use the word *fundamental* to communicate that the discipline should be critical. All theology, like all knowledge, begins with the traditions and narratives of particular religious communities. To this extent, all theology (like all knowledge) is born out of faith. Although faith, tradition, and confession characterize the beginning moments of theology, a fundamental practical theology is willing to advance reasons that maximize the rational plausibility of its confessional beginning points.

David Tracy, in *Blessed Rage for Order*, has advanced proposals for a fundamental theology, calling it a "revised or critical correlational theology." By this he means a theology that enters into critical conversation with the full range of prominent alternative interpretations of experience that modern cultures have advanced. Such a correlational conversation looks for identities, nonidentities, and analogies between the Christian witness and other interpretations of cultural experience. It not only listens to the questions of alternative interpretations (as did Tillich's correlational theology) but also critically engages the answers advanced by these alternatives.[12] A revised correlational theology is willing to advance reasons for the plausibility of its interpretations of both the Christian classics and their meaning for life.

There is a difference, however, between Tracy's view of fundamental theology and my view of fundamental practical theology. I am saying that theology as a whole, and not just strategic practical theology, is practical through and through. Because Tracy has been influenced profoundly by Gadamer's hermeneutics, he probably would not object to

197

this formulation. But Tracy concentrates so decidedly on the task in fundamental theology of determining transcendental or metaphysical truth-claims that the potentially practical character of fundamental theology is obscured. My view of a fundamental practical theology that is also correlational is close to the "praxis correlational" models of theology proposed by Matthew Lamb and Rebecca Chopp.[13] It should be pointed out that the practical questions that a fundamental practical theology brings to the classic texts of the faith are always theory-laden. Buried within them, therefore, is the full range of cognitive and moral-validity claims that Tracy is concerned to address. Nonetheless, Gadamer is right that existential-practical interests dominate all understanding, even theological understanding. When we recognize this, the structure of theology looks different and suggests, I believe, the priority of a fundamental practical theology.

Descriptive Theology and Congregational Studies

The view of fundamental or critical practical theology I propose holds within it a definite place for descriptive theology, including congregational studies. Descriptive theology is interested, of course, in *all* situations—occupational, familial, educational, governmental, legal, military—that are part of life and that engender practical questions to be addressed by Christian action. But congregations and synagogues are the principal carriers of Christianity and Judaism, the communities that introduce and socialize their members to the classic texts of these faiths. Hence descriptive theology will have a special interest in congregations as situations for fundamental practical theological thinking and action.

In this connection, a congregational case study should serve as a helpful illustration. The case of Wiltshire Methodist Church, recorded in *Building Effective Ministry* (1983), edited by Carl Dudley, can illustrate the meaning of descriptive theology, show what it contributes to congregational studies, and place such studies within the larger framework of fundamental practical theology.

Wiltshire Church is the fictitious name of a Methodist church located in the suburbs of a New England city given the name of Springfield. The team of researchers who studied it was convened by the Lilly Endowment in the early days of its interest in congregational studies. Made up of three sociologists, two psychologists, two cultural anthropologists, two church development consultants, and one practical theologian (myself), the team was told that our purpose was to help our audiences understand the "full richness" of congregations and to illustrate what the different disciplines that had been assembled could contribute to such an understanding.

This was a worthy objective, but one thing was missing: provision for an explicitly theological perspective. The practical theologian was charged with the responsibility of integrating the various perspectives, none of which was originally theological. The leaders of the team eventually recognized this and invited two theologians to join the project. But the omission of a more complete theological perspective in the beginning was telling. It suggested that the description of congregations was a task solely for social scientists. The idea of a theological description of a congregation had not occurred to either the leaders or most of the members of the team. Did this mean that theology was a discipline that studied God but could not describe life, even the life of a Christian congregation?

If Bellah is correct that all the social sciences are shaped by tradition and that tradition always has a religious horizon, then to some extent all social sciences have descriptive theological dimensions. This may seem an outrageous statement. But several recent studies have uncovered religious dimensions in both the psychological and sociological disciplines.[14] In light of these studies and the discussions in *Habits of the Heart*, the idea of descriptive theology is not so outlandish.

Description within a hermeneutical model of understanding is never neutral and objective. Description in Gadamer's theory of understanding as dialogue has a situated and value-laden character. A researcher can take certain cognitive steps to gain partial distance from embeddedness in his or her own traditions, but these maneuvers are never absolute. Total descriptive objectivity is a myth. Honesty rather than objectivity should be the major goal, and self-awareness on the part of the person doing the description is the only objectivity achievable. Such self-awareness permits dialogue and mutual criticism to proceed more freely.

The research team's multiple perspectives on Wiltshire Church help illuminate what I mean by descriptive theology. Descriptive theology helps grasp the contextual richness of the basic questions implicit in situations—in this case, the situation of Wiltshire Church. These questions in their full contextuality animate practical theological reflection. The vision of descriptive theology that I propose makes a place for the special foci of the human sciences. These sciences are treated as moments within a larger structure of understanding conceived as dialogue and conversation.

This attempt to enrich the dialogical structure of understanding by the special foci of the different social or human sciences is crucial for a proper understanding of both hermeneutic social science and practical theology. Both Ricoeur and Bellah attempt to retain, in contrast to Gadamer, a dialectical relation between explanation and understanding (*Verstehen*).[15] The explanatory interests of certain forms of psychology, sociology, or anthropology have a place within both a hermeneutical social science and a hermeneutical descriptive theology. It is very useful for descriptive theology to gain insight into the psychobiological pressures studied by psychology; the pressures of class, occupation, race, and technical rationality studied by sociology; or the systems of codes and signs that make up a group's unconscious meanings, as studied by cultural anthropology. But these are explanatory submoments within a broader structure of understanding as dialogue. The model of descriptive theology I propose uses the explanatory interests of specific social sciences but places them within a structure of dialogue that explicitly and critically acknowledges its beginning point in the Christian message and narrative.

As we examine the contributions of the four disciplines (psychology, sociology, cultural anthropology, and theology) to the description of Wiltshire Church and its surrounding community, we will see how each of the secular disciplines lapsed at times into the outer edges of descriptive theology. In each case a representative of theology could have integrated into theology's broader framework the special explanatory interests of the social sciences. Had this happened, we would have seen a genuine example of what I mean by descriptive theology—the first movement of a fundamental practical theology.

The Story of the Wiltshire Church

Wiltshire Methodist Church was located in the community of Wiltshire, a suburb of a large New England industrial and commercial center. Most of the people of Wiltshire made their living in this larger community, which we called Springfield. The mayor of Wiltshire called Wiltshire a "Shangri-la." It was located in a lush valley between two ridges several miles from the bustle and confusion of Springfield. At the time of our study in the early 1980s, it was a community of 21,000. It had grown rapidly in the previous two or three decades. The community had been founded in the 1600s. In the 1800s, a textile firm owned by the Adams family had moved to Wiltshire and become its principal employer. Its policy was to pay low salaries but to take care of its people. The owners of the Adams Company had built and paid for most of the present Methodist church and had imported its Anglican architectural design directly from England. The patriarch of the Adams family helped balance the church's annual budget at the beginning of every fiscal year by writing a check in the presence of the church board.

In the 1970s, Sid Carlson became the new minister. The congregation was stagnant, but the community was booming. Its population had quadrupled over the last twenty years. Once a company town in a rural setting, it was now a residential haven for executive-level families. Before making his decision to come to Wiltshire Church, Sid had disguised himself and visited the schools, and other leading institutions of the town. He concluded that because the town was growing, there was a good chance for the church to grow as well. Immediately upon arriving at his new charge with his wife and two daughters, Sid made some dramatic changes. He removed 221 nonparticipating members from the rolls that had totaled over 700. He reduced the Sunday morning worship services from two to one. He reduced the size of the official church board. He significantly raised the average giving of the church. He placed a strong emphasis on the church school and the music program. He began attracting young families. He established a reputation for being a good preacher and a decisive leader. Wiltshire Church was called "the best show in town." People joked that if a family could not afford a country club, Wiltshire Church was a good substitute.

Sid Carlson characterized his church as full of "wistful hearts"—people who were largely agnostic but who wanted something solid for their children. They were not biblically literate. Many of his congregation, he thought, were disillusioned with the American dream of the "two-car garage and the house in the country. Divorce—kids drinking and using pot—job conflicts—the plumbing leaking and your husband in San Francisco—the family needs are monumental." In the years directly before our study, the community and Wiltshire Church began to slow down. The population began to decline, and with it, school enrollments. Sid reached fifty and began working on a Doctor of Ministry degree. He later confessed that he failed his doctoral examinations. His ties with the wider Methodist church declined. He became concerned with his retirement and whether he could afford the college education of his daughters. Some members of the congregation became concerned about its "country club image." Two proposals that Sid was pushing were meeting resistance by the official board. One had to do with enabling Sid to move out of the parsonage and buy his own home—a move against the rules of the Methodist church. The other proposal had to do with the renovation of the Christian education building. This building always had been considered noticeably inferior to the more elegant, Anglican-styled building containing the sanctuary. Sid was deeply disappointed by this resistance. Charges and countercharges were flying. People were resigning from the official board. Some were leaving the church. Accusations about Sid's manipulative and arbitrary style of leadership were beginning to surface. At the time our study concluded, the church was in a crisis.[16]

The psychological, sociological, and anthropological scholars who studied this congregation have something in common. They claim to be, on the whole, objective and value-free. Barry Evans and Bruce Reed of the psychological team say, "our approach is . . . to *describe* the realities of the situations rather than to *evaluate* them."[17] Sociologists Jackson Carroll, William McKinney, and Wade Clark Roof write, "Sociological analysis will not prescribe to the church what it should be or do. . . ."[18] The two scholars functioning as cultural anthropologists are not as explicit. James Hopewell reveals his theological commitments in his *Congregation: Stories and Structures* (1987), but he does not mention them in his article on Wiltshire in *Building Effective Ministry*.[19] Only Melvin Williams acknowledges that ethnographical research is basically practical and "should be useful" to the groups the researcher studies.[20] But even here, Williams does not comprehend fully the dialogical and historically situated character of the ethnographic model he employs.

These social scientists do not conceive of their work as hermeneutic social science. A close reading, however, of their essays reveals hermeneutic leanings in all. Psychologists Evans and Reed concentrate on what group-dynamics specialist W. R. Bion calls the emotional "basic assumptions" of Wiltshire Church. They show how the church shifted from a basic assumption of "dependency" during the dominance of the Adams family to one of "expectancy" during the early days of Sid Carlson's ministry.[21] During the period of expectancy, Sid was endowed with almost superhuman qualities; he led the church to consolidate its values around those of the secular community of Wiltshire—the values of hard work in one's vocation, relaxation in one's private life, wealth, education, and safety. In spite of their avowals of neutrality as researchers,

Evans and Reed soon reveal their hermeneutical beginning point. They call the religion of Wiltshire Church a "pseudofunctional" religion. It is pseudofunctional because it only consolidates and legitimates the values of the Wiltshire community; it does not inject a genuinely reflective and self-critical process into the life of that church—their criterion of a genuinely functional religion.[22] Such remarks reveal that Evans and Reed have religious commitments that go beyond their alleged neutrality and what is implied by their use of functional models of religion. To them, Wiltshire Church is not the church that it should be. Their view of Wiltshire Church is informed by a vague horizon of normative religious commitments. Their focus on the basic psychological assumptions of Wiltshire find their meaning within this larger structure of understanding. Although there is a hermeneutical fringe to their interpretation of Wiltshire, it is not a genuine hermeneutical dialogue. Wiltshire Church never gets a chance to enter into the dialogue and respond. Only one party to the dialogue actually speaks for the public record, and that is the team of Evans and Reed. It is all too easy to say that this happens because Evans and Reed are Christians. But if the hermeneutical model of the social sciences is correct, something like this will happen in any description of that church or any other human community, whether the researchers are Christian or not. The effective history of the researchers shapes the structure of understanding they bring to the descriptive task.

This happens as well with the sociological team that studied Wiltshire Church. Carroll, McKinney, and Roof emphasize the various ways the external social-systemic and cultural characteristics of the community of Wiltshire influenced the inner life of Wiltshire Church. They do not take a hard deterministic point of view. They do not assert that the external social and cultural factors are so powerful that no generative elements whatsoever come from the inner religious beliefs, piety, and worship life of Wiltshire. But they do hold that the external factors are powerful and that Wiltshire Church largely reflects them. Among these are the rapid growth of the community, its infusion with executive-level people who work hard in their vocations but seek relaxation, refuge, and support in their private lives. Such people want their churches to support their private rather than their public lives.

This sociological team had its precommitments just as did the psychologists. Although they do not intend to "prescribe to the church what it should be or do," they clearly have an evaluative perspective. They do not like the privatism of the Wiltshire community and church. They are not excited by its preoccupation with familial and "private" issues like "drugs in the schools, tension and divorce in families, alcoholism for particular persons." [23] In addition to using a descriptive and explanatory focus to look at the external factors influencing the life of Wiltshire Church, this sociological team also functions out of a structure of understanding that measures Wiltshire Church against a Christian vision and finds it lacking. But the team does little to expose this larger structure of understanding or its situated character. Nor does it try to take critical responsibility for its precommitments in the way Bellah believes is necessary for the social sciences.

Williams and Hopewell, although both use the tools of cultural anthropology, take vastly different approaches. Williams applies the distinction between *structure* and *communitas* developed by the late Victor Turner. [24] He believes that Wiltshire Church overemphasizes structure at the expense of a *communitas* of intimate relationships. In doing so, the church follows the bureaucratic ethos of the occupational world of its executive-class membership. Williams clearly has a preference for *communitas*, but he never reveals the grounds of his own precommitments—his own association of *communitas* with the heart of the Christian message.

Hopewell, on the other hand, uses the semiotic theory of literary critic Northrop Frye to uncover a deep and unconscious myth functioning in the life of Wiltshire Church: the myth of Zeus, who liberated the gods by slaying the old and saturnine Chronus. [25] In doing this, Zeus established a new moral order and inaugurated an era of happiness, joviality, and progress. Hopewell argues that, at an unconscious level, Sid Carlson played the role of Zeus in the minds of the new members of Wiltshire Church. Slaying the old, dull, and saturnine rule of the Chronus-like Adams Company, Carlson inaugurated an era of progress that defied time and old age and established a community of joviality and optimism. But now Carlson (Zeus) was himself getting old, and the mythical defeat by him of aging and dullness was being exposed as superficial and incomplete.

Hopewell's creative interpretation raises several issues. First, how does this interpretation relate to the explicit self-understanding of Wiltshire Church? How does this latent mythic narrative relate to the Christian narrative preached from its pulpit? Does the latent myth corrupt the Christian story? Does the Christian story transform the latent myth? For that matter, why try to capture the latent myth of a church? Is the purpose similar to that of psychotherapy? If a church understands its unconscious story, will it be better able to control and direct itself? Hopewell does not address these issues adequately in "The Jovial Church," his essay for the Dudley volume, though he does address them to some extent in his 1987 work, *Congregation*. In "The Jovial Church," however, Hopewell makes clear his belief that the latent myth was the dominant narrative of Wiltshire Church and that this was not good. Hopewell too was in an implicit hermeneutical conversation with Wiltshire Church.

A Theological Description of Wiltshire Church

Each of these social science perspectives on Wiltshire Church thus displays a vague but still discernible religious horizon. The idea of an explicitly theological description should therefore seem less offensive, and perhaps even necessary. If all the social science perspectives actually bordered on theological interpretations, it seems reasonable to ask them to make their assumptions explicit and, indeed, perhaps even attempt to justify them critically.

This, then, should be the task of descriptive theology. Such a description can use the special foci of psychology, sociology, and anthropology as long as they are understood as submoments of a hermeneutic dialogue between interpretations of the Christian narrative and the interpretations Wiltshire explicitly uses about itself. Organizing the perspectives hierarchically in this way makes possible the descriptive theology I am proposing.

Such an integration is almost achieved in Joseph Hough's theological interpretation of the Wiltshire Church. In Hough's view, Sid Carlson presented God as a source of love and courage that Christians could tap into during times of crisis and stress. Jesus was seen primarily as a moral example, an example of courage and faith in a time of trial. Jesus does not challenge the present order but gives us the strength to face the trials of life.[26]

Hough's description of the operative theology of Wiltshire Church is informed by his own view of the Christian narrative, especially what it means for the concept of the church. The church for Hough is a human community that is also the body of Christ. As the body of Christ, the church must be a "community for the poor," a "community for the world."[27] Jesus became human, according to Hough's view of the gospel, not just for human beings but for the whole world. From this standpoint,

Wiltshire's message of love and courage to individuals facing stress is part of the story, but only part. Identification with the poor and care for the natural world are downplayed if not absent at Wiltshire.

Even though Hough's interpretive perspective is directly theological, he makes some use of the social sciences, particularly sociology. He is fully aware of the demographic trends of the Wiltshire community. He is aware of what the influx of executive-level families means for the cultural ethos of the Wiltshire community. But he does not handle these trends deterministically. In fact, for a descriptive theology to use the social sciences deterministically would be a contradiction in terms. Descriptive theology is interested primarily in describing the potential dialogue between the narrative tradition of the researcher and the narrative tradition of the person or group being described. The contributions of the special social sciences should be handled as relative and nondeterministic submoments within this larger structure of understanding. In a loose, unsystematic, yet insightful way, Hough's description of Wiltshire Church is a suggestive illustration of descriptive theology. This would have been even truer had he found ways to integrate the other submoments of psychology and cultural anthropology.

We should not be surprised, then, that Hough's description of Wiltshire Methodist Church was the most charitable and optimistic of the interpretations. Although Hough saw a great distance between his understanding of the Christian narrative and the one heard at Wiltshire Church, he believed that elements of grace and new hope could be found there.[28] Wiltshire's concern for the education of its children, its pastoral care, its love of the eucharist, and indeed the very controversy then besetting its life—all these indicated to Hough that the Holy Spirit was working in subtle ways in the life of that congregation. The controversy indicated sufficient tension between its ideals and the reality at Wiltshire Church for self-criticism and possible transformation to begin taking place. Christian theology, in all its forms, depicts an open world where grace and transformation are possible. For this reason, it may be better equipped than the other sciences to detect signs of these realities.

The Tasks of Descriptive Theology within Practical Theology

The primary task of descriptive theology is to render a thick description of situations. From its particular angle of vision, it should attempt to grasp the psychological, sociological, and religiocultural meanings that shape the life of the community being studied. But hermeneutically oriented description is done for a purpose: to help formulate the deep questions implicit in a situation. In this case, the purpose is to grasp the deep question coming forth from the life of Wiltshire Church. Descriptive theology describes this question with as much richness as possible and then brings it to historical and systematic theology. Application guides the interpretive process from the beginning, as Gadamer insists.

But descriptive theology has another function. It attempts to capture this deep question in its concreteness so that it can be addressed by the rest of the hermeneutical circle—especially strategic practical theology. Strategic practical theology faces the task of communicating back to the world described by descriptive theology, of trying to make contact with this world, its psychosocial forces, and its latent symbols. It does this so that the Christian message—its unique message for this situation—can be heard. The world described by descriptive theology is important also for the verification tasks of strategic practical theology. The reasons advanced by strategic practical theology will have to make logical and rhetorical sense in relation to the world of meanings and forces uncovered by descriptive theology. Congregational studies as a part of descriptive theology are essential if the transformational goals of strategic practical theology are to be achieved.

The question for Wiltshire Church can be stated simply, but it has great depth and richness: *How does a church balance the needs of its own leaders and members with the needs of others?* This is the question that Sid Carlson is asking in wanting to own his home and wanting to earn real estate equity as the members of his church do. This is the question the church is asking in trying to determine whether the children of the church deserve a building as attractive as the sanctuary enjoyed by the adults. In both cases, the needs being balanced are perceived as internal to the life of Wiltshire Church. But there are vague feelings among some members that in preoccupying itself with this question, Wiltshire Church is overlooking the needs of those beyond its boundaries.

This abstract formulation of the question, however, does not capture the richness of what descriptive theology should grasp. It is one thing to ask how the needs of the self are balanced with the needs of others. It is another thing to ask how an affluent community whose people experience a split between their public and private worlds; who feel beleaguered by the strains of success; who are concerned about their families; who have had dim and unconscious expectations about a life of never-ending expansion; who have heard that God will support them in this expansion; who secretly have hoped that their minister would consolidate this expansion but are now confronting both the limitations of life and the limitations of their minister—how these people can balance the needs of their leaders and members with the needs of others.

This thicker sense of the question provides much more contextuality for the interpretive steps in historical and systematic theology. It provides a richer, more concrete world for strategic practical theology to address. It makes it possible to discern the strengths and weaknesses of Wiltshire in more detail. It makes it possible for strategic practical theology to have a richer dialogue about the identities, nonidentities, and analogies that exist between Wiltshire's present interpretation of its situation and a deeper interpretation that might come from a more honest confrontation with the scriptural classics that allegedly rule its life.

The completion of that task in fundamental practical theology is beyond the scope of this paper, but the case of Wiltshire Church does help us locate the place of congregational studies within a critical or fundamental practical theology.

Strategic Practical Theology and Congregational Studies

Congregational studies are a natural part of descriptive theology's job of describing situations. They are also useful for helping us understand how congregations carry out in practical thought and action their transformative missions to the world. Stated in philosophical terms, these missions aim toward the practical reconstruction of life in light of the meanings and demands of a transcendent reality. It is my claim that congregational studies can help us better understand how religious communities do their thinking and acting. Or, to put it differently, congregational studies can help us understand how strategic practical theology actually takes place in congregations. Furthermore, these studies can help us see congregations as communities that sometimes exercise forms of practical reason, or *phronesis*, in ways that can be recognized by contemporary moral philosophy.

Narrative and Formalist Understandings of Practical Reason

In both theological ethics and moral philosophy, the nature of practical reason is currently being debated. Kantians and utilitarians, who have held the dominant position in modern times, have claimed that practical reason can be expressed in terms of a principle—for Kantians, the universalization principle, for utilitarians, the principle of bringing the greatest good to the largest number of people. Such formalist perspectives have influenced theology. Moral philosopher Alan Donagan has claimed that Christian ethical thinking has strong Kantian components, and philosopher Ronald Green has used the neo-Kantian moral philosophy of John Rawls to give powerful interpretations of both Jewish and Christian moral theology.[29] Utilitarianism has been used in the situation ethics of Joseph Fletcher.[30]

In recent years, these positions have been opposed by thinkers who claim that practical reason follows no single rational principle but rather is formed by the narratives of communities of tradition and memory. Alasdair MacIntyre has been the foremost proponent of this position in philosophy, and Johann Baptist Metz, Stanley Hauerwas, and James McClendon have been the major voices in theology.[31] Practical reason, according to this view, generalizes and applies stories to particular situations. Practical reason in a Christian community generalizes and applies the Christian narrative and tries to live according to its demands and promises.

It is my conviction that congregational studies can give us insight into how congregations actually do their practical moral and theological thinking. Although congregations do not all think alike, these studies can throw light on the process. And what we learn may be both morally suggestive and instructive for the improvement of the strategic practical theological thinking of congregations. An illustration of strategic practical theology is available in the case of the Church of the Covenant, a conservative Presbyterian church that became a sanctuary congregation. In this case, elements of both the narrativist and the formalist perspectives are combined. A study of them will not solve the philosophical debate, but it may raise new questions and give us insights into the practical rationality of congregations.

The Story of the Church of the Covenant

The Church of the Covenant was a conservative Presbyterian church located in a conservative midwestern community. When in 1964 its pastor returned from marching in Washington with Martin Luther King, Jr., he was asked to resign. In January 1983, the church held a retreat of its official board and invited Paul Williams to speak. Williams was a graying Republican businessman and a committed Christian. He had become concerned with the refugee problem created by the civil war in El Salvador. He challenged the church to become "involved in loving its neighbor by reaching out to the world." Shortly after the retreat, Williams asked the church to "provide hospitality" for a group of refugees from El Salvador who might be traveling through the country speaking on the sanctuary movement. The Session referred the issue to the Mission Committee.

The Mission Committee was chaired by Nan Carr. Carr asked Hilda Mann, a professor at a nearby university who had interests in liberation theology and Martin Luther, to join the committee. The committee soon concluded that there were political refugees whose lives were being threatened in El Salvador by death squads and guerrillas. They also concluded that the U.S. Immigration and Naturalization Service may have been in contradiction with its own legal framework and established international traditions pertaining to the treatment of political refugees.

Nan Carr and Hilda Mann had long discussions over the phone about the issues. They agonized about the suffering refugees. They were aware of the laws against Americans aiding, transporting, or housing illegal aliens. They thought together about how breaking the law could lead to prison, fines, embarrassment, and the disruption of life plans. They wrestled with what the gospel seemed to demand. They discussed the relation of law to gospel. Shortly after the Mission Committee began its work, one male committee member resigned. Mann herself, after an initial period of enthusiasm, resigned in response to gossip and innuendo that began circulating about the committee. She later rejoined the committee. Carr and Mann read Bonhoeffer's *Cost of Discipleship* (1949).

In June 1983, the committee asked the Session to inform the attorney general of the United States that Covenant supported other churches that had become sanctuary churches. The sanctuary movement was gaining ground throughout the country. These churches were following an ancient tradition of providing hospitality and sanctuary to political refugees. The committee then began formulating a plan for educating the congregation on the sanctuary issue. Hal Roberts, the minister of the congregation, asked the committee to plan a careful program of education that would involve the entire church and would present a balanced review of the issues. The committee hoped to involve both adults and youth. (Covenant Church had a large youth program involving approximately 150 young people each Thursday evening for a program and dinner.) Not only were the adults and youth invited but also interested outsiders from the community of Centerville. Many responded.

The program was called "Latin America—Paradise Lost." It consisted of a ten-week series of lecture-discussions presented at 10:00 on

Sunday morning with discussion continuing during coffee hour after church. The committee attempted to achieve balance between different points of view but was never sure it adequately represented more conservative views. Pastor Roberts was invited to preach on the subject, but he declined, reporting that he was following the lectionary. In addition, for three years he had been centering his preaching on God's grace and the tensions between law and gospel. The associate pastor, Carl Gordon, did preach one sermon on the sanctuary issue. Taking as his text Matthew 2:1–18, he drew a connection with the "civil disobedience" of the Wise Men who ignored the instructions of authorities and returned home another way in order to protect the life of the infant Jesus. The major text for the ten-week study was Bonhoeffer's *Cost of Discipleship*. It emphasized that the grace and forgiveness of God were designed to empower followers of Jesus to accept the demands of self-sacrificial love and the way of the cross.

Before the ten-week program concluded, Paul Williams brought three Salvadoran refugees to Centerville—Rosa, Juan, and Oscar. A few members of Covenant Church extended unofficial help to the refugees, and many members met and socialized with them.

A new study committee was formed immediately after the ten-week program. It formulated a resolution that Church of the Covenant become a sanctuary church and extend official hospitality to Rosa, Juan, and Oscar. At a congregational meeting the resolution was passed with a vote of 151 to 91.[32]

The study from which this summary is drawn is reported in *Tensions Between Citizenship and Discipleship: A Case Study* (1989), written by a team of scholars called the National Faculty Seminar on Religious Education. Although the study contains a variety of analyses of Covenant's struggle with the sanctuary issue, I focus here on the church's educational process, on its practical theological thinking, and on how it did this thinking as a group.

Covenant Church and the Five Levels of Practical Reasoning

In several essays and books I have been devising a model of practical reasoning that mediates between formalist and narrativist theories and also between classical deontological and teleological perspectives.

Within this model I identify five levels of practical reasoning. (I now call it *practical reasoning*, rather than *practical reason*, to emphasize that it involves several different logics and several different kinds of reasoning.)

I call the five levels the *visional,* the *obligational,* the *tendency-need,* the *contextual,* and the *rule-role* levels.[33] The *rule-role* level, made up of the patterns of practices that organize everyday behavior, is the most concrete, and it is where one should begin in analyzing situations. The practices themselves, however, are theory-laden and thick. They have within and around them a rich set of meanings that can be analyzed using the remaining four dimensions. The *visional* level is made up of narratives and deep metaphors that tell individuals and communities the meaning of life and the nature of its ultimate context; narrativists are most concerned with this level. The *obligational* level is influenced by the visional level, but in some circumstances it achieves a quasi-independence; formalists are most concerned with this level. The *tendency-need* level entails assessments of what humans really want and need. The sheer existence of these needs does not mean that they are morally justified, but our attempts at the visional and obligational levels to define and properly order our moral obligations always assume the existence of these needs and some theory about them. Finally, practical reasoning has a *contextual* dimension entailing judgments about the constraints, pressures, and limits of our social and ecological environments. At this level we make judgments about which of all our needs and tendencies can be actualized justly within the limits of our institutional and environmental settings.

These five levels of practical reason are functioning, I believe, in the strategic practical theology of Covenant Church. Furthermore, we can identify the different groups and voices in the church that contributed to one or another level. No single, dominant person was doing the practical reasoning at Covenant Church: ministers, lay leaders, even outsiders contributed to the total gestalt of religiously informed practical reason there. An examination of the patterns of practical reasoning at Covenant Church demonstrates that congregations do have recognizable forms of rationality. In addition, it suggests the wisdom of both the narrativist and formalist theories of practical reasoning as well as a model for bringing them together.

In setting forth the case of the Church of the Covenant, I already have recounted its concrete practices, rules, and roles. I now turn directly to the thick layers of meaning that surround them.

The Visional Level. This level of Covenant's practical thinking on sanctuary came from different places. The ministerial leadership, especially the senior minister, made an important but limited contribution. Hal Roberts refused to take a direct stand on the sanctuary issue, yet he strongly supported the congregation's moral dialogue about the issue and vigorously urged that all voices be heard. Roberts held what Jürgen Habermas would call an implicit *discourse ethic*.[34] He had an ethical idea about how a hermeneutical dialogue on sanctuary should take place. Outside that, however, he confined himself to preaching on grace and forgiveness and the law-gospel dialectic.

Roberts's message provided an incomplete narrative context for the functioning of practical reason at Covenant, but it accomplished at least three important things. First, it provided, in psychiatrist Donald Winnicott's terms, a *holding environment* for the discussion.[35] Roberts communicated to the discussion participants that they were justified by their faith in God and not by which side of the controversy finally proved successful. Second, his preaching relativized the law: it gave little content to the law and little general content to issues of right and wrong, but it did say that the law as such was not the grounds for salvation and that some expressions of the law were more justifiable than others. This was relevant as the congregation members were assessing U.S. law against aiding illegal aliens. Third, although the law was relativized, the seriousness of moral issues and questions of justice was still upheld. Admittedly, this was done abstractly. But this move had the virtue of liberating the congregation to make an inquiry. Roberts did not assume he had the right answer. He did not assume, at the start of the discussion, that anyone in particular had the right answer. But his preaching on the law-gospel dialectic did imply that some answers were better than others and that the congregation had a moral obligation to inquire into what the morally right answer might be.

Another aspect of the narrative context of Covenant's practical deliberations was connected to the lay leaders of the inquiry—specifically Nan Carr and Hilda Mann. These two women, in their moral conversations with one another, most directly confronted the issue of the cost of discipleship. They thought deeply about the legal consequences of breaking the law. They were informed and inspired by Bonhoeffer's theology of the cross in *The Cost of Discipleship*. They were responsible for adopting this book as the basic text for the ten-week educational course. This study supplemented Hal Roberts's emphasis on the narrative of God's love and redeeming grace in Jesus, which saves those who trust in God regardless of their moral failures. The emphasis on the cross contributed significantly to an extension of practical reason that focused on the principle of neighbor love.

The Obligational Level. The more specific content of moral obligation, however, came from neither Roberts nor Carr and Mann. It came from the first references to the principle of neighbor love by Paul Williams at the board retreat. Williams said there that Christians were to reach out and love the neighbor. He further made reference to the parable of the Good Samaritan and identified the neighbor as "the person abandoned on the roadside."[36] Williams's juxtaposition of the principle of neighbor love and the story of the Good Samaritan gave expression to a particular form of practical reason. It suggested that the neighbor was anyone who was in need. Neighbor love tells us to love our neighbor as ourselves (Matthew 19:19; 22:29). As we would want assistance and hospitality were we abandoned at the roadside, so too do others; we should therefore treat others as we would wish to be treated. Williams applied this principle to the situation of the political refugees of El Salvador: we should not abandon them but reach out to them and give them a helping hand.

In injecting this principle into the life of Covenant Church, Williams was developing a particular theory of moral obligation and a particular interpretation of the moral meaning of Christian love. He was moving close to what moral philosophers would call a Kantian or neo-Kantian view of moral obligation. Kantian and neo-Kantian principles of obligation emphasize the logics of reversibility and universalizability. The principle of reversibility holds that any claim I make on the other person I must permit that person to make on me. And the principle of universalizability suggests that I must be willing to generalize this to all other similar cases. The work of John Rawls on the conditions for generalizability (the veil of ignorance) and Lawrence Kohlberg on the nature of reversible moral thought are two powerful articulations of these related concepts.[37] Kohlberg explicitly sees the principles of neighbor love and the Golden Rule as exemplifications of this kind of thinking. Ronald Green has thoughtfully applied Rawls to the interpretation of neighbor love and the Golden Rule in both Judaism and Christianity.[38] Paul Williams was involved in just such moral rationality when he spoke before the board of Covenant Church, and what he said evidently stimulated the moral thinking of the board accordingly.

Narrativists like Hauerwas and Metz often attempt to deny the functioning of a general principle of obligation in the Christian message. I take the position that it is better to acknowledge the presence of the principle in the narrative and its continuities with Kantian philosophical positions (as well as the presence of similar principles in almost every advanced culture and religion of the world).[39] It is also important to acknowledge that this principle functions uniquely within the Christian narrative. It assumes, for instance, certain features of the narrative that witness to the goodness of creation and the sacrality of all humans in view of their status as bearers of the image of God. This is the Christian way of stating what Kantians claim under the more secular-sounding belief that all humans are ends and never only means. We earlier saw ways in which doctrines of grace, forgiveness, and the law-gospel dialectic could liberate the functioning of reversible and universalizable practical reason by freeing people from the belief that their justification depends on being "right" or winning the vote. The emphasis on the cross and the cost of discipleship added something further to Williams's principle of obligation. The theology of the cross says that we are to extend the mutuality and reversibility of neighbor love even in situations of difficulty, rejection, or hostility. We are to exercise the practical rationality of neighbor love even if it costs. The principle of neighbor love as such does not say this; it just tells us to love the neighbor as ourselves. But the cross tells us to do this even if we must pay a price. This is the contribution of Nan Carr and Hilda Mann to the narrative context of practical reason as it functioned at Covenant Church.

The Tendency-Need Level. Thinking at the tendency-need level of practical reasoning was attended to by the early research of the Mission Committee members, who attempted to establish whether persecution was actually taking place. Were people suffering? Were people hungry, cold, without homes, without sources of income? Were people dying? These innocent-sounding questions actually exhibit the teleological substratum of practical reasoning. They try to establish the nonmoral or premoral goods at stake. In concluding that Salvadoran refugees *were* suffering these losses, the committee was saying in effect that something should be done to restore these basic goods to their lives. Frequently in issues of this kind, questions about basic human nature and fundamental human needs are not difficult to establish. There is little debate that humans need food, water, clothes, health, and shelter. But in situations involving medical care, family and sexual ethics, biomedical engineering, or reproductive technology, these issues are both fundamental and difficult to settle. Questions about fundamental human needs and how they are known are thus an important dimension of practical reasoning—a dimension pursued at this church.

In attending to teleological questions about the premoral good, the Covenant members follow a logic that is both theologically and philosophically defensible. Their teleological concerns about the good are subordinated to their deontological concerns about justice, reversibility, and equal regard. I believe that they are close to Paul Ricoeur's interpretation of the Golden Rule. Ricoeur interprets the words "Do unto others as you would have them do unto you" to mean that we should "do *good* unto others as we would have them do *good* unto us."[40] Judgments of justice, reversibility, and equal regard are formal and empty unless they distribute basic human goods and meet genuine human needs. Judgments about the good are an essential dimension of practical reasoning, especially the practical reasoning that functions within the Christian narrative.[41]

The Contextual Level. The contextual level of practical reasoning is not problematic in this situation. Judgments about the social systemic situation were made in a variety of settings: judgments about the conflict of social forces in El Salvador between guerrillas and government forces and the intolerable situation in which it placed some Salvadorans, judgments about U.S. government policies, judgments about the resources available to Covenant Church. Did the church have the resources to care for these refugees? Although the judgments in this case were attained relatively easily, in other situations they could have been more difficult. What if Covenant Church had been poor? What if there had been a famine in the United States? What if Covenant Church itself had been under siege? Or again, what if as the U.S. government had claimed, the Salvadorans were not being persecuted and were not, indeed, even political refugees?

This case study alone cannot settle the issues between narrativist and formalist views of practical reason. But with the introduction of additional philosophical insights, the case is suggestive. It suggests first that both positions in their pure forms are extreme and one-sided. In particular, the monolithic view of the currently fashionable narrativist position in theology needs to be loosened. This view goes too far, collapsing practical reasoning completely into narrative. I see instead an outer envelope and an inner core to our practical reasoning. The outer envelope is the background beliefs that narrative traditions transmit to communities of memory. Yet the inner core of practical reasoning cannot be forgotten. It is into this inner core that formalist Kantian and utilitarian positions have had some insight. The narrativists are right that this inner core of practical reason always is shaped to some extent by the outer narrative envelope of practical reason. But our capacity for practical thinking in Kohlberg's sense interacts with human experience and can gain relative independence from our narrative traditions. We must remember that Covenant Church decided to become a sanctuary church after Rosa, Juan, and Oscar had already arrived in Centerville. Many members of the church met them, experienced their humanness, and became acquainted with their needs. The actual physical presence of these refugees must be seen as part of the educational experience. Learning about the refugees in this way doubtless influenced the practical thinking and practical reasoning of the Covenant members.

Kantians would say that Covenant's actual experience of these refugees was secondary to reason's a priori judgment that it can act without self-contradiction only if it follows the maxim of universalization. Narrativists and the cultural-linguistic school headed by George Lindbeck would say that our experience of the refugees is secondary to the narrative and linguistic categories we bring to our interpretation of this experience.[42] On the other hand, radical empiricists like William James, Nancy Frankenberry, and William Dean, although acknowledging how cultural-linguistic and narrative traditions form our interpretive categories, would say that Covenant's actual experience of the personhood, agency, and humanness of these refugees further affected the inner core of that church's practical reason.[43] It may have led the people of Covenant to say, "We notice that these three refugees seem to have many of the same feelings, the same thoughts, the same fears, and the same capacities that we do. Since they seem to be human like us, we should treat them as we would want them to treat us." The radical empiricist would say that our experience of the "otherness" of others precedes and informs our rational capacities for inference, generalization, and noncontradiction—capacities that the Kantians and neo-Kantians understand so well.

This raw experience of the "otherness" of others at times also breaks through and enriches our narrative construals of persons. Not all narrative traditions are morally elevated. Some are seriously lacking. Nonetheless, we often find people transcending aspects of their immediate tradition. It is for this reason that the narrative and cultural-linguistic schools need to be broadened to account for the ways the givenness of experience sometimes breaks through our interpretive categories and brings genuine surprises. If this broadening occurs, narrative and cultural-linguistic approaches to practical theology can move closer to what I have called a revised correlational or fundamental practical theology. A revised correlational approach assumes more genuine interaction between narratives and experience; neither totally dominates the other. This is why interpretation and understanding are a dialogue. And this is why theology must be confessional in its starting point, dialogical in the middle, and critical and apologetic in the end as it turns toward the future.

In summary, the latent practical purpose behind the recent turn to congregational studies needs to be made clearer. Congregational studies can be seen as part of a more inclusive fundamental practical theological project, contributing to both descriptive and strategic practical theology. Within descriptive theology, such studies are one example of the many tasks of describing the situations of practical theological reflection and discerning the thickness of meaning behind the questions these situations generate for historical, systematic, and strategic practical theology. Congregational studies can also help us understand the strategic practical theological thinking that congregations actually do (sometimes well and sometimes poorly) and can reveal the range, levels, and types of rational thinking they enact. This understanding in turn can throw light on the current controversy between narrativist and formalist theories of practical reasoning. Narrativists have insights into the outer envelope of practical reasoning, but even within Christian ethics there is an inner core that has similarities with philosophical, especially neo-Kantian, models of practical rationality as well as patterns of moral thinking internal to some other religions around the world.

NOTES

1. Stephen Warner, *New Wine In Old Wineskins: Evangelicals and Liberals in a Small-town Church* (Berkeley: University of California Press, 1988); Jack Werthei-mer, ed., *The American Synagogue* (New York: Cambridge University Press, 1987); Carl Dudley, ed., *Building Effective Ministry* (San Francisco: Harper and Row, 1983).

2. Robert Bellah et al., *Habits of the Heart* (Berkeley: University of California Press, 1985), pp. 297–307; Jürgen Habermas, *Theory of Communicative Action*, vol. 1, *Reason and the Rationalization of Society* (Boston: Beacon Press, 1984), and idem, *Theory of Communicative Action*, vol. 2, *Lifeworld and System: A Critique of Functionalist Reason* (Boston: Beacon Press, 1987).

3. David Tracy, *Blessed Rage for Order* (Minneapolis: Seabury Press, 1975), pp. 49–52; *The Analogical Imagination* (New York: Crossroad, 1981), pp. 73–75.

4. Hans-Georg Gadamer, *Truth and Method* (New York: Crossroad, 1982), p. 289.

5. Richard Bernstein, *Beyond Objectivism and Relativism* (Philadelphia: University of Pennsylvania Press, 1983); Richard Rorty, *Philosophy and the Mirror of Nature* (Princeton: Princeton University Press, 1979).

6. Thomas Kuhn, *The Structure of Scientific Revolutions*, 2d. enl. ed. (Chicago: University of Chicago Press, 1970).

7. Bellah, *Habits of the Heart*, p. 330.

8. Gadamer, *Truth and Method*, p. 273.

9. Bellah, *Habits of the Heart*, p. 301.

10. Johannes van der Ven, "Practical Theology: From Applied to Empirical Theology," *Journal of Empirical Theology* (1988), 1:7–28.

11. Edward Farley, "Theology and Practice Outside the Clerical Paradigm," in *Practical Theology*, ed. Don Browning (San Francisco: Harper and Row, 1983); idem, "Interpreting Situations: An Inquiry into the Nature of Practical Theology," in *Formation and Reflection*, ed. Lewis Mudge and James Poling (Philadelphia: Fortress Press, 1987), pp. 1–26; Don Browning, *Practical Theology: The Emerging Field in Theology, Church, and World* (San Francisco: Harper and Row, 1983).

12. Tracy, *Blessed Rage for Order*, pp. 45–47.

13. Matthew Lamb, "The Theory-Praxis Relationship in Contemporary Christian Theologies," *Catholic Theological Society Proceedings* (1976) 31:149–78; Rebecca Chopp, "Practical Theology and Liberation," in *Formation and Reflection*, ed. Lewis Mudge and James Poling (Philadelphia: Fortress Press, 1987), pp. 120–38.

14. Don Browning, *Religious Thought and the Modern Psychologies* (Philadelphia: Fortress Press, 1987); Clarence Karier, *Scientists of the Mind* (Urbana: University of Illinois Press, 1986); Lewis Brandt, *Psychologist Caught* (Toronto: University of Toronto Press, 1982); Robert Fuller, *Americans and the Unconscious* (New York: Oxford University Press, 1986).

15. Paul Ricoeur, *Freud and Philosophy* (New Haven: Yale University Press, 1970), pp. 5–7, 160, 431–39; Robert Bellah, "Social Science as Practical Reason," in *Ethics, Social Sciences, and Policy Analysis*, ed. Daniel Callahan and Bruce Jennings (New York: Plenum Press, 1983), p. 59.

16. Dudley, *Building Effective Ministry*.

17. Barry Evans and Bruce Reed, "The Success and Failure of a Religious Club," in Dudley, *Building Effective Ministry*, p. 41.

18. Jackson Carroll, William McKinney, and Wade Clark Roof, "From the Outside In and the Inside Out," in Dudley, *Building Effective Ministry*, p. 99.

19. James Hopewell, "The Jovial Church: Narrative in Local Church Life," in Dudley, *Building Effective Ministry*.

20. Melvin Williams, "The Conflict of Corporate Church and Spiritual Church," in Dudley, *Building Effective Ministry*, p. 58.

21. Evans and Reed, "Success and Failure," pp. 50–51.

22. Ibid., pp. 52–53.

23. Carroll, McKinney, and Roof, "From the Outside In," p. 99.

24. Williams, "Conflict of Corporate Church," p. 59.

25. Hopewell, "Jovial Church," p. 73.

26. Joseph Hough, "Theologian at Work: Theological Ethics," in Dudley, *Building Effective Ministry*, p. 114.

27. Ibid., p. 126.

28. Ibid., p. 130.

29. Alan Donagan, *The Theory of Morality* (Chicago: University of Chicago Press, 1977); Ronald Green, *Religious Reason* (New York: Oxford University Press, 1978).

30. Joseph Fletcher, *Situation Ethics* (San Francisco: Harper and Row, 1966).

31. Alasdair MacIntyre, *After Virtue* (Notre Dame: University of Notre Dame Press, 1981), and idem, *Whose Justice? Which Rationality?* (Notre Dame: University of Notre Dame Press, 1988); Johann Baptist Metz, *Faith in History and Society* (New York: Crossroad, 1980); Stanley Hauerwas, *A Community of Character* (Notre Dame: University of Notre Dame Press, 1982); James McClendon, *Biography as Theology* (Nashville: Abingdon Press, 1974), and idem, *Systematic Theology: Ethics* (Nashville: Abingdon Press, 1986).

32. Nelle Slater, ed., *Tensions Between Citizenship and Discipleship: A Case Study* (New York: Pilgrim Press, 1989).

33. See Don Browning, *A Fundamental Practical Theology* (Minneapolis: Fortress Press, 1991), chaps. 5, 6, and 9, for a detailing of the justifications and respective logics for each of these five levels. Here, I will illustrate where these levels of practical reasoning can be found in the deliberations of the Church of the Covenant. See also Don Browning, *Religious Ethics and Pastoral Care* (Philadelphia: Fortress Press 1983); *Religious Thought and the Modern Psychologies* (Philadelphia: Fortress Press, 1987); "Religious Education as Growth in Practical Theological Reflection and Action," in *Education for Citizenship and Discipleship*, ed. Mary Boys (New York: The Pilgrim Press, 1989); "Religious Education for Practical Theological Thinking and Action: Discipleship and Citizenship in the Ecology of Faith," in Slater, *Tensions*.

34. Jürgen Habermas, *Moral Consciousness and Communicative Action* (Cambridge: MIT Press, 1990), pp. 196–98.

35. Donald Winnicott, *The Maturational Processes and the Facilitating Environment* (London: Hogarth Press, 1965).

36. Slater, *Tensions*, p. 3.

37. John Rawls, *A Theory of Justice* (Cambridge: Harvard University Press, 1971), pp. 136–42; Lawrence Kohlberg, *The Philosophy of Moral Development* (San Francisco: Harper and Row, 1981), pp. 193–201.

38. Green, *Religious Reason*, p. 189.

39. Kohlberg, *Philosophy of Moral Development*, p. 100.

40. Paul Ricoeur, "Entre Philosophie et Théologie: La Règle D'Or Question," *Revue D'Histoire et de Philosophie Religieuses* 69 (1989): 3–8.

41. This is close to the "mixed-deontological" theory of practical reason held by William Frankena in *Ethics* (Englewood Cliffs: Prentice-Hall, 1973), p. 52.

42. George Lindbeck, *The Nature of Doctrine* (Philadelphia: Westminster Press, 1985).

43. William James, *The Varieties of Religious Experience* (New York: Mentor Books, 1958); Nancy Frankenberry, *Religion and Radical Empiricism* (Albany: State University of New York Press, 1987), pp. 68–82, 98–106; William Dean, *American Religious Empiricism* (Albany: State University of New York Press, 1986).

PART THREE

CONGREGATIONS AND LEADERSHIP

SEVEN

Patterns of Leadership in the Congregation

JAY P. DOLAN

IN AN IMPORTANT ESSAY published in 1956 Sidney Mead pointed out that the key to understanding the evolution of ministry in the United States was adaptation. But adaptation was not only the key organizing principle in the evolution of ministry, it was also the principal shaper of the patterns of congregational ministry.[1] Those Europeans who first permanently settled what is now the United States in the early seventeenth century were compelled to adapt their Old World ways to the challenges posed by the New World's geographical, social, and political environment.

Over the course of time different patterns of congregational leadership have appeared on the American landscape. Along the nineteenth-century Minnesota frontier, women were the leaders in local Episcopal parishes. In Pittsburgh's immigrant neighborhoods men who spent their days toiling in steel mills occupied their evenings planning the future of Lutheran or Catholic congregations. In twentieth-century New York rabbis ruled over the synagogue. This essay will examine such diverse patterns of congregational leadership among Protestants, Jews, and Catholics in the United States from colonial times to the middle of the twentieth century. The essay will focus on those individuals, both ordained and nonordained, who were the key decision-makers in the congregation and thus had the most influence in shaping the development of the congregation.

It is clear that no one type or model of leadership prevailed in American congregations. In some instances the political environment encouraged a democratic polity, but clerical autocracy was also very widespread. Women were most often relegated to minor leadership roles in the parish, but for many Protestant denominations this began to change substantially in the early twentieth century. As is true in so many aspects of the American experience, adaptation was the norm and diversity the central feature insofar as leadership in the congregation is concerned.

The First Settlements

When English colonists settled in Virginia in the early seventeenth century, one of their first tasks was to organize parish religious life. They wanted their church to be in conformity with the church in England "as neere as may be." The phrase "as neere as may be" was a concession to the realities of the Chesapeake region. In other words, from the moment they set foot on the shores of America these transplanted English settlers had to adapt their Old World understanding of church to the environment of the New World. They ended up by establishing "an Episcopal church without bishops." As a result, a pattern of congregational life developed in which the laity became more powerful than was the case in the mother country. Given the absence of bishops and a scarcity of priests, lay vestrymen took control of church affairs at the local level; even in a place like Petsoe Parish in Gloucester County, where there was an Anglican priest for over thirty years, the vestry exercised a considerable amount of control over the affairs of the parish.[2]

Across the Potomac River in Maryland another colony was taking shape and there the realities of the North American environment were also transforming the shape of the local church. Unlike in Virginia there was no officially established state church in Maryland. Protestants and Catholics were urged to tolerate one another and they did, most of the time, until the 1690s. But Catholics clearly had the upper hand for much of the seventeenth century, since the proprietor of the colony, Cecil Calvert, was Catholic and Jesuit priests were a persistent presence in the colony. As in Virginia, the environment of the Chesapeake shaped the development of the local church. People lived at great distances from one another and a "typical neighborhood" in rural Maryland consisted of twelve to twenty families who lived within two miles or so of each other. Given the scarcity of clergy and the dispersed pattern of settlement, congregational life was nonexistent. Catholics did stick together and practice their religion, but most often it was without the benefit of clergy. Unlike Virginia, which did have Anglican parishes, no Catholic parishes existed in seventeenth-century Maryland; the center of church life was the Jesuit farm that served as the home base for itinerant priests who visited Catholic families scattered throughout southern Maryland;

the farm chapel was also a gathering place for nearby Catholics on religious feast days.

In Massachusetts the founding generation of settlers had to invent something new to take the place of the Anglican church polity that they had left behind in England. For them the congregation became the heart of the church, and it was clear that the lay people, the visible saints who made up the congregation, had a great deal of influence in affecting the development of the congregation. Much the same pattern of lay involvement characterized the seventeenth-century Jewish community in New York. Soon after their arrival in 1654 the pioneer generation of Jews founded a synagogue. As in New England, the congregation was the heart of the Jewish community, and in the absence of a rabbi lay leaders held firm control over every aspect of congregational life.

This brief glimpse of the pioneer generation of the seventeenth century suggests that Jews, Protestant, and Catholics had to rethink their understanding of the congregation in the context of the New World. Among all three groups two features stand out. First, each of them adapted their Old World understanding of the local congregation to the situation in the New World and something new resulted. Second, in each tradition the lay people occupied a central position in the local congregation. This was especially true in Jewish and Protestant settlements, but even among Maryland Catholics religion took on a decidedly lay character because of the scarcity of clergy and the domestic nature of religious life. In the next three hundred years each of these major religious traditions would continue to adapt and adjust to a changing social and political environment. As these traditions evolved over time, leadership at the congregational level also changed. Protestant pastors became as authoritarian as the pope, rabbis took control of synagogue life, and priests gained unlimited power in their parishes. Lay leadership did not disappear, however. It took on new shapes as new denominations came into existence and religious revivals awakened the people in the pews. Eighteenth-century New England provides a fine example of how leadership in the local congregation would change over time.

1700–1776

There was always a strong populist strain in New England Congregationalism. The minister was the "creation of the individual church." This meant that except in rare cases a person could not be ordained unless the local congregation or community called this individual to be their pastor. Unlike the hierarchical tradition of Roman Catholicism where the priest was selected, approved, ordained, and appointed by the hierarchy, the New England Protestant tradition was rooted in the theory of congregationalism and the notion of a covenanted community. The people in the local community conferred the office upon the individual, and, once ordained, the minister became a central figure in that community. He was the glue that held the community together, "the mainstay of communal order" as the historian Donald Scott has put it. In fact, he was so central to the community that his presence effectively "transformed a mere settlement into a genuine, organic community."[3]

With the passage of time, religious leadership in New England changed. According to J. William T. Youngs, Jr., three stages of development had occurred by the middle of the eighteenth century. In the founding generation the ministers were the "mainstay of communal order" and occupied a position of respect and prestige. By the beginning of the eighteenth century clericalism began to set in. Ministers increasingly viewed themselves as special people set apart from the rest of the community, and even an informal clerical hierarchy developed. Within a given region certain clergymen were recognized as the leaders and some even received an informal title such as "bishop"; in the Connecticut River valley the venerable pastor of Northampton, Massachusetts, Solomon Stoddard, was known as the "Pope." Another indication of this growth in Congregational clericalism was the formation of ministerial associations throughout the four New England colonies. These associations reinforced the clergy's sense of separateness from the rest of the community. This clericalism was so strong that Youngs contends that if there had not been the Great Awakening "the Congregational clergy might have acquired the hierarchy, the ceremonies, and even the Arminian doctrine associated with the Anglican clergy." The growth of clericalism, however, did not signal an increase in ministerial authority. On the contrary, it suggested just the opposite. Congregations continued to wield authority over their ministers and the clergy began to perceive "themselves as an embattled remnant whose misfortune it was to labor at a time when popular respect for God's ministers had sadly declined."[4]

The Great Awakening of the 1730s and early 1740s radically altered the popular understanding of religious leadership. A populist strain entered the sanctuary and challenged the tradition of clerical superiority and authority. A converted heart, not a clever mind, became the measuring rod for the religious leader. Without it the minister quickly became eligible for unemployment. Many people turned their backs on unconverted ministers and went off to organize new congregations.

The revivals of the 1730s and 1740s forced the clergy to acknowledge that their power and prestige did not come from ordination or membership in a ministerial association; rather it came from their ability to work effectively with their people as pastors. The closer they were to their people, the more power and authority the clergy enjoyed. A country ideology, based on "the idea of the leader who was close to his people," replaced the courtly ideology of the early eighteenth century. The populist strain of early nineteenth-century Protestantism reinforced this tendency as it became the norm for the clergy in the United States. The closer the minister or priest was to the people, the more esteemed he would be.[5]

Religious leadership in eighteenth-century Catholic Maryland differed substantially from that in the earlier era. The principal reason for this was a series of penal laws to prevent "the Growth of Popery" that were enacted in Maryland in the first two decades of the century. The laws sought to curb the public pastoral activities of the Jesuit clergy and limit the political involvement of Catholic laity. These laws were successful insofar as they did force Catholics to practice their religion in a very private and discreet manner. With the prohibition of public worship, the idea of a public congregational life became foreign to the Catholic mind. Nonetheless, Catholics adjusted, and the Jesuit farm or plantation once again became the institutional center of Catholic life.

Many more Jesuits worked in Maryland in the 1700s but their pastoral work did not differ very much from that of their predecessors in the previous century. Sunday was the principal day for religion at the Jesuit farm, and at least twice a month people who lived in the surrounding area would gather at the farm for religious services. On weekdays and other Sundays the missionaries traveled fifty to sixty miles to visit remote settlements of Catholics. At each of these places "everything is done more or less in the following manner," wrote one missionary: "from early morning until 11 o'clock they hear confessions: then they celebrate Mass, and distribute holy communion: once Mass is finished they preach to the congregation, and Christian doctrine is explained."[6]

By the 1760s congregational life began to change significantly. New churches were built on some of the Jesuit farms; parish registers for baptism, marriage, and death appeared and lists of parishioners were compiled and maintained. Parish devotional societies were also organized. Thus, at a time when Catholics were still legally discriminated against, denied the ballot, and allowed to have only private worship services, the church was going public by building "publick meeting places of divine worship" and organizing parish communities.

The pattern of religious leadership among Maryland Catholics was quite traditional. According to Catholic theology, ordination set the priest apart from the rest of the community; he was a new person, ontologically superior to the unordained mass of humanity. Unlike the New England pastor, the Jesuit missionary was not "the creation of the individual church." He was the creation of the institutional church in Europe. Ordained in Europe, he was sent by his Jesuit superior to the Maryland mission regardless of the people's wishes to have him or not. In Maryland the missionary was primarily a circuit rider who visited rural Catholic neighborhoods a few times a year. Since he never stayed very long in any one place, his influence in the rural communities was limited and intermittent. His role was to celebrate Mass, administer the sacraments, preach, and then move on. Such a pattern of ministry significantly limited the priest's sphere of influence. In addition, Maryland's penal laws forced him to remain a private person. He could not assume the public role of leadership that his Congregational counterpart exercised in New England. Undoubtedly this helps to explain why no one Jesuit priest stands out in the prerevolutionary period. Even when the first blush of parish life emerged in the 1760s, the clergy still remained very much in the background. Sixty years and more of the penal laws conditioned them to live and work in the shadow of the public arena. As parishes matured, the clergy still remained the sacramental and catechetical ministers that they had been throughout the entire colonial era. Though Maryland Catholics could boast of a good number of leaders, the most famous of them being Charles Carroll of Annapolis and his son, Charles Carroll of Carrollton, these people worked in the social and political arena. In the realm of religion there was a visible vacuum of leadership until after the Revolution.

The Maryland Catholic situation also differed from that in Virginia where the lay Episcopal vestry continued to control the clergy. In Maryland the laity did not control the clergy. Like the priests in Anglican Virginia, the Jesuits were clerical aristocrats, set apart from the rest of the community by their ordination. As was the case in Virginia, the clergy's sphere of influence was very limited. Nonetheless, within the religious arena they were quite independent from the laity. They answered to their Jesuit superiors in Europe, not to the farmers in Maryland.

In the small Jewish communities of colonial America the synagogue served all the needs of the Jewish people; it was synonymous with the community. As one historian put it, "the local synagogue virtually exercised a monopolistic control over every Jew within its ambit."[7] Since no rabbis were present in these communities, there was no doubt about who controlled the synagogue. Laymen ruled these congregations and they appointed the necessary cantors or ministers to lead the religious services. Such a prominent role for the laity resembled the ecclesiastical pattern in Virginia Anglicanism and New England Congregationalism.

1790–1840

The American Revolution ushered in a new age for both the nation and its churches. On one side of the divide was an age of privilege, deference, and authority. On the other side was an era of democracy, equality, and freedom. The new republic exalted the will of the people, and the people's choice became the highest tribunal in the land. Onto the American stage walked a new type of person; they called this individual a republican, "the inheritor of a revolutionary legacy in a world ruled by aristocrats and kings."[8] The uniqueness of this revolutionary change became even more apparent more than two centuries later when Communist-ruled nations in Eastern Europe caught the fever of democracy and sought freedom and equality for all the people of their nations. These were cultural and political earthquakes which left many observers in the Western world in a state of disbelief. Yet, the political and cultural changes sweeping through twentieth-century Eastern Europe pale in comparison to the first democratic revolution of 1776. "In a world ruled by aristocrats and kings" the people rose up and commenced a "new order of the ages" in which the voice of the people became the voice of God.

Such profound changes altered the religious landscape once and for all. Just as people sought to gain control over their political life so they also sought to determine their spiritual destiny. Common people refashioned their religion and "molded it in their own image." In this new age they wanted "their leaders unpretentious, their doctrines self-evident and down-to-earth, their music lively and singable, and their churches in local hands."[9] The urge for change and the irresistible attraction of a more populist understanding of ministry caused havoc in many congregations. People quarreled over the meaning and style of ministry. In fact, according to historian Nathan Hatch, "the fundamental religious quarrel of the late eighteenth century was not between Calvinist and

Arminian, orthodox and Unitarian, evangelical and freethinker, but between radically different conceptions of the Christian ministry."[10]

A clear example of the democratization of congregational leadership in the early nineteenth century was the reform movement known as "Christian" or "Disciples of Christ." Four men dominated the movement—Elias Smith, James O'Kelly, Barton Stone, and Alexander Campbell. Each one marched to his own tune and in his own peculiar style, but they all came to a similar conclusion. As Hatch put it, for these men and their followers "the priesthood of all believers meant just that— religion of, by, and for the people."[11] They despised church hierarchy and the idea of a clerical elite. For them clergy and laity must be "on an equal footing"; in other words, they wanted to abolish the traditional distinction between clergy and laity and this meant that in the local church the will of the people would be supreme. In a sense each believer was his or her own minister. Moreover, people had the "unalienable right" to study Scripture for themselves and follow its inspirations wherever these might lead. It was an age that "exalted the right of the people to think for themselves."

These Christian leaders were radical to be sure, and clergy and laity of a more traditional ethos cringed when they read the manifestos of Smith or Campbell. Nonetheless, populism had once again invaded the sanctuary, and an American style of ministry, first noticed in the colonial period, became more firmly rooted in the religious landscape.[12]

The early history of the Baptists in Alabama provides a clear example of the egalitarian nature of the local church in the early nineteenth century. In August 1819 a group of seven men and five women established Mt. Hebron Baptist Church near Leeds, Alabama. A distinctive feature of this antebellum congregation was the strong sense of community. As a Baptist, the individual believer had an identity only within the church community; beyond the community was the barren land of exile. Leadership resided in the community and not in an individual. This can be seen in the way the congregation went about defining itself. The Baptists in Leeds first established a set of theological principles that bound them together in a covenant of faith. Then they formulated a disciplinary code and this action reflected the spirit of democracy that was sweeping the country at that time. At their monthly congregational meetings the church members voted on issues affecting the congregation. At these gatherings the congregation stipulated that a simple majority vote would win the day. In other words, they wanted the same type of democracy in their church that prevailed in secular society.[13]

Given the type of church government among Baptists, this concern for congregational democracy in Mt. Hebron Church was to be expected. Nonetheless, other Protestant denominations whose style of church government was less egalitarian than the Baptists' showed a similar impulse toward democracy in the local congregation. Terry Bilhartz's study of church and society in Baltimore clearly demonstrates this. The religiously competitive environment of the early nineteenth century encouraged some churches in Baltimore to portray themselves as more democratic than others while the cultural preoccupation with issues of government made even the most authoritarian churches defenders of republicanism. This concern for democracy and republican government pushed the issue of leadership in the congregation to the foreground of public debate, and according to Bilhartz it was a central concern of Baltimore's Protestants.

As in most regions of the United States Maryland law placed the responsibilities for the welfare of the church in the hands of a board of trustees. Since the franchise was limited to white male pew-holders or contributors, the task of electing the leaders in the congregation was "exclusively a middle-to-upper class, adult, white-male affair."[14] The men elected as trustees were also from the upper class and this was as true of the working-class Catholic congregation as it was of the prestigious First Presbyterian Church. Thus, concludes Bilhartz, "church leadership was clearly an upper-class affair. Baltimore church life reflected a traditional conservative society in which the masses of nominal churchgoers deferred without complaint to the leadership of the most respectable classes."[15] This hardly meant that church leaders exercised their authority with genteel politeness. On the contrary, the power of the lay trustees was very real and they did not hesitate to dismiss incompetent pastors.

In his study of the village of Rockdale, located near Philadelphia, Anthony F. C. Wallace arrived at conclusions similar to those of Bilhartz. Rockdale was a small village in the early nineteenth century and when it came to organizing churches laymen were the key leaders. As in Baltimore they came from the upper classes; as Wallace put it, the "mill owners and manufacturers . . . were the leaders in building new religious institutions in the community."[16]

Democracy, voluntarism, and a concern for republican government were clearly important influences in shaping the government of the local congregation in the early national period, but pragmatic realism was also operative. Churches could not keep pace with the growth and distribution of the population and there were too few clergy to meet the needs of people settling in the villages of rural America. This was a dilemma that confronted Catholics as well as Protestants and into this vacuum stepped the laity.

As important as lay leadership was in this era of the Second Great Awakening, the star clergyman remained a very real presence in the churches. The quintessential example for this period would be Lyman Beecher. More than a gifted speaker, he was a national institution; when he spoke, people listened. As pastor of the Second Presbyterian Church in Cincinnati he had to resolve some serious financial problems, and so he mounted the pulpit one Sunday and told the congregation that "the debt must be cancelled before they left church. The doors were then closed, and the money was raised before he would allow them to open."[17] Clearly no one had to ask who was in charge at Second Presbyterian Church.

A major development in the local church in this era was the increasing activity of women. For many women religion now became a virtual profession. The key catalyst for this was the Second Great Awakening. Not only did it bring many women converts into the churches but it inspired them to become active in the service of the Lord. They held prayer meetings to promote revivals and acted as evangelists within their own families. They worked as Sunday school teachers; they organized missionary societies and benevolent organizations; and they distributed tracts and visited prisons and almshouses. Women had taken on new roles in the church and had carved out an area in which they could exercise leadership.[18]

Another important development was the emergence of the independent black church. This began in Philadelphia in the 1790s and eventually spread to other cities. The independent church, free from the control of whites, provided blacks with the opportunity for leadership in the church. But there was a certain irony to this. While the laity were gaining more power in the white congregation at this time, the minister was becoming the central figure in the black church. Endowed with an extraordinary ability to pray, preach, and sing, charismatic individuals stepped forth from the community to organize new churches in black urban neighborhoods. Ordinary men, some of whom were former slaves, they provided their parishioners with a sense of self-esteem in a society that was becoming increasingly racist. From this movement came "'The Preacher,' a figure that W. E. B. DuBois later praised as 'the most unique personality developed by the Negro on American soil.'"[19] In many instances these preachers became powerful leaders who commanded the loyalty and respect of their followers.

Though the democratization of religion acquired a strange twist in the black church, it followed a more predictable pattern in the Catholic and Jewish communities. Among Catholics the most notable sign of this democratic impulse was the popular support given to the trustee system of church government.

Because of the scarcity of Catholic clergy in these years, lay people had to organize the church themselves, and the trustee system provided the legal machinery that made this possible. Wherever Catholics settled, the trustee system appeared. What this meant was that laymen were elected each year as parish trustees by the dues-paying members of the congregation. These elected representatives of the people assumed a major leadership role in the local church. Nor did this cease when a priest took up residence in the parish. In most instances priest and people worked together in guiding the affairs of the parish. This pattern of parish government received its most sustained support in the 1820s and 1830s in the Carolinas and in Georgia, where Bishop John England had the trustee system incorporated into the diocese's written constitution. The trustees met regularly throughout the year with the pastor of the parish acting as president at these meetings. Their principal concern was financial: collection of pew rents, salaries of clergy, purchasing a new organ, managing the cemetery, and paying off church debts. They also supervised the work of such church personnel as organist, choir director, and maintenance men. In such an arrangement laity and clergy learned to work together for the benefit of the local church.

According to the Catholic tradition the clergy ran the parish, and in the United States there were many parishes where that was the accepted arrangement. But with the lack of clergy in the new nation and the enthusiasm for democracy, a more populist type of leadership developed through the lay trustee system. By encouraging lay leadership in the local congregation the trustee system established a very important precedent for American Catholics.

In the early nineteenth century the Jewish community in the United States was still very small. In 1820 there were only seven Jewish synagogues in the United States and they were all located along the east coast. Nonetheless, this small religious community did not escape the pervasive impact of the democratic revolution. Eager to be accepted as Americans, Jews adopted prevailing Protestant customs of behavior in their synagogues and pledged their loyalty to the new nation. They organized their synagogues "on democratic principles" and as was true in earlier days, laypeople were the primary leaders. Such a pattern of lay leadership would set important precedents for the future of congregational life among American Jews.[20]

1840–1940

The first half of the nineteenth century witnessed important changes in the shape of American society. Chief among these was the emergence of an industrial economy. The factory replaced the home as the principal place of work. With this development came increased specialization as individual factories concentrated on specific products and workers acquired a particular trade. Such specialization not only separated the home from the workplace, it also separated workers from each other. Eventually different craftsmen organized themselves into separate unions or associations and this sealed the divisions within the work force. In these decades the urban population grew significantly, and as cities expanded they became increasingly segregated along the lines of race, class, and ethnicity. What these and other changes suggest is that a new social order was taking shape in the mid-nineteenth century. The communalism of the eighteenth century was disappearing and the social order was now viewed "as a set of separate domains." As Donald Scott put it, "distinctions between sacred and secular, domestic and economic, masculine and feminine, private and public took on an indelibility and significance they had not possessed in the eighteenth century."[21]

Such a fundamental change in society influenced the realm of religion. The most notable effect was the separation of the public and private spheres of religion. "By the mid-nineteenth century," concluded Scott, "the church had become almost exclusively a devotional center . . . a private organization for the nurture and worship of a self-selected group of Christian believers."[22] Religion still influenced public discourse, but it did so most often through a new form, the voluntary association. Organized locally as well as nationally, these associations took over many of the tasks that the local congregation had once performed. As the congregation changed so did the nature of congregational leadership.

As congregational leadership developed in various Protestant denominations during the late nineteenth and early twentieth centuries, certain trends emerged. Because the congregation became more focused on its devotional purpose, leadership in the congregation remained limited to the sphere of religion. Washington Gladden and other advocates of the social gospel sought to correct this tendency by urging the clergy to expand their horizons and reach out to the world beyond the parish so as to achieve a "social salvation." As one Episcopal bishop put it, "the Gospel must be brought to bear directly upon society, as well as the individual."[23] This tension between focusing on the salvation of the individual or the redemption of society sparked a good deal of debate on the nature of the congregation and congregational leadership in the late nineteenth and early twentieth centuries. It fostered the development of the institutional church which sought to extend the scope of the parish's mission by meeting the social and economic needs of the congregation as well as their religious needs. It also encouraged the clergy to become leaders in the community as well as in the church. This development suggested one very important point—different types of congregations demanded different styles of leadership.

The tension between the social gospel and the individual gospel continues to challenge the understanding of ministry in the modern world. Nonetheless, it is clear that from 1840 to 1940, and indeed right up to the present, the overwhelming majority of Protestant congregations and ministers remained committed to nurturing the salvation of the individual. This certainly was the conclusion of Robert and Helen Lynd's study of Middletown (Muncie, Indiana) in the 1920s. In Middletown the focus of the congregation was decidedly devotional or religious. As was true in the 1840s, religion entered the public realm through such voluntary associations as the ministerial association or the Rotary Club.[24] Liston Pope's study of Gastonia, North Carolina, in the 1930s came to a similar conclusion. The sermons of the preachers could be summed up in the following manner: "The mission of the church is to do the will of Jesus and to seek to save lost souls. It brings men hope of heaven and comforts them in their sorrows and distresses."[25] As Pope so thoroughly documented, the church in Gastonia was concerned about the salvation of the individual and it remained indifferent to the economic affairs of the community. In such an environment the church was primarily a devotional center, and leadership in the congregation was limited to nurturing the salvation of the individual.

A second development during this era was the professionalization of the clergy. The ministry became a profession as well as a calling. This meant that education and learning became increasingly more important for those who entered the ministry. For the clergy there has always been a tension between learning and piety, and it is clear that in the late nine-teenth century learning was gaining the upper hand. The contrast with earlier years was especially noticeable among the Methodists. In 1800 the typical Methodist preacher "had a horse, Bible, Book of Discipline, and hymnal and preached at dozens of stations on a far-flung circuit. By 1900 he pastored an urban church and had a library in the parsonage and at least a college degree."[26] The emergence of the modern seminary was a major reason for this development, along with the increase in education among the general population. Nevertheless, the tension be-tween piety and learning remained. Holiness and Pentecostal churches rebelled against this trend toward professionalization and encouraged the common folk to come forth and lead the congregation. Eventually they too succumbed to the demand for an educated ministry. Nonethe-less, even today many congregations still prefer a "converted" minister to an "educated" one.

A significant result of the professionalization of the clergy and the emergence of the seminary was that now the clerical profession was tied to the denomination rather than the community. The privatization of religion that was already evident in the mid-nineteenth century also en-couraged this development. Congregational leadership ceased to have the public dimension that it possessed in the colonial era in the Protes-tant settlements.[27]

A third development in this period was the strengthening of the clergy's control over the congregation. In the colonial period the tension between laity and clergy as regards congregational leadership was very clear. This became more pronounced in the democratic era of the early nineteenth century as the laity sought to democratize the church. But by the middle of the nineteenth century the clergy were beginning to gain the advantage in this quest for power. A study of the Presbyterian Church in the South clearly indicated this; the same pattern was evident among Lutherans. Lynd's study of Middletown painted a similar pic-ture. The congregation was the devotional center for the people, and not surprisingly the chief person in the congregation was the devotional professional. Even in the institutional church, where a wide array of organizations and services existed, the minister was the principal leader who set the tone and determined the agenda for the congregation. This development was more pronounced in such denominations as the Pres-byterians, Methodists, and Episcopalians, where the clergy are more central to church polity than among Baptists and Congregationalists.

Over the course of the hundred years from 1840 to 1940 there were many instances, especially in the formative years of congregations, where the laity took on important leadership roles in the governance of the parish, but the overall pattern, in stark contrast to the early decades of the nineteenth century, was the pervasiveness of clerical dominance.[28]

A final feature of congregational leadership in this era was the increased involvement of women. In the nineteenth century women were most active in the area of missions, both foreign and domestic. Women had begun to organize themselves into missionary societies before the Civil War and by 1882 there were sixteen such societies. "By 1900 the women's societies were supporting 389 wives, 856 single women missionaries, and 96 doctors. They were responsible for numerous orphanages, hospitals, schools and dispensaries around the world."[29] This was the area of ministry where women made their mark. Women's activity in the local church did increase in these years, but this was in such areas as music and education. In the frontier region women did assume important leadership roles in the congregation, but they were clearly exceptions. Control of the congregation still remained in the hands of men.[30]

This pattern began to change in the early twentieth century as more women became ordained ministers. Women pastors were common in Holiness and Pentecostal congregations in the formative years of these denominations. In the Church of God, based in Anderson, Indiana, "women pioneered and carried on missions in impoverished and crime-ridden areas of cities, evangelized rural regions, established strategic urban congregations, engaged in foreign missionary work, conducted a publishing ministry for the blind, and were active in publishing other Christian literature." By 1925 as many as one-third of the Church of God congregations had women pastors. A similar pattern was evident in the Church of the Nazarene. From its very beginning the Church of the Nazarene ordained women, and by 1908 one of five Nazarene pastors was a woman. The Moody Bible Institute, founded in 1889, trained dozens of women as preachers, pastors, and evangelists. The mainline denominations, however, did not follow suit.[31]

After World War I the ordination of women began to slow down. In the late nineteenth century women had aspired to larger public roles and began to enter typically male professions, including the clergy. This pattern continued up until 1920 when, as historian Michael Hamilton suggests, women increasingly began to favor "domestic roles, and the ideology supporting their movement into male professions collapsed. The number of women moving into traditionally male professions—including the clergy—levelled off, as much because women did not aspire to these professions as because men sought to prevent their entry."[32] Only after World War II and the emergence of the modern women's movement would significant numbers of women once again aspire to become church pastors. Until then control of the congregation continued to be exercised by men.

Like American Protestantism, Judaism in the United States is a very diverse phenomenon. Each of the three major branches or "denominations" of Judaism—Reform, Orthodox, and Conservative—developed its own type of synagogue and its own style of congregational leadership. Nonetheless, certain general trends in that leadership stand out that parallel the Protestant experience.

In the early years of the nineteenth century the model of the "synagogue-community" still prevailed in most American Jewish communities. This type of institution "controlled all aspects of Jewish life and commanded allegiance from every Jew dwelling or sojurning within its ambit." As new immigrants arrived and the Jewish population increased, the model of the "synagogue-community" broke down and competing synagogues were soon established. Under such pressure the synagogue was no longer able to unite the community. Once the model of the synagogue as a total community institution began to dissolve, it ceased being coterminous with the Jewish community; it now became a center of devotion and ritual, much like its Protestant counterpart. In addition, it also became a voluntary association, and synagogues began to compete for members much like other American congregations. Then in the early twentieth century the synagogue underwent another transformation. It changed from a house of worship into a synagogue-center. In a sense it was an attempt to return to an earlier era and to make the synagogue once again the central institution of Jewish life. As Mordecai Kaplan, a proponent of this change put it, the synagogue must be "reconstructed to meet the new needs which have arisen in Jewish life. . . . It should be a neighborhood center to which all Jews to whom it is accessible should resort for all religious, cultural, social and recreational purposes." The synagogue-center fostered a variety of clubs and organizations for all ages and in doing so it resembled the "institutional church" development that was taking place in American Protestantism.[33]

By encouraging a variety of ministries in the synagogue and the need for professionals in these positions the synagogue-center limited the influence of the rabbi. Moreover, as the Jewish community gained educational stature in the twentieth century, leaders emerged in the business and academic arenas and this development further limited the authority and prestige of the rabbinate. In the immigrant era the rabbi had been a powerful spokesperson for the community, but in the post–World War I period this was no longer true. By then he had many rivals in the community.[34]

The issue of gender has its own history among American Jews. The Jewish tradition emphasized the home as the proper place for women; this was their "synagogue" where they sought to nurture the religious life of the family. The real synagogue remained a male preserve. By the end of the nineteenth century this began to change as Jewish women joined together to form sisterhoods or ladies' auxilaries. Sponsored by the synagogue, these organizations sought to do good works and in doing so they provided women with the opportunity for leadership roles in the synagogue. In Cincinnati's Rockdale Temple a sisterhood was organized early in the century and it "quickly grew into one of the most active contributors to temple activities." It soon "assumed responsibility for temple, school, communal, and Reform movement-wide activities, including fund-raising."[35] In Reform and Conservative synagogues women also gained increased involvement in liturgical services and in time Reform and Conservative synagogues became increasingly feminized.[36] This paralleled the increased activity of women in various ministries in Protestant congregations. In spite of this development, men continued to have control over the synagogue and its affairs.

These general trends among American Jews and Protestants show how complex the issue of congregational leadership was during the 1840–1940 period. Despite the similarities, diversity remained the major feature of congregational leadership for the simple reason that both Protestantism and Judaism became much more pluralistic during these years. New denominations emerged within Protestantism and Judaism and each of them carved out its own distinctive history and tradition. To do justice to this issue of congregational leadership during this period it will be useful to look at one denomination in an attempt to understand how leadership in the congregation developed over the course of a century.

Roman Catholicism and Congregational Leadership, 1840–1940

During the course of the nineteenth century the Catholic Church in the United States changed substantially. The reason for this was immigration. Catholicism went from being a small denomination heavily concentrated in the border states to the single largest denomination in the country with a population concentrated in the industrial cities of the northeast. In the early decades of the century people of Irish or German descent were the major ethnic groups; by the end of the century at least twenty-eight different ethnic groups worshiped in Catholic parishes. During this period the role of the laity in parish government diminished significantly and the priest took over control of the parish. But this did not happen all at once. It took place in stages over the course of time and proceeded more slowly with some immigrant groups than with others.

The first stage of this development took place during the formative years of a parish's organization. Once the immigrants settled in the cities of the New World they began to organize their own churches. First the immigrants would establish a mutual aid society or a devotional confraternity. Then, when the community was numerically and financially strong enough, they would begin the process of founding a church and parish community. After buying the land they would plan the construction of the church. At some point the local bishop would become part of the process and most often he would affirm the work of the immigrant community. The Germans in Cincinnati followed this pattern in the 1840s, and they met numerous times to discuss such issues as the cost of the land, the size of the windows in church, and even the thickness of its walls. When time came to lay the cornerstone of the new church, the laity planned the festivities. Forty years later the Slovaks in Pittsburgh followed the same pattern, and, as with the Germans, the laity were the major actors in the organization of the immigrant church. What took place in Cincinnati and Pittsburgh was repeated in many immigrant Catholic communities throughout the nineteenth century. Even in the twentieth century new immigrant groups such as the Ukrainians manifested the same pattern of lay involvement during the formative years of a parish. In other words, such lay leadership was not limited to any particular decade or time period but was evident in the founding era of a parish whether this was in the 1840s, 1890s, or 1920s.[37]

In this first stage the laity, especially those men who were elected as parish trustees, were important leaders in the congregation. During these years a primary function of the immigrant parish was social. It provided the immigrant newcomers with the sense of identity and belonging that they needed in the New World. Another major purpose of the congregation was to nurture the religion of the people. This was not so dominant in the formative years, when brick and mortar were major concerns, but once the congregation was established its religious function became all-important. Since the priest was the essential religious figure in the parish, his role increased in importance as the parish moved from its formative, organizational stage to the next stage of development when religion became the dominant feature of the congregation.

Religion was always the raison d'être of the parish, but this became more real and substantial in the second half of the nineteenth century when a devotional revolution transformed Roman Catholicism throughout the world. The parish was the primary locale where this devotional revolution took place and it meant that the priest, more than ever before, became the central figure in the parish, because without him a public devotional life was not able to exist. In the early years of the century the priest was mainly a celebrant of the Catholic mass. By the end of the century his role had expanded considerably; more than just a mass priest, he conducted numerous devotions for the people and presided over an elaborate array of religious services. By this time Catholics had also begun to attend Sunday mass more regularly and to receive the sacrament of confession and eventually the Eucharist more frequently. Clearly "a priest-centered piety" was developing among Catholics and this enhanced the prestige of the priest.[38] This devotional revolution took place just about the time that many immigrant parishes were moving from the formative stage of their development to the consolidating stage when religion became more central to their existence. For this reason the devotional revolution reinforced the shift to religion and substantially strengthened the authority and role of the priest in the parish. As this took place the leadership role of the laity weakened and the priest gained an importance that he did not possess in the formative years of the immigrant parish. As the clergy gained prestige and status as devotional leaders of the local church they also sought to increase their control over the parish by weakening or even eliminating any structure that encouraged lay leadership.

The history of nineteenth-century Roman Catholicism in the United States encompasses a multitude of issues. The emergence of the parochial school, the need to build churches, increasing financial debt, conflicts between bishops and clergy, the struggle of women religious to maintain their independence in a male, clerically controlled institution, and the desire to fashion an American style of Roman Catholicism were some of the more critical issues. But at the local level one issue stood out above all others and that was the question of power. Who would control the local parish, the priest or the people?

This question of power caused a great deal of conflict during the immigrant era. The issue generally arose as the parish moved into the second stage of its development, the devotional era. In the formative period a congregational model of the church in which the laity shared power and authority with the clergy prevailed. Nevertheless, many clergy desired a hierarchical model of the church in which the priest possessed supreme authority in the parish. This became more possible as the role of the priest became more central to the parish in its devotional era, but it did not take place without challenges from lay leaders. Such challenges led to serious conflict and no immigrant group was exempt. Congregational battles were especially fierce in the Polish immigrant community. Many parishes broke off their allegiance to the Roman Catholic church rather than submit to the authority of the priest and his bishop. The situation had become so serious that in 1904 a number of independent parishes joined together to form the Polish National Catholic Church. This was the first major schism among Catholics in the United States, and it resulted to a large degree from the struggle over the issue of democracy in the government of the local church. French-Canadian, Slovak, and Lithuanian parishes waged similar battles, and in some instances individual congregations declared their independence from the Catholic church.

Despite such widespread conflict the American hierarchy remained adamant in its opposition to lay involvement in the government of the local church. As a result the hierarchical model of church gradually and decisively became the norm, and the local parish developed into a clerical preserve. By the early twentieth century the clergy controlled the parish, and the tradition of lay people participating in the organization and government of the local church had come to an end. Once the clergy gained control over the parish, a distinct style of leadership began to emerge.

The theology of the priest that was current at this time offered an exalted view of the priest. He was the mediator who stood between God and the people, another Christ who opened the door to salvation for the laity. As one priest put it in a sermon to a Dearborn, Michigan, congregation, "the priest is God's representative in our midst . . . on the altar and in the confessional, he is simply omnipotent, simply divine."[39] Enveloped in such a supernatural aura, the priest, solely by virtue of his ordination, stood head and shoulders above the rest of the congregation. Once he was robed in the aura of a religious superman it was but a short step to omnipotence in other areas. A parish bulletin explained this very clearly. The priest was a person "who knows everything, who has the right to say anything, from whose hallowed lips words of divine wisdom are received by all with the authority of an oracle, and with entire submission of faith and judgment."[40] Such an exalted and comprehensive understanding of the priest did not leave much doubt as to who was supposed to rule and lead the congregation.

Enhancing this high theological view of the priest was his social position in the immigrant community. More than just a priest, the immigrant pastor was a representative of the community. Being one of the more highly educated persons in the neighborhood, he was often called on to represent the group and speak on its behalf.

Such a lofty view of the priest fostered a style of leadership that was rather autocratic. In this era the pastor was the supreme authority in the parish and his word was law. Vincent Barzynski, pastor of Chicago's St. Stanislaus Kostka parish from 1874 to 1899, was very representative of this type of one-man rule. Born and raised in the Polish regions of Eastern Europe, Barzynski came to the United States as a priest. After a brief stay in Texas he moved to Chicago and St. Stanislaus Parish. For a quarter of a century he presided over the parish and gained a national reputation for his work in the Polish community. A brick-and-mortar pastor, he turned St. Stanislaus into one of the premier Polish parishes in the country. A banker as well as a builder, he founded a bank for the Polish that had over a half-million dollars in deposits in the 1890s. He was an educator as well and built a complex of elementary and secondary schools. Barzynski ruled with an iron will and in many respects was the Polish pope of Chicago as well as the pastor of St. Stanislaus. His opponents compared him to the tsar of Russia, a despot who hid behind the mask of religion.[41] Barzynski was not unusual. Just about every city with a sizable Polish population had a similar figure. In Buffalo, New York, his name was Jan Pitass and in New Britain, Connecticut, it was Lucyan Bojnowski. Daniel Buczek, a historian who has studied many of these priests, described them as "priest titans," men whose authority in the Polish community rivaled that of the bishop. Not surprisingly, many people resented such an autocratic style of parish leadership, and conflict became a standard feature of the Polish parish.[42]

The Irish also nurtured a clergy of benevolent autocrats. For centuries the Irish had held their priests in high esteem because the English had turned them into martyrs by banishing them from the land. A tradition of deference to the clergy grew up among the Irish, and the immigrants transplanted this to the United States.[43] As a result, the Irish pastor reigned like the lord of the manor. His will was law and people accepted it. One such colorful figure was Maurice J. Dorney of Chicago.

Dorney was an American-born Irishman, and in 1880 he founded the parish of St. Gabriel, near the Union Stockyards on the South Side of the city. Known as "King of the Yards," he was a legend in the neighborhood and in the stockyards. A priest-builder, he put up a church as well as a grammar school, high school, rectory, and convent. His authority was such that he was called on to arbitrate labor strikes; he acted as an employment agent and single-handedly kept the saloons off residential streets in the neighborhood.[44]

Even though Dorney and Barzynski stood out because of their flamboyance and their powerful personalities, their style of leadership had become accepted by the late nineteenth century. They were not inventing something new. Rather they were following a standard that had been set in place and would become more normative with each passing decade. Obviously the personality of the pastor was an important element in shaping the style of leadership in a congregation. Some pastors were benevolent and avuncular; others were irascible and dictatorial. But regardless of personality differences, they all followed the same model in terms of leadership. The local church boss, they enjoyed the prerogatives of one-man rule.

In the late nineteenth and early twentieth century the Catholic parish moved into the third stage of its development. This was the era of the comprehensive parish, or the total parish, and it was very noticeable by the 1920s. The parish was not only to provide for the traditional spiritual needs of the people, but it also sought to satisfy their educational, recreational, social, and cultural needs as well. Parallel developments were taking place in both Jewish and Protestant congregations with the emergence of the synagogue-center and the institutional church. In this stage of development parish societies began to increase and an emphasis on youth became especially obvious. Some Catholic parishes had as many as eleven or more social events a year; dances, plays, minstrel shows, card parties, parish bazaars, and picnics became commonplace. In New York, parish social life was so hectic that the local Catholic newspaper even published a weekly column, "What's Going On in City Parishes," to keep people abreast of the activity. The parish had become such a total institution that for many Catholics it was the center of their lives from the cradle to the grave.

Jeffrey Burns's study of St. Peter's Parish in the Mission District of San Francisco underscores this dimension of the parish. Both the neighborhood and the parish were insulated from the rest of the city and the world by the "tightly knit, highly localized basis of community life." Parishioners fondly recounted how their lives were centered in the parish and the neighborhood—rarely was there a need to venture beyond the Mission District. As one resident said, "our neighborbood was our world." Reinforcing this insular quality of parish life was the prevailing Catholic ideology that viewed the world as evil and pernicious.[45]

In the early twentieth century Catholicism was viewed as more than just "a creed, a code, or a cult" in the words of a group of educators. As they put it, Catholicism "must be seen as a culture."[46] Understood in this manner as a total culture, Catholicism encouraged the development of a comprehensive parish which would fully encompass the lives of its parishioners. An integral element of this ideology was a pervasive dualism that viewed the world beyond Catholicism as evil. Thus, the task of the parish was not only to nurture the piety of the people and meet their many needs, but also to protect them from the evil influences of the world. When a San Francisco pastor wanted to build a new parish hall, the reason he gave for the huge expenditure was to keep the young people of his parish "away from the dance halls, pool rooms, and decrease their frequent visits to the movies by giving them a meeting place where they can enjoy themselves according to their tastes in an innocent way."[47]

In this third stage of development the parish had gone beyond the social function of the formative period and the devotional focus of the late nineteenth century and encompassed a wide variety of functions. As a comprehensive cultural institution, the parish had become the most important institution in the neighborhood as far as most Catholics were concerned. But its horizons did not reach outside the neighborhood and the Catholic realm because beyond this world was the kingdom of evil. In many respects the Catholic parish of the early twentieth century resembled the fundamentalist congregation of the late twentieth century. Both of them were the major institutions of a religious subculture, and they aspired to absorb totally the lives of their parishioners and thus protect them from the evils of the secular world.

In the comprehensive parish of the early twentieth century the style of leadership did not change very much from previous decades. The priest enjoyed a monopoly of power and the more comprehensive the parish, the wider his influence. He was not just the spiritual leader, but the educational, moral, and cultural oracle as well. One such individual was Peter C. Yorke, the Irish-born pastor of the Irish parish of St. Peter in San Francisco. Yorke followed in the footsteps of other builder-priests and enlarged an already sizable parish complex of buildings. Like many twentieth-century pastors he concentrated a great deal of energy on the education of youth and had separate elementary and high schools for boys and girls; he also organized a successful Sunday school program for those children who did not attend the parish schools. As the devotional leader of the parish he nurtured a very active devotional and liturgical life among the people. Yorke was also a highly regarded figure in the Irish community and was an ardent supporter of Irish nationalism. When he took his evening walk in the neighborhood, people greeted him with affection, and many individuals, the children especially, regarded him with "awe."[48]

As in previous years the prevailing theology of the priesthood supported such a lofty view of the priest. According to the theologian the power of the priest was "equal to the power of Jesus Christ" and people revered him as a man "set apart."[49] A new development took place in the early years of the century which would greatly reinforce this sublime view of the priest. This was the emergence of the modern seminary. The seminary trained young men to become priests, and a key component of this training was the encouragement of a clerical culture. Priests were supposed to be men set apart from the rest of the Catholic community lest the secular world somehow contaminate them. Such a mentality resulted from the dualistic view of the world that divided reality into good and evil, Catholics and non-Catholics, clergy and laity. The seminary also sought to encourage a sense of solidarity among the priests and this nurtured a clerical culture that emphasized the differences between the people and the priest; the growth of this clerical culture served to enhance the authority of the pastor.[50]

This period was the golden age of the American Catholic priesthood. The priest was the key figure in the Catholic subculture; he was put on a pedestal by a lofty theology of the office and kept there by the culture of clericalism. The vast majority of Catholics accepted this high view of the priest and revered him with affection and deference. In her study of Catholicism in Detroit Leslie Tentler referred to the many instances when people went out of their way to express affection for their pastor. Crowds would greet him when he returned from European trips, and his death sparked a general outpouring of affection.[51] I can still remember standing alongside the railroad tracks at the train station as a very young boy clinging to my mother's hand while waving good-bye to the priest from my parish who was going off to serve in World War II as a chaplain. He was a hero going off to war and perhaps the ultimate sacrifice. This is the only memory I have of going to the train station to say good-bye to anybody. Obviously the priest was a special person in the community. Hollywood also thought he was special, and in these years many movies featured stories involving heroic priests. There was none more famous than Father O'Malley, played by Bing Crosby, in *Going My Way*. Such movies served to increase the popular affection of Catholics for their priests.

Although one-man rule was the standard style of leadership in the Catholic parish in these golden years prior to World War II, there were many exceptions to the norm. The new immigrant communities, especially those from Eastern Europe, tried to keep alive the tradition of lay leadership in the local church, and this persisted into the 1940s. In rural states such as Kansas where the institutional church was underdeveloped and clergy were scarce, laypeople often organized themselves into worshiping communities and looked after the affairs of the congregation. In Washington and Oregon similar patterns developed because the shortage of priests forced the laity to assume many of the responsibilities of parish life. The Mexican community had a different relationship with the clergy than most other ethnic groups. The laity were traditionally very active in the parish and assumed leadership roles in the devotional life of the community; because of the scarcity of Spanish-speaking clergy they also took responsibility for other aspects of parish life.[52]

Aside from these exceptions the laity seldom exercised any leadership role of significance in the parish. By this third state of parish development they had been relegated to the devotional and fraternal activities of the parish. They joined confraternities and sodalities, women much more than men, and within this sphere they enjoyed some leadership functions. But the priest was always the final authority, and he presided over these aspects of parish life with the same aura of power that he enjoyed in other areas.

Sisters were key actors in the parish, but they generally confined their work to the parish school. This was the center of their universe. But the headmaster of the school, the local superintendent of education, was the pastor. Since he held the sisters in a state of economic dependency, he wielded great power over them. The culture of the cloister which separated the sisters from the secular world did not allow them to go beyond the convent and the school, and thus they confined their leadership roles to that sphere.

In summary, then, the Catholic experience of leadership in the congregation mirrored most of the general patterns present in the Protestant denominations. In this era the parish became a devotional center and most often isolated itself from the larger society. As it became a more comprehensive institution, it continued to be insular and parochial in its vision. The clergy became more professional and the development of the seminary encouraged a clericalism and denominationalism that was also evident among Protestants. Because of the hierarchical model of church and the male dominance of the clerical state, where celibacy was the mandated norm, women were not encouraged to take on leadership roles in the congregation. They limited their involvement to the educational and devotional areas of parish life. Given the opposition of church authorities to the ordination of women, they never took on the leadership roles as church pastors that some of their Protestant sisters eventually assumed.

During this century, 1840–1940, different patterns of congregational leadership were evident in Roman Catholicism. The most clearly remembered and celebrated model was the one-man rule that emerged in the late nineteenth and early twentieth centuries. This remained in place until the post–World War II era when social, educational, and religious forces brought about the dissolution of the Catholic subculture. With this dissolution everything Catholic came under the scrutiny of reform, and from this has emerged new styles of congregational leadership that have challenged the clerical autocracy of the recent past. Once again adaptation and diversity have begun to transform the American religious landscape.

Conclusion

In looking back over three centuries of American history it becomes very obvious that different patterns of congregational leadership were present. Most frequently individuals ordained to the ministry were the recognized leaders in the congregation; this was most obvious among Roman Catholics, but even within this hierarchical institution unordained lay persons stepped forward from time to time to become leaders. This was most noticeable in the formative years of a Catholic community. In eighteenth-century New England the laity had a powerful voice in the affairs of the congregation and the clergy had to be sensitive to the will of the people. The dismissal of Jonathan Edwards, clearly the most distinguished theologian of the eighteenth century, from his parish in Northampton was a striking example of such power and authority. In colonial Jewish communities the laypeople were in control of the affairs of the synagogue. Most often the leaders in the congregation were men, not women. But this pattern had its exceptions as well. Along the nineteenth-century frontier women had assumed leadership roles in Episcopal congregations; by the middle of the twentieth century such female leadership in the congregation was becoming more common among Protestants. In fact, some denominations were already ordaining women by this time. Another distinguishing feature of congregational leadership was class. Very frequently leadership roles went to individuals in the middle and upper classes, but in immigrant communities factory workers and laborers took on the responsibility for the welfare of the congregation. Thus, just as the congregation has changed over the centuries and taken on different roles in different ages so has the pattern of congregational leadership changed. No one pattern commanded the landscape. What was normative for one age was not always accepted as normative by the succeeding generation. There were several reasons for such diversity and change.

One important influence on congregational leadership was the geographical environment. In settled towns and cities leadership took on different patterns than in frontier areas. Tradition and the weight of the past had an important influence in old urban congregations, whereas along the frontier everything was starting from scratch. As a result the exceptional sometimes became the norm; women, not men, became leaders and the laity rather than the clergy very often organized the congregation on the frontier.

Another key reason for diversity in congregational leadership was the spirit of democracy that inspired the new nation in the course of the early nineteenth century. With democracy came a wave of religious populism. The first surge of this populist wave appeared in the eighteenth century with the Great Awakening. The democratic revolution unleashed by the war for independence intensified this wave and encouraged the democratization of the local church. Not only did this challenge the clerical traditions of the past, but it also encouraged the formation of new denominations whose theology was very egalitarian. This democratic spirit still influences the shape and style of congregational leadership.

The voluntary principle in religion was another influential force in shaping leadership patterns in the congregation. Voluntarism meant that no one church would dominate the religious landscape. People were free to choose their own religion and even to create their own congregation. Freedom of religion also gave people the liberty to select the style of religious leadership that suited their needs. In addition, it allowed people to establish styles of leadership that differed from the norm.

Class also influenced the style of congregational leadership. This was most evident in the nineteenth century when class lines became more clear and differentiated. In addition, gender began to take on more importance in religion as the nineteenth century developed, and by the twentieth century it was clearly influencing the area of congregational leadership. Women were no longer limited to educational or missionary work, but were now present in the sanctuary as recognized congregational ministers.

A final reason for the diverse patterns of congregational leadership was the professionalization of the clergy. This began to take place in the second half of the nineteenth century and has continued to the present time, with congregational leadership becoming more and more limited to the professionals. Egalitarianism and democratization could go only so far and with each passing decade of the nineteenth century they gave way to professionalism. The emergence of professionalism had another important effect on the congregation; as much as any other force it helped to reduce the public role of the congregation.

In the colonial period the congregation was the heart and soul of the community. In that age church and society were bound together like Siamese twins and the leaders in the congregation were the leaders in the community as well. This public dimension of the church began to dissolve in the middle of the eighteenth century, and a century later the congregation had become a devotional institution with very little connection to the public sphere. The professionalization of the clergy, accompanied by seminary training and a burgeoning clerical culture, intensified this narrowing of the congregation's role in society. By the end of the nineteenth century ministers had become religious professionals, and lay people were now the recognized leaders in other areas of community life. Only in rare instances did a congregational leader emerge as a community leader.

In the period after World War II significant changes took place in American society that challenged the prevailing style of congregational leadership. The rise of suburbia, the women's movement, the intensification of bureaucracy, and the expansion of higher education were just some of the forces that led to a major realignment of religion in the United States.[53] These changes have rivaled those presented by the Great Awakening and the subsequent democratic revolution of the eighteenth and early nineteenth centuries. It is clear that in the 1990s a new understanding of the congregation is developing and that from this have emerged new patterns of congregational leadership. Once again adaptation and innovation are sweeping across the religious landscape.

NOTES

I want to thank Professor George Rawlyk whose careful reading of this essay was most helpful and constructive.

1. Sidney E. Mead, "The Rise of the Evangelical Conception of the Ministry in America: 1607–1850," in *The Ministry in Historical Perspectives*, ed. H. Richard Niebuhr and Daniel D. Williams (New York: Harper, 1956), p. 210.

2. William H. Seiler, "The Anglican Parish in Virginia," in James Morton Smith, ed., *Seventeenth Century America: Essays in Colonial History* (Chapel Hill: University of North Carolina Press, 1959), p. 123, and Daniel J. Boorstin, *The Americans: The Colonial Experience* (New York: Vintage Books, 1958), p. 123.

3. See Donald M. Scott, *From Office to Profession: The New England Ministry, 1750–1850* (Philadelphia: University of Pennsylvania Press, 1978), pp. 1, 12, and 16.

4. J. William T. Youngs, Jr., *God's Messengers: Religious Leadership in Colonial New England, 1700–1750* (Baltimore: Johns Hopkins University Press, 1976), pp. 68–69 and 138; Harry S. Stout, *The New England Soul: Preaching and Religious Culture in Colonial New England* (New York: Oxford University Press, 1986), p. 159.

5. See Youngs, *God's Messengers*, pp. 138–39, and Stout, *The New England Soul*, p. 211.

6. Quoted in Robert Emmett Curran, S.J., ed., *American Jesuit Spirituality: The Maryland Tradition, 1634–1900* (New York: Paulist Press, 1988), p. 12.

7. Quoted in Abraham J. Karp, "Overview: The Synagogue in America— A Historical Typology," in *The American Synagogue: A Sanctuary Transformed*, ed. Jack Wertheimer (New York: Cambridge University Press, 1987), p. 2.

8. Sean Wilentz, *Chants Democratic: New York City and the Rise of the American Working Class, 1788–1850* (New York: Oxford University Press, 1984), p. 61.

9. Nathan O. Hatch, *The Democratization of American Christianity* (New Haven: Yale University Press, 1989), p. 9.

10. Ibid., p. 44.

11. Ibid., p. 69.

12. Ibid., pp. 71, 76, 77, and 81.

13. Wayne Flynt, "A Special Feeling of Closeness: Mt. Hebron Baptist Church, Leeds, Alabama," in James P. Wind and James W. Lewis, eds., *American Congregations*, vol. 1, *Portraits of Twelve Religious Communities* (Chicago: University of Chicago Press, 1994), pp. 107–11.

14. Terry D. Bilhartz, *Urban Religion and the Second Great Awakening* (Rutherford, N.J.: Fairleigh Dickinson University Press, 1986), p. 33.

15. Ibid., pp. 36–37.

16. Anthony F. C. Wallace, *Rockdale: The Growth of an American Village in the Early Industrial Revolution* (New York: Alfred A. Knopf, 1978), p. 323.

17. James W. Fraser, *Pedagogue for God's Kingdom: Lyman Beecher and the Second Great Awakening* (Lanham, Md.: University Press of America, 1985), p. 166.

18. See Martha Tomhave Blauvelt, "Women and Revivalism," in Rosemary Radford Ruether and Rosemary Skinner Keller, eds., *Women and Religion in America*, vol. 1, *The Nineteenth Century* (San Francisco: Harper and Row, 1981), pp. 1–9, and Mary P. Ryan, "A Women's Awakening: Evangelical Religion and the Families of Utica, N.Y., 1800–1840," *American Quarterly* 30, no. 5 (Winter 1978): 602–23; also Wallace, *Rockdale*, pp. 312–18.

19. Quoted in Hatch, *The Democratization of American Christianity*, p. 107. See also Gary B. Nash, *Forging Freedom: The Formation of Philadelphia's Black Community, 1720–1840* (Cambridge: Harvard University Press, 1988) for an excellent study of the black church.

20. Jonathan D. Sarna, "The Impact of the American Revolution on American Jews," in Jonathan D. Sarna, ed., *The American Jewish Experience* (New York: Holmes and Meier, 1986), pp. 25–27.

21. Scott, *From Office to Profession*, pp. 150–51.

22. Ibid., p. 149; also very suggestive for this time period was the essay by E. Brooks Holifield, "The Historian and the Congregation" in *Beyond Clericalism: The Congregation as a Focus for Theological Education*, ed., Joseph C. Hough, Jr. and Barbara G. Wheeler (Atlanta: Scholars Press, 1988), pp. 94–98.

23. Henry Anstice, *History of St. George's Church in the City of New York* (New York: Harper and Brothers, 1911), p. 327.

24. Robert S. Lynd and Helen Merrell Lynd, *Middletown: A Study in Contemporary American Culture* (New York: Harcourt, Brace, 1929), pp. 332–412.

25. Liston Pope, *Millhands and Preachers: A Study of Gastonia* (New Haven: Yale University Press, 1942), p. 177.

26. Charles E. Hambrick-Stowe, "The Professional Ministry," in *Encyclopedia of the American Religious Experience*, ed. Charles H. Lippy and Peter W. Williams, vol. 3 (New York: Macmillan, 1988), p. 1575.

27. See Martin E. Marty, "The Clergy," in *The Professions in American History*, ed. Nathan Hatch (Notre Dame: University of Notre Dame Press, 1988), pp. 80–83.

28. See Ernest Trice Thompson, *Presbyterians in the South* (Richmond: John Knox Press, 1973), vols. 2 and 3; Hugh George Anderson, *Lutheranism in the Southeastern States, 1860–1887: A Social History* (The Hague: Mouton, 1969); Anstice, *History of St. George's Church;* and Lynd, *Middletown*.

29. Virginia Lieson Brereton and Christa Ressmeyer Klein, "American Women in Ministry: A History of Protestant Beginning Points," in *Women of Spirit: Female Leadership in the Jewish and Christian Traditions*, ed. Rosemary Ruether and Eleanor McLaughlin (New York: Simon and Schuster, 1979), p. 306.

30. See Joan R. Gunderson, "The Local Parish as a Female Institution: The Experience of All Saints Episcopal Church in Frontier Minnesota," *Church History* 55, no. 3 (September 1986): 307–22, and "Parallel Churches? Women and the Episcopal Church, 1850–1980," *Mid-America* 69 (April–July 1987): 87–97.

31. Letha Dawson Scanzoni and Susan Setta, "Women in Evangelical, Holiness, and Pentecostal Traditions," in Ruether and Keller, *Women and Religion in America*, 3 : 1900–1968, pp. 225–29.

32. Michael S. Hamilton, "Women, Public Ministry, and American Fundamentalism, 1920–1950," *Religion and American Culture: A Journal of Interpretation* 3, no. 2 (Summer 1993): 185; Hamilton bases this interpretation on the study by Nancy F. Cott, *The Grounding of Modern Feminism* (New Haven: Yale University Press, 1987).

33. See Jonathan D. Sarna and Karla Goldman, "From Synagogue-Community to Citadel of Reform: The History of K. K. Bene Israel (Rockdale Temple) in Cincinnati, Ohio," in Wind and Lewis, *Portraits*, pp. 161, 185.

34. See Daniel J. Elazar, "The Development of the American Synagogue," in Alexandra Shecket Korros and Jonathan D. Sarna, *American Synagogue History: A Bibliography and State-of-the-Field Survey* (New York: Markus Wiener Publishing, 1988), pp. 44–49; also the essays in Jacob Neusner, ed., *Understanding American Judaism* (New York: Ktav Publishing House, 1975).

35. Sarna and Goldman, "From Synagogue-Community to Citadel of Reform," p. 187.

36. See Jenna Weissman Joselit, "The Special Sphere of the Middle-Class American Jewish Woman: The Synagogue Sisterhood 1890–1940," in Wertheimer, *The American Synagogue*, pp. 206–30.

37. Jay P. Dolan, *The American Catholic Experience; A History From Colonial Times to the Present* (New York: Doubleday, 1985), pp. 158–94.

38. Leslie Woodcock Tentler, *Seasons of Grace: A History of the Archdiocese of Detroit* (Detroit: Great Lakes Books, 1990), p. 142.

39. Quoted in ibid., p. 143.

40. Quoted in Joseph J. Casino, "From Sanctuary to Involvement: A History of the Catholic Parish in the Northeast," in *The American Catholic Parish: A History From 1850 to the Present*, ed. Jay P. Dolan, vol. 1 (New York: Paulist Press, 1987), p. 58.

41. See Joseph John Parot, *Polish Catholics in Chicago, 1850–1920* (Dekalb: Northern Illinois University Press, 1981), pp. 59–94.

42. See Daniel S. Buczek, *Immigrant Pastor: The Life of the Right Rev. Msgr. Lucyan Bojnowski of New Britain, Connecticut* (Waterbury, 1974), and idem, "Three Generations of the Polish Immigrant Church: Changing Styles of Pastoral Leadership," in *Pastor of the Poles: Polish American Essays Presented to Right Reverend Monsignor John P. Wodarski*, ed. Stanislaus A. Blejwas and Mieczyslaw B. Biskupski (New Britain: Central Connecticut State College, 1982), pp. 20–36.

43. See Patrick Corish, *The Irish Catholic Experience: A Historical Survey* (Wilmington, Del.: Michael Glazier, 1985), pp. 190–91, and S. J. Connolly, *Priests and People in Pre-Famine Ireland, 1780–1845* (New York, St. Martin's Press, 1982), pp. 56–58 and 269–71.

44. Dolan, *The American Catholic Experience*, p. 171.

45. Jeffery M. Burns, "¿Qué es esto? The Transformation of St. Peter's Parish, San Francisco 1913–1990," in Wind and Lewis, *Portraits*, p. 398.

46. Quoted in Dolan, *The American Catholic Experience*, p. 351.

47. Burns, "¿Qué es esto?" p. 403.

48. Ibid., p. 402.

49. Quoted in R. Scott Appleby, "Present to the People of God: The Transformation of the Roman Catholic Parish Priesthood," in Jay P. Dolan, R. Scott Appleby, Patricia Byrne, and Debra Campbell, *Transforming Parish Ministry: The Changing Roles of Catholic Clergy, Laity, and Women Religious* (New York: Crossroad, 1989), p. 8.

50. See Tentler, *Seasons of Grace*, pp. 366–402, for a fine analysis of the seminary culture in the Detroit archdiocese; also Joseph M. White, *The Diocesan Seminary in the United States: A History From the 1780s to the Present* (Notre Dame: University of Notre Dame Press, 1989), for a thorough study of the topic.

51. Tentler, *Seasons of Grace*, pp. 153–54.

52. See Tentler, *Seasons of Grace*, p. 425 for examples of Eastern European independence in the twentieth century; see the essays by Jeffrey M. Burns, "Building the Best: A History of Catholic Parish Life in the Pacific States," and Carol L. Jensen, "Deserts, Diversity, and Self-Determination: A History of the Catholic Parish in the Intermountain West," in Dolan, *The American Catholic Parish*, vol. 2 (New York: Paulist Press, 1987), for examples of lay leadership in regions sparsely populated with Catholics.

53. Robert Wuthnow analyzes these changes in his *The Restructuring of American Religion* (Princeton: Princeton University Press, 1988); I have applied Wuthnow's analysis to recent Roman Catholicism and in particular to the parish, in Dolan et al., *Transforming Parish Ministry*, pp. 281–320.

EIGHT

The Safest Place on Earth:
The Culture of Black Congregations

ROBERT MICHAEL FRANKLIN

THE UNITED STATES HAS PROVEN to be fertile soil for a fascinating variety of religious communities and theological visions, as is evident in the stories told throughout the first volume of *American Congregations*. Among the most enduring and significant of them have been African-American congregations. Although they are American religious expressions, and ought to be viewed as part of a mainstream heritage, they tend to be understood as marginal or exotic addenda. Consequently, few Americans are aware of their extraordinary history and importance for understanding religion in the U.S.

In response to horrific conditions of racial and economic oppression, black congregations emerged as alternative cultures wherein their affirmations of God, community, and selfhood provided the strength to resist exploitation and to love others. I am convinced that as white, Asian, Latino, and other people examine the stories of black congregations, they will discover valuable insights and lessons on what it means to be *homo religiosus* in a postmodern world.

One of the primary lessons that this chapter presents to those outside the black church tradition is that congregations are places where alternative cultures may be nurtured, prophetic language and action shaped, and liberating visions celebrated. The liberating culture that developed within black congregations empowered ordinary people to resist dehumanization, to struggle for social change and justice, and to celebrate the presence of God in their midst, even when they sometimes felt abandoned. Every song, prayer, sermon, and gesture reflected some awareness both of hard times in this world and of the certainty that God was on their side. But black congregations were not content merely to survive the horrors of the past; they also made claims upon the nation's identity, conscience, and moral obligation to practice fairness and mercy toward its most disfranchised citizens. Their public mission was to compel America to become America for everyone. Hence the African-American religious narrative may offer clues to all sorts of congregations about how to renew hope and energize ministries that can positively transform society.

In order to understand the genius of black congregations, it is important to understand how the congregation's entire culture does the work of empowering parishioners for mission. Central to that cultural work is the pivotal role of pastoral leadership in its manifestation of theological convictions, rhetorical skills, and practical wisdom. Most portraits of black congregations emphasize the role of clergy. This is understandable, given the elevated office of ministry in most black communities. A more careful examination of black congregational culture, however, requires attention to the array of practices that are sustained by the *laity*—style of worship, singing, ecstatic rituals (shouting, altar prayer), and politically relevant religious education. Effective congregational mission actually flows from the dynamic *interaction* between qualified, gifted leadership and an empowering congregational culture. Black clergy are, in the first instance, servants called to nurture and maintain a healthy congregational culture. Once progress in this task has been demonstrated, then they may be authorized to exert leadership that mobilizes the congregation for ministry in the public arena. (We see this illustrated in Lawrence Mamiya's chapter in the first volume of *American Congregations* on the Bethel A.M.E. congregation in Baltimore.)

Charismatic leadership alone, it must be stated, is ineffectual. Such styles of leadership may even be pernicious, as an apathetic community looks to messianic figures for magical solutions to problems. While dramatic sermons and an attractive presence can easily degenerate into mere entertainment, *authentic* leadership helps to create a community that is vital, hopeful, and unified. Even in the absence of gifted leadership, the wisdom and work of community members themselves often generate significant ministry in the public arena. But the potential for such ministry may go untapped without an overarching vision compelling people to self-committing action. And in the case of the church, that vision must be faithful to the Christian revelation. Hence the preacher as theologian is authorized to present, interpret, and apply the symbols of Christian faith in ways that equip people for service.

Let us begin, then, first by examining the structure and dynamics of black congregational culture, and then by analyzing the leader's task of maintaining and mobilizing the congregation for ministry. In that connection, the catalytic and sustaining function of preaching is particularly important. It then may be helpful to look at four dominant leadership styles assumed by black clergy who have successfully mobilized congregations for public mission: those of consensus builders, crusaders, commanders, and campaigners.

The Culture of Black Congregations

As numerous interpreters of black religion have already reminded us, there is no monolithic, undifferentiated social institution that can be labeled "the black church."[1] Rather there are varieties of black congregations which share a common core culture. This culture is an amalgam of symbols, practices, and ideas drawn from numerous traditions, including traditional African religion, Islam, Catholic popular piety, Protestant evangelicalism, and American civil religion. Over time, these elements have been forged into the dynamic spiritual expression encountered in most black congregations. Notwithstanding differences in polity, dogma, or socioeconomic levels, that expression is vibrant and consistent in nearly all black congregations. Even predominantly white congregations with a substantial black membership have been transformed by the infusion of this tradition's dynamism.[2]

In an excellent case study of black congregational culture, anthropologist Melvin D. Williams provides an illuminating summary of its many functions.

> [Zion Holiness Church, a pseudonym for a Pentecostal congregation in Pittsburgh] is a huddling place where members take refuge from the world among familiar faces. It is a source of identity and a matrix of interaction for the members it recruits. It is a subculture that creates and transmits symbols and enforces standards of belief and behavior. It allocates social status, differentiates roles, resolves conflicts, gives meaning, order, and style to its members' lives, and provides for social mobility and social rewards within its confines.[3]

Williams reminds us that local congregational cultures are complex, multidimensional phenomena. Black preachers and pastors are expected to be familiar with this variety of social functions and insure that they are carried out with dignity and seriousness. Among the most significant constitutive practices of the culture are the full engagement of the

senses in worship, intimate prayer, cathartic shouting, triumphant singing, politically relevant religious education, and prophetic preaching.[4]

Full Engagement of the Senses in Worship

One of the most significant and fascinating legacies of slavery is the
ritualized manner in which African Americans organized their nonwork
lives in order to experience interior liberation. Although their hard work
on the plantation was uncompensated and was emotionally and intellectually unstimulating, African slaves created sacred space in which the
mind, emotions, and all of their senses were engaged in transcending
the banality of evil. Knowing that they would soon return to the bore-
dom and dread of field work, they threw themselves into the worship
experiences.[5]

This legacy has shaped contemporary black worship wherein one
receives (and co-creates) a full sensory experience. The sacred drama
and motion of call-response preaching and colorful choir robes are
seen; the rhythmic power of choirs, drums, tambourines, horns, and
electric keyboards is heard; the wafting aromas of Sunday dinner being
prepared in the church kitchen are often taken in; touching, hugs,
and holy kisses are exchanged; and one's inner core is deeply satisfied
to know that in this crowd of loving people, one is in the safest place
on earth. For oppressed people, such worship has always been valued
as providing a glimpse of God's commonwealth. But beyond its sensory value, this worship-induced glimpse has significant theological
content.

The milieu of black church worship seeks to mediate the felt sense
of God as revealed through the social outcast Jesus Christ, and made
available through the operation of the Holy Spirit. Theologically, black
worship coheres around a strong doctrine of God's sovereignty in the
universe. Most black worshipers affirm that God is both omnipotent and
compassionate toward humanity. The suffering of the righteous and innocent are held to be mysteries that will be understood better "by and
by." Although the horrors of slavery were sufficient to cause some black
people to forsake Christianity, skillful black preachers helped congregations to interpret slavery within the context of God's unfolding plan,
in which they somehow stood at the center. Preachers reminded listeners that God chose to enter the human race bearing the social status of a
marginal, oppressed person. As James Cone and other black theologians
have maintained, black perceptions of God tend to be filtered through

One of Kunjufu's insights regarding public education is relevant to [t]he educational component of black congregational culture. He suggests [th]at in order to increase levels of student retention and achievement [e]specially among black boys), "coaches" rather than mere instructors [ar]e needed. He argues: "Instructors specialize in dispensing informa-[tio]n. Coaches have the ability to combine subject matter and learning [sty]les with identity and self-esteem."[13] In black congregations, the most [eff]ective teachers are coaches, and their degree of involvement in the [cha]racter development of children may exceed that of many parents. [Thi]s is especially important for single-parent families, in which the re-[mai]ning parent (usually the mother) is often nearly overwhelmed by [oth]er responsibilities. Such mentoring by Christian educators not only [enh]ances the self-esteem of young people but also nurtures the capacity [for c]ritical thinking and political consciousness.

Prophetic, Imaginative Preaching

[I]n the context of worship that stimulates the senses, preaching [is a] central sacred act and may be the chief mobilizing catalyst for [actio]n activity. In his examination of African-American folk culture, [histori]an Lawrence W. Levine highlights historian of religion Mircea [Eliade]'s definition of the sacred. Eliade has taught us that "for people in [traditio]nal societies religion is a means of extending the world spatially [upward] so that communication with the other world becomes ritually [possible], and extending it temporally backward so that the paradigmatic [time of] the gods and mythical ancestors can be continually re-enacted [is indef]initely recoverable."[14]

[Thi]s comment illumines the genius of black sacred rhetoric. Each [black] preacher is charged with the priestly responsibility of *mediating* [encoun]*ter with the holy* through the spatial and temporal extension of [time. W]hile most interpreters of black preaching understand the [preacher] to be a prophet who is a moral teacher, I am calling attention [to the] dimension of sacred rhetoric that has been inadequately ex-[plored. O]ne of the foremost scholars of black preaching, Henry Mitch-[ell, al]erted us to this function by observing that "at his best, the [prea]cher must be not only a teacher and mobilizer, a figure and [..., but also a *celebrant*" (emphasis mine).[15]

[The b]lack preacher—through the anointing of the Holy Spirit, [and th]e virtuosity of imaginative, narrative, lyrical, and poetic

the lens of historical oppression. This makes a transcendent God humanly trustworthy.

But it is through the life of Spirit that blacks come to experience the power of a transcendent Creator and the empathy of an immanent Christ. Through the careful coordination of auditory, visual, olfactory, and tactile stimuli, good worship facilitates the dilation of the human spirit in order that one may feel God's Spirit and thereby know God. Hence, contrary to the reductionistic, materialistic interpretations often applied to experiential religion by social scientists, feeling the Spirit during worship is a profoundly theological moment which those explanations are inadequate to illumine. Rather, we must consult the discipline of theology to get at the heart of black worship. Authentic worship is, in Paul Tillich's terms, a theonomous encounter wherein we meet a God who reconciles the rational and the emotional, sacred and secular, right brain and left brain, yin and yang.[6]

Intimate Prayer

In the black church tradition, the altar prayer or pastoral prayer is a significant therapeutic moment. In the absence of a formal ritual of confession, this moment permits congregants to have their personal and collective sinfulness named and absolved by the pastor or prayer leader. Such moments are never rushed; people are given time, as Howard Thurman said, to "center down" and remove themselves from the turbulence and traffic of their lives. In addition to the time and space for intimate communion with God, emotional license is given to each praying person to experience God's response of liberation. Persons may do grief work, weep, express vulnerability, and make moral resolutions to do the right thing in the future.

Ironically, and fortunately, such intimate, private, personal spiritual work is done in the communal, public context so that one is discouraged from conceptualizing her or his prayer needs nonrelationally. Communal prayer challenges religious privatization as it gathers up the cares of the entire community and articulates them as the common existential expression of the people.

Cathartic Shouting

Elsewhere I have provided a brief sketch of the core culture of most black congregations, noting that shouting is the most controversial feature of that culture.[7] Shouting includes emotionally liberating, ecstatic expressions of adoration, praise, and triumph. During designated moments of formal worship, shouters may stand, walk, dance, leap for joy, speak in tongues, or fall to the floor in response to an overwhelming encounter with the mysterium tremendum.[8]

This license provides persons with the opportunity to release positive and powerful energies in exclamatory expressions. Also, disturbing dynamics may be worked through or purged in this ritualized form of radical unmasking. Persons who shout report that they feel better and that something therapeutically significant has occurred.

An interesting feature of "shouting" black congregations is the presence of uniformed nurses stationed strategically near the altar to supervise the cathartic ritual. The nurses insure that the process unfolds in a healthy manner; when problems occur, they intervene to arrest any dysfunctional or nonspiritual behaviors. Along with the pastor, they supervise the delicate process of what anthropologist Victor Turner refers to as *reincorporation* of the ecstatic, "liminal" agent back into the life of the community. Ultimately, the pastor seeks to insure that ecstasy will have some ethical consequences.[9]

Most black pastors try to foster a creative relationship between the two dominant movements of a healthy moral life, identified by American psychologist William James long ago: ascetic striving for justice and mystical disengagement from the stresses of modern life.[10] Black pastors understand that personal conversion, gradual reformation, and equipping for witness and service are part of the normative socialization process within a congregation. Consequently, people can shout if they feel led to, but they must also be prepared to act as responsible moral agents when the shouting is finished.[11]

Triumphant Singing

I grew up in a congregation whose impressive music ministry included a choir that moved to well-choreographed steps and was clad in magnificent robes, and a band in which I played the drums. The idea of drums in worship may upset the equilibrium of some, but we felt that the organ, drums, and guitar helped people to experience and move to the rhythms of the holy. The God who created the rhythms of the heartbeat, the ebb and flow of ocean waves, and the changing of nature's seasons was a God of rhythm. Hence the drums had a *conjuring* function: when they were properly played, the Spirit fell.

The songs of the choir were carefully orchestrated to inspire hope

and triumphant faith among persons on the margins of so power in society. Such songs as "I'm a Soldier in the Army and "Victory Shall Be Mine" empowered black people to s fully for justice in a racist society.

Not all of the music in the black church tradition quick-paced. The organ and the soft chants of the choir calm the worship atmosphere after it has been ecsta These chants mediate the return from a mystical mount dane milieu.

Concerning the therapeutic and preparatory fun cred music, communications theorist Molefi Kete As observed that

singing sets the stage or mood by preparing the au ally and physically for the preacher, whose comm made easier because of the audience receptivity though instructive, is much more palliative; it tions and draws the congregation together. inherits an attentive audience by virtue of the c

Politically Relevant Religious Edu

Since the time of the civil rights and black po black congregations have revised their educati aim of being more relevant to the cultural new generation. Many congregations have education literature provided by white educ that facilitate worshiping God while celebra gious educators now publish a wide variety materials.

In Chicago, Pastor Jeremiah A. Wrigh Church of Christ, is explicit in his desire to ture that is "unashamedly Christian an phrase also prominent in Baltimore's Betl end, he requires all clergy and memb classes. He teaches the clergy group an logians who advance a liberation age tone of political relevance and persp the congregation. In addition, he is tion's members, Jawanza Kunjufu, tional consultant.

26

language, and through co-creativity with a responsive congregation— brings together sacred and human realms. The preacher calls down the Spirit and calls the masses up to the mountaintop. Because the preaching moment is antiphonal, inviting the response of the congregation, the word of God is experienced as a dialogue in which God is a trustworthy conversation partner. Hence the word does not belong to the elite (male and middle-class) preaching guild, the possessors of specialized knowledge, but is a gift in which all the people share.

Black people expect the sermon, as a word inspired by God and located within the community, to be spiritually profound, politically relevant, socially prophetic, artistically polished, and reverently delivered. I have heard many white preachers express some envy, and not a little intimidation, at the prospect of such congregational investment in, and quality control over, their weekly proclamations.

In a stimulating essay on African-American oral culture, Molefi Kete Asante has noted that blacks have developed "consummate skill in using language to produce communication patterns *alternative* to those employed in the American situation" (emphasis mine).[16] Asante argues that black sermons illustrate the peculiar transformative power inherent in the spoken word, a dynamism he refers to as *nommo*. Commenting on the complexity of the "religious interactive event" between preacher and audience, he also reminds us that not all black preachers have mastered the tradition.

> Every speaker does not possess the assurance that he will be successful in provoking a total response. In fact, some preachers never succeed in moving an audience to the total interactive event, which is necessary for them to consider their speeches successful. These preachers must be satisfied with the occasional feedback expressed by an "Amen" or a "Lord, help," offered by several members as the sermon is presented. Other preachers, through a delicate combination of vocal manipulations, characterized by rhythm and cadence, and vital thematic expression, usually developed in narrative form, can easily produce a creative environment when message is intensified by audience response. . . .
>
> In mounting the platform to speak . . . the black preacher does not challenge *nommo* but uses it, becomes a part of it, and is consumed in the fire of speech and music. The perfect force of the moment is sensual, giving, sharing, generative, productive, and ultimately creative and full of power. Hallelujah![17]

Such transformative preaching temporarily transports black worshipers into a realm where they are assured of God's care and affirmation of their being despite a society that denies their claims to equal dignity. In that realm they are addressed as responsible moral agents who are charged to work for a just society.

A significant amount of moral education occurs within the preaching moment. "Preaching moment" is an oxymoron because preaching in the black community claims a large portion of worship time. Preachers employ a wide variety of rhetorical styles (especially the narrative art form) in order to lift up and embody Christian virtues and values. Martin Luther King, Jr., used this strategy brilliantly during his early sermons in Montgomery, Alabama, in order to rally bus boycotters to new levels of courage and personal power.

> We are here this evening because we are tired now, but let us say that we are not here advocating violence. We have overcome that. I want it to be known throughout Montgomery and throughout this nation that we are a Christian people. We believe in the Christian religion. We believe in the teachings of Jesus. The only weapon that we have in our hands this evening is the weapon of protest. . . . This is the glory of America, with all of its faults. . . . The great glory of American democracy is the right to protest for right.[18]

It was precisely King's mastery of the black preaching tradition that transformed him into the symbol and principal interpreter of the movement. The extraordinary manner in which he worked the tradition (especially in his "I have a Dream" address) earned him a place in nearly every American's consciousness as the greatest preacher of the twentieth century.

The six features of black congregational culture identified here are by no means exhaustive. But they are defining ritual practices found in the vast majority of black congregations and, as such, they constitute a distinctive religious culture.[19]

Maintaining and Mobilizing the Congregation

Black pastors are given the priestly authority to nurture these practices in black congregational culture. They cannot easily mobilize the congregation for risky social action unless they have attended to these antecedent responsibilities. Presumably, the new pastor was charismatic enough to be chosen as pastor: he or she possessed the desired rhetorical and interpersonal qualities necessary for getting a second interview. The more difficult task is to become the "people's pastor" and not merely the congregation's employee. New pastors often rely upon wise elders in the congregation to orient them to those aspects of the local congregational culture that are especially "sacred" and merit attention.

In a discussion of the "strategic qualities employed to gain and maintain power," Melvin Williams offers a list of leadership abilities that have some relevance for our discussion of how pastors are granted permission to mobilize for mission. He observed that the ministers at the "Zion Holiness Church" had to be able to

1. create emotional excitement in the congregation by integrating experiential empathy with religious aspirations and biblical accuracy in a sermon that begins with a text and ends in emotional frenzy,

2. interact with the members so that they demonstrate their love for "everybody" yet maintain the appropriate social distance concomitant with their position,

3. create an air of distinctiveness around their individuality by appearances, wealth, education, political astuteness, glibness, intellectual prowess in recognition of the Zion idiom, ease of interaction and identification among various subcultures.

4. jest and entertain the congregation within the limits of propriety determined by Zion,

5. motivate the congregation to work to maintain the physical plant and to raise money; to organize,

6. appreciate the symbols and values in Zion so as to be upwardly mobile without undue threat to the vested interests of superiors,

7. conduct their personal lives so that they do not create church or public scandal,

8. withstand gossip, the threat of schism, feminine guile, and the pressure groups within Zion and in the international organization,

9. support the international and state organization in membership and finances,

10. attract new members, whether within programs or personal appeal.[20]

Readers will perhaps pause at his reference to "feminine guile," which reflects the sexist assumptions of a patriarchal culture. As increasing numbers of women occupy pulpits, however, it will be necessary either to attribute guile to all humans or to revise our way of thinking about interpersonal and sexual relations within congregations. Furthermore, his reference to international and state organizations reflects a connectional polity that is less relevant to free-church traditions.

Although Williams reports that these qualities are thought to be important for maintaining a preacher's personal power in the congregation, they may also be viewed as means by which a pastor helps to maintain the internal ethos of the congregation. Black pastors help to nurture and maintain congregational culture by two principal practices, preaching and pastoral care. By verbal endorsement from the pulpit, and by their physical presence in group meetings or special worship services, pastors give value to dimensions of the congregation's life that might be undervalued by some parishioners. When the pastor commends a subgroup's ministries to prison inmates or the homeless, everyone realizes that these are important to the life of the church. Every ministry in the congregation covets such favorable public mention from the pastor. Similarly, when the pastor stands up and rejoices in response to the gospel choir's renderings, that mere gesture indicates that the chief inspector of quality in worship is pleased.

The pastor who successfully maintains this internal ethos may be rewarded by having the congregation embrace his or her social vision and political commitments. But such mobilization, it must be stressed, grows out of a relationship of trust and common experience. Dynamic things can happen when a healthy congregational culture and charismatic pastoral leadership work together smoothly.

This was the case when the Reverend Adam Clayton Powell, Jr., pastor of what was once the largest black congregation in America, Abyssinian Baptist Church, mobilized the congregation to boycott discriminatory businesses and housing policies in Harlem. A successful boycott led to his successful bid for city council and, in 1944, his election to Congress. But Powell understood that he had to help maintain the congregation's culture, and his own power base, before and while becoming involved in secular politics. He did this by returning periodically to preach in Harlem.

Similarly, when Martin Luther King, Jr., began his ministry at Montgomery's Dexter Avenue Baptist Church, he did not have long to work on maintaining the local culture before he was swept into the national spotlight. But through his personal example of discipleship (even when it endangered his own life), spellbinding preaching, and diligence in not allowing his public visibility to compromise his pastoral duties, he mobilized an impressive segment of his staid, middle-class congregation to support the Montgomery bus boycott along with other activities of the civil rights movement.

I see an important relationship between the preaching of these two prominent pastors and the social movements they helped to lead. But what is the relationship between preaching and action for social change? It is clear to most observers that the relationship is exceedingly complex and rarely simple, direct, and causal. Indeed, Powell, King, and other preachers availed themselves of the entire culture while calling for concerted action in the public realm. And it was their preaching that functioned as the chief catalyst to move people from reflection and celebration to life-endangering action in the cause of Jesus Christ.

Preaching as a Catalyst

In order to understand the relationship between preaching and social action, it may be helpful to consider the structure of effective sermons advocating social change. The model I offer is necessarily a modest effort toward the impossible task of distilling the genius of black preaching into discrete steps.[21] Five steps are identified: naming the demon, analyzing the crisis, describing a solution, prescribing a specific action plan, and offering hope.

First, the phrase "naming the demon" is borrowed from the New Testament's depiction of Jesus' authority over evil spirits which enables him to ask their names. After knowing the name of the opponent, Jesus is able to vanquish him. In black preaching, this "naming" refers to a particular manner of framing the crisis that faces the community. Often people are overwhelmed by perceiving problems to be so large and complex that ordinary people are incapable of approaching them. Preachers who skillfully frame such crises in ways that empower people are moving congregations a step closer to engaging and, perhaps, overcoming the problems.

For instance, inner-city parishioners daily experience the massive assault of violent crime, addictive drugs, economic depression, and social chaos. How are these demons to be named? King illustrated the black sermonic style of framing crises in a sermon titled "Antidotes for Fear."

In these days of catastrophic change and calamitous uncertainty, is there any man who does not experience the depression and bewilderment of crippling fear, which, like a nagging hound of hell, pursues our every footstep?[22]

By employing the picturesque simile "like a nagging hound of hell," the preacher renders that which began as vast and seemingly unconquerable into something familiar and more manageable. After hearing this rhetorical device, people can identify and deal with the fear they feel. He goes on to suggest that fear can be "harnessed and mastered" through honest confrontation, courage, love, and faith. He concludes with an empowering poem:

> Fear knocked at the door.
> Faith answered.
> There was no one there.[23]

Sometimes the mere title of a sermon begins the process of naming and framing in an empowering way. Consider King's sermon of May 17, 1956, titled, "The Death of Evil Upon the Shore," in which evil is given a persona and is vanquished.[24] Or Harlem pastor Carolyn Ann Knight's sermon, "The Survival of the Unfit," which subverts Darwin's axiom by heralding the work of Christ in behalf of an unfit humanity.[25] Black preaching aimed at mobilizing the congregation for action must reveal that evil can be overcome and that there are no unredeemable situations.

Second, skillful preachers analyze the crisis using biblical categories and language. Christian social preaching explores and interprets the contradictions and possibilities of human existence in light of the Good Friday/Easter event. The preacher places community and world events into a framework that assumes the existence of God, a God who acts in history and has special compassion for the poor, the stranger, and the victim. The preacher is unafraid to employ the powerful ensemble of biblical categories like sin, exodus, crucifixion, and resurrection in order to help people step outside, imaginatively and literally, the modern framework of commercialism and popular psychology into an alternate way of viewing the human condition. Literature scholar Hortense Spillers notes that the black preacher "weaves analogy and allegory into the sermon, comparing and juxtaposing contemporary problems in morality with and alongside ancient problems in morality."[26] Thus black preachers have employed the exodus motif (the most famous in black sermonic discourse) to portray the African-American struggle for justice as continuous with, and parallel to, ancient Israel's struggle to make exodus from Egypt.

Consider King's analysis of the great conflict of good and evil in history, in the sermon "Our God Is Able."

> Christianity contends that evil contains the seed of its own destruction. History is the story of evil forces that advance with seemingly irresistible power only to be crushed by the battering rams of the forces of justice. There is a law in the moral world—a silent, invisible imperative, akin to the laws of the physical world—which reminds us that life will work only in a certain way. The Hitlers and the Mussolinis have their day, and for a period they may wield great power, spreading themselves like a green bay tree, but soon they are cut down like the grass and wither as the green herb.[27]

Using the theological categories and poetic imagery of the Bible, King sets the struggle against racism and segregation into a grand philosophy of history which assures the ultimate conquest of righteousness. Victory is assured because his doctrine of God posits a compassionate, personal, and powerful agent. This conception of God functions as the normative theological and ethical warrant in black church culture. God's action makes human agency possible and worthwhile. King concludes the sermon with words designed to mobilize and sustain public activism:

> Let this affirmation [Our God is able] be our ringing cry. It will give us courage to face the uncertainties of the future. It will give our tired feet new strength as we continue our forward stride toward the city of freedom. When our days become dreary with low-hovering clouds and our nights become darker than a thousand midnights, let us remember that there is a great benign Power in the universe whose name is God, and he is able to make a way out of no way, and transform dark yesterdays into bright tomorrows. This is our hope for becoming better men. This is our mandate for seeking to make a better world.[28]

Coming after naming and analyzing, the third step involves describing the resolution or solution by using symbols from the Christian and black folk idioms. In this step a moral vision for the public is developed, and in this mode of discourse the black church has sought to point America and the world toward a better future. In perhaps the best-known sermon of the twentieth century, King spoke to the heart and the imagination of the nation on August 28, 1963.

I have a dream that one day on the red hills of Georgia, sons of former slaves and sons of former slave-owners will be able to sit down together at the table of brotherhood.

I have a dream that one day, even the state of Mississippi, a state sweltering with the heat of injustice, sweltering with the heat of oppression, will be transformed into an oasis of freedom and justice.

I have a dream my four little children will one day live in a nation where they will not be judged by the color of their skin but by the content of their character.

I have a dream that one day, down in Alabama, with its vicious racists, with its governor having his lips dripping with the words of interposition and nullification, that one day, right there in Alabama, little black boys and black girls will be able to join hands with little white boys and white girls as sisters and brothers. I have a dream today!

I have a dream that one day every valley shall be exalted, every hill and mountain shall be made low, the rough places shall be made plain, and the crooked places shall be made straight and the glory of the Lord will be revealed and all flesh shall see it together.

With this faith we will be able to work together, to pray together, to struggle together, to go to jail together, to stand up for freedom together knowing that we will be free one day.

Dr. King concludes with a majestic, panoramic vision of the vast beauty of America, hinting at the nation's indebtedness, and responsibility, to God.

So let freedom ring from the prodigious hilltops of New Hampshire.
Let freedom ring from the mighty mountains of New York.
Let freedom ring from the heightening Alleghenies of Pennsylvania.
Let freedom ring from the snow-capped Rockies of Colorado.
Let freedom ring from the curvaceous slopes of California.

Then, in the middle of this driving refrain and sensuous portraiture, his eye takes a dramatic turn southward, which introduces tension and upsets the equilibrium of the celebrating audience. How might he juxtapose the brave and free territories of the north and west with the segregationist south?

But not only that.
Let freedom ring from Stone Mountain of Georgia.
Let freedom ring from Lookout Mountain of Tennessee.
Let freedom ring from every hill and molehill of Mississippi,
from every mountainside, let freedom ring.

And when we allow freedom to ring, when we let it ring from every village and hamlet, from every state and city, we will be able to speed up that day when all of God's children—black men and white men, Jew and Gentile, Protestants and Catholics—will be able to join hands and sing in the words of the old Negro spiritual, "Free at last, free at last; thank God Almighty, we are free at last."[29]

King's moral vision of a renewed American republic was inspiringly inclusive and drew upon images and symbols from the Bible, from Negro spirituals, and from common American experience. His idiom of inclusiveness established the still unfinished agenda of the civil rights movement. This vision became the social manifesto for most black churches, and black preachers across the country restated and reinterpreted its contents within their local contexts. It is a vision more ethical than eschatological: King and other black clergy were determined to translate this vision into political reality in the not-too-distant future, within the lifespan of their children. The political revolution would be the outgrowth of human effort as well as divine grace. This was the optimism that celebrated the signing of the Voting Rights Act of 1965, finally granting suffrage to all people of color.

After sketching a general moral vision, social-change sermons in black churches typically move toward prescribing a specific action plan for a particular congregation. In this part of the sermon, listeners are reminded that although they may not be able to remedy large-scale crises, they can do something about the local manifestations. Calvin O. Butts, currently pastor of the Abyssinian Baptist Church in Harlem, reminds parishioners that even though they cannot stop the flow of drugs across national borders or stop the manufacture of products harmful to health, they can stop the irresponsible corporate advertising of some products in poor black ghetto communities. Recently, after preaching on the subject and specifying what ordinary people of conscience should do, he led parishioners with paintbrushes and ladders to whitewash all the alcohol and tobacco advertisements in Harlem. In response to a CNN news reporter's question about the legality of this initiative, and as New York police looked on impassively, he responded that he was willing to go to jail for this defiant act of trying to save lives in the face of bad corporate citizenship.

The fifth component of preaching that catalyzes in response to crisis is simply offering hope. Henry Mitchell refers to this as the climactic moment of celebration in black preaching. It is here that the congregation is offered a word of assurance that God is on the side of those who struggle and suffer for righteousness' sake. Again King is exemplary. During the last three years of his ministry, the theme of hope was the most prominent in his efforts to mobilize congregations and all citizens to march on Washington in order to call attention to the plight of poor people in 1968. But my favorite illustration comes from his sermon "Our God Is Marching On," delivered before the state capitol building at the conclusion of the famous march from Selma to Montgomery, March 21–25, 1965.

> So as we go away this afternoon, let us go away more than ever before committed to the struggle and committed to nonviolence. I must admit to you that there are still some difficulties ahead. We are still in for a season of suffering in many of the black belt counties of Alabama. . . .
>
> I must admit to you there are still jail cells waiting for us, dark and difficult moments. We will go on with the faith that nonviolence and its power transformed dark yesterdays into bright tomorrows. We will be able to change all of these conditions.
>
> I know you are asking today, "How long will it take?" I come to say to you this afternoon however difficult the moment, however frustrating the hour, it will not be long, because truth pressed to earth will rise again.
>
> How long? Not long, because no lie can live forever.
>
> How long? Not long, because you will still reap what you sow.
>
> How long? Not long, because the arm of the moral universe is long but it bends toward justice.
>
> How long? Not long, 'cause mine eyes have seen the glory of the coming of the Lord, trampling out the vintage where the grapes of wrath are stored. He has loosed the fateful lightning of his terrible swift sword. His truth is marching on.[30]

Or consider the hopeful sermonic resolution of Caesar A. W. Clark of Dallas, one of the nation's most eloquent black preachers. His sermon is titled "Christ, the Center of History."

In Christ we have:
A life that can never be forfeited.
A relation that can never be abrogated.
A righteousness that can never be tarnished.
An acceptance that can never be questioned.
A title that can never be clouded.
A standing that can never be disputed.
A justification that can never be reversed.
A seal that can never be violated.
A wealth that can never be depleted.
A possession that can never be measured.
A peace that can never be destroyed.
A joy that can never be suppressed.
A service that can never be unrewarded.
An intercessor who can never be disqualified.
A victor who can never be vanquished.
A glory that can never be dimmed.
A hope that can never be disappointed.
A resurrection that can never be hindered![31]

No matter what the scale of the crisis, whether discriminatory social policies or the advertising of harmful products in communities of despair, effective preaching can mobilize people by naming the issue, analyzing it in light of Christian faith commitments, pointing toward a solution, directing specific moral action, and offering hope through celebration.

Black Clergy Leadership Styles

In his Pulitzer Prize–winning book, *Leadership,* James MacGregor Burns has noted that

leadership is a process of morality to the degree that leaders engage with followers on the basis of shared motives and values and goals. Leadership over human beings is exercised when persons with certain motives and purposes *mobilize,* in competition or conflict with others, institutional, political, psychological, and other resources so as to arouse, engage, and satisfy the motives of followers. (Emphasis mine.)[32]

Burns also distinguished transactional from transformational leadership. The former makes temporary contact with people for the purpose of exchanging valued things (jobs for votes, goods for money, or hospitality for a listening ear), but the latter engages with others in such a way that the leader and followers "raise one another to higher levels of motivation and morality."

> Transforming leadership ultimately becomes *moral* in that it raises the level of human conduct and ethical aspiration of both leader and led, and thus it has a transforming effect on both. Perhaps the best modern example is Gandhi. . . . Transcending leadership is dynamic leadership in the sense that the leaders throw themselves into a relationship with followers who will feel "elevated" by it and often become more active themselves, thereby creating new cadres of leaders.[33]

Although I find Burns's social-scientific definition of leadership somewhat thin with regard to the deep passions and motivations that religious experience and identity may stir, his discussion of transformational or transcending leadership suggests the sort of emotional and rational bonds that connect pastor and people, people and God. Although I imagine that most Christian pastors think of themselves as transformational leaders, Burns helps us to discern transactional leadership patterns of behavior in the church. Also, his notion that transformational leaders help to create new leaders follows the logic of Jesus' practice of making disciples, a model of empowerment rather than of dependence and manipulation.

I note that my typology is intentionally noncomprehensive. I am interested only in clergy-persons who are already persuaded of the social and political dimension of the gospel and who care to enhance American public life through the practice of ministry. I will not discuss the relatively small numbers of black clergy and faith communities that avoid or condemn ministry in the public arena. Such leaders may be interesting because of the rich and robust congregational culture they help to maintain, but their interpretations of Christian ministry (especially of the Great Commission) and of the black church liberation tradition are regrettably parochial, and tragically irrelevant.

When a crisis emerges in the community, laypeople and clergy gather facts and begin to develop opinions about its scope and nature. Is the crisis a monumental problem or a trivial matter? Will it persist and require attention, or is it a passing annoyance that may be ignored? Who should be responsible for resolving the crisis, and at what cost? Such questions are debated in barbershops and beauty parlors, over food, drink, and sport, and everywhere on the street until Sunday morning arrives. Persons who attend the Sunday worship service expect the preacher to frame the crisis in biblical and theological terms. Earlier, I illustrated the typical mode of sermonic discourse employed by black clergy seeking to mobilize for mission. But not all black clergy-persons mobilize in the same way. Leaders differ in temperament, organizing skill, and knowledge, just as congregational cultures vary.

First, there are *consensus builders*, who mobilize by educating, persuading, and seeking to build unity around a commonly desired goal. Consensus builders rely on decision-making structures and committees within the church to pave the way for concerted, united action. For them, mobilization occurs only after careful study, debate, and negotiation about strategies, goals, and rationales. Because mobilizing the entire congregation is an objective, they invite everyone to participate in some manner, and they work hard to resolve potentially divisive disagreements. In the end, the people come to feel that the public mission is the result of their efforts rather than of the pastor's.

One of the best-known consensus-building mobilizers in the nation is the Reverend Leon Sullivan, pastor of the Zion Baptist Church in Philadelphia. Sociologists C. Eric Lincoln and Lawrence Mamiya report that Sullivan organized a Selective Patronage Campaign which successfully boycotted several corporations that employed inadequate numbers of African Americans. This effort was supported by four hundred black ministers in Philadelphia. At Zion Church, he developed a plan known as the "10-36." Church members were urged to "contribute $10 for 36 months to support the Philadelphia Community Investment Cooperative. The group of 227 original subscribers grew to over 5,000 with about 400 black churches participating." This enterprise culminated in the construction of the Progress Plaza Shopping Center, the "first and largest black-owned and operated shopping complex in the United States."[34]

In 1964, Sullivan founded the Opportunities Industrialization Centers of America, which became a national job-training program operating in seventy cities. Sullivan is best known, however, as the first black to be appointed to the board of directors of General Motors. In an effort to bring an end to apartheid in South Africa, he introduced the "Sullivan

Principles," challenging American corporations to use their power for social change. The principles were embraced by many American companies and even received cautious endorsement from the Reagan administration. More recently, Sullivan has convened hundreds of people of African descent for a Pan-African conference in West Africa. All his mobilization efforts entail identifying themes and goals that enjoy wide consensus in the community. Even his personal manner combines fiery oratory with a disarming charm that makes him easy to approach.

Some clergy mobilize congregations through personal, charismatic authority which is put in the service of a righteous cause. I refer to them as *crusaders*, leaders who act first and debate later. Often when they begin, they act almost alone. They have faith in the capacity of small, highly disciplined groups to initiate social change. Crusaders rely upon the self-evident correctness of the cause and the power of their personal example to pull and invite others to follow them into the crusade. Crusaders are comfortable initiating action in the absence of congregational consensus, because they believe that leaders are supposed to be in the front lines of battle. Often they resort to crusading after frustrated efforts to build consensus. Crusaders think of themselves as realists who recognize that their own congregations are not ready or able to join them in a particular struggle. Consequently, they appeal to the conscience of the wider community beyond their congregations. Calvin Butts, mentioned above, is a prominent example of such a style. Butts knew that his socially prominent middle-class congregation was not inclined to join him, en masse, in breaking the law by defacing advertisements in the community. He did, however, win a following in the city and nation by his bold initiative. These initiatives were modeled on the radical activism of his mentor and former pastor, Adam Clayton Powell, Jr.

Another example of a crusader is a Chicago Catholic priest, Father George Clements, the former pastor of Holy Angels Church. Clements received national attention when he adopted a child and urged other priests, parents, and churches to solve the crisis of abandoned black children. Clements was branded a maverick and a crusader, but tangible results followed. His example inspired the Illinois Department of Family Services to develop a cooperative program with black churches in which "black families adopt black children through their churches." Since 1981, the "One-Church One-Child" program has reduced a backlog of more than 700 black children in Chicago awaiting adoption to fewer than 60.[35] The crusading Clements is not discouraged by the fact that very few other priests have followed his example. His most recent crusade, similar to Butt's effort, has targeted and boycotted neighborhood drug paraphernalia shops.

Third, some pastors are *commanders* who enjoy a degree of institutional authority, respect, fear, or loyalty that permits them simply to order congregations and individuals to become involved in mission activity. Little time is spent in debate, and rarely do they get involved directly in the mission activity themselves. Rather, they seize opportunities for doing ministry and command others to respond, often not without other motives (like entrepreneurship or concern for popularity). This authoritarian, quasi-military style was once common in the black church but is now being replaced by more consensus-oriented, managerial leadership.

One example of such a style is provided by the late Joseph H. Jackson, president of the National Baptist Convention from 1953 to 1982, and pastor of the historic Olivet Baptist Church in Chicago. During the civil rights movement and the ascendance of Martin Luther King, Jr., Jackson was an ideological foe of the movement who espoused a more conservative, self-help approach to black liberation. It was Jackson's organizational gifts and ability to cultivate strong loyalty from followers, no doubt inspired by his friend Mayor Richard J. Daley, that enabled him to hold the presidential office for an unprecedented twenty-nine years.[36] In the end, Jackson was able to command his "forces" in a way that forced King and other younger, educated, and politically progressive clergy to depart and organize the Progressive National Baptist Convention in 1961.

Finally, there are *campaigners,* clergy who seek to mobilize congregations along with the wider community. They understand themselves to be pastors for the entire community and seek to translate Christian values into more widely embraceable public values (nonviolence, self-sacrifice, and so on). They do this by campaigning in behalf of a public vision (like a welfare state or democratic socialism), a partisan political platform, or even their own bid for public office. At the risk of oversimplification, one could say that this leadership style invites the congregation to become more worldly and the world to become more churchly. The campaigner blends some of the elements of the crusader who initiates action in the public arena and the consensus builder who seeks to consolidate support around him- or herself.

The most prominent example of this style is the Reverend (and former congress-person) William H. Gray of Philadelphia. Like Adam C. Powell, Jr., Walter Fauntroy, and Floyd Flake, Gray served in Congress while continuing to pastor a congregation. Although he was a successful pastor before running for elective office, Gray believed that campaigning for his vision of a just society in the larger community could be best done through political channels. He proved so effective in this role that he became the majority whip for Democrats in the House of Representatives, thereby making him the most influential black politician in the nation. In order to get there, he used the skills of a consensus builder. With the influence of his office, he gained the authority of a commander. But in 1991 he announced that he would resign from Congress to become president of the United Negro College Fund. Gray suggested that politics was too slow and ineffectual in bringing about the urgent change he believed necessary for the poorest members of society. A career in education seemed a better investment of his time.

This typology should expose as a stereotype the conception of the authoritarian black pastor who is unaccountable to the surrounding church culture. A variety of leadership styles—consensus building, crusading, commanding, and campaigning—have actually proven effective in mobilizing congregations (and others) for public mission. Institutionally, some clergy (consensus builders and commanders) focus internally on the congregation's welfare and are maintenance-oriented as they survey readiness for public ministry. Other clergy (crusaders and campaigners) are more outer-directed and concerned aggressively to mobilize people whether the congregation is ready or not. Some clergy (consensus builders) are closely engaged with the lives of their parishioners and, according to my anecdotal data, are perceived by them to be authentic, caring, and "good" pastors. Other clergy (campaigners) enjoy the appearance of closeness but prefer to maintain social distance in order to avoid becoming too parochial. They are usually perceived by parishioners to be "busy" or "popular" pastors. Some clergy are loners by virtue of the nature of the office (commanders) or the rigor of their chosen lifestyle (crusaders). Parishioners in congregations led by commander-style pastors refer to them as "important and powerful but intimidating." They appreciate the political influence of the pastor but resent the fact that their personal needs are not priorities for the commander. Parishioners in congregations led by crusaders characterize them as "serious" pastors who take a no-nonsense approach to social justice concerns but also subordinate the personal, spiritual needs of parishioners to the social agenda.

It is important to note that although the characterizations I have selected may sound rather masculine, the growing number of women pastors assume many of these same styles. For illustrative purposes, I have selected widely known examples, and they happen to be men. Notwithstanding Lincoln and Mamiya's report that "fewer than 5 percent of the clergy in the historic black denominations are female," these women are in the process now of challenging rather than conforming to pastoral models created by men and are beginning to offer new styles for the future.[37]

In the absence of research data, I hesitate to make a judgment about which of these styles is more transformational, especially in regard to enabling people to become leaders themselves. However, the evidence from Martin Luther King's biography and the history of the civil rights movement suggest that the combination of leadership styles typical of a crusader and a consensus builder holds special promise for those interested in effecting social change and creating new leaders. As pastor of Dexter Avenue Baptist Church, King proved himself a consummate consensus builder. He was called out of this relatively comfortable place to become a crusader. By temperament, many colleagues report, he would not have chosen this lifestyle or leadership style. Nor would he have been comfortable as a campaigner, as many of his clergy disciples have been, including Jesse Jackson, Andrew Young, John Lewis, Walter Fauntroy, and Hosea Williams.

Conclusion

The entire culture of the black church thus works to create the sensibilities necessary for public mission. Black church culture is a rich and vibrant ensemble of practices that offer praise to God and hope to oppressed humanity. Clergy are expected first to maintain and then to mobilize this culture for Christ's mission in the world. Maintenance and mobilization are dialectically related.

Preaching is the ecclesial practice most central to the sacred oral culture of African Americans and most essential for mobilizing and sustaining people for public action. Good black social preaching names and frames crises creatively, analyzes them in biblical perspective, describes solutions using indigenous symbols and images, prescribes specific action plans, and offers hope via celebration.

Congregations have extraordinary potential for transforming and enhancing human existence in both the personal and public zones of our lives. In order to tap that potential, pastors must understand and work with congregational cultures. In many respects, the practices of

African-American pastors illustrate how this may be done effectively. The challenge for leaders in black churches is to continue in this rich tradition. The challenge for leaders from other ethnic communities is to examine carefully the culture of their own congregations. Different communities will value particular liturgical practices differently; celebrating the Eucharist, for example, may be more important than preaching in some congregations. Despite such differences, pastors must seek to identify and preserve those practices that renew hope and energize socially transformative ministry.

NOTES

1. As a descriptive label, "the black church" calls attention to the homogeneous aspects of African-American ethnoreligious identity while obscuring its many varieties. This "problem of the one and the many" is a theme illustrated in a volume edited by Milton C. Sernett, *Afro-American Religious History: A Documentary Witness* (Durham: Duke University Press, 1985), p. 5.

2. The best example is Atlanta's rapidly growing Cathedral of the Holy Spirit, a charismatic congregation led by a white pastor, Bishop Earl Paulk. The church is admirably intentional about its mission to be multiracial.

3. Melvin D. Williams, *Community in a Black Pentecostal Church: An Anthropological Study* (Prospect Heights, Ill.: Waveland Press, 1974), p. 157.

4. I refer to this ensemble of practices as *defiant spirituality*. Robert M. Franklin, "Defiant Spirituality: Traditions of Care and Discipline in Black Churches," paper presented at a conference on Congregational Care and Discipline at Christian Theological Seminary, Indianapolis, March 2, 1990.

5. For a discussion of the impulses underlying black worship, see Edward P. Wimberly, "The Dynamics of Black Worship: A Psychosocial Exploration of the Impulses that Lie at the Roots of Black Worship," *The Journal of the Interdenominational Theological Center* 14 (Fall 1986–Spring 1987), nos. 1 and 2, pp. 195–207. Wimberly identifies three impulses: (1) the need for a positive self-image; (2) the need to be whole and to grow in mind, body, and spirit, and in relationship to others and God; and (3) the need to respond to a God who affirmed blacks in the midst of oppression. This volume, edited by Melva Wilson Costen and Darius Leander Swann, contains a variety of outstanding essays on black Christian worship.

6. The concept of theonomy is elucidated by Paul Tillich in *Systematic Theology* (Chicago: University of Chicago Press, 1967), pp. 85ff.

7. Robert Michael Franklin, "Church and City: Black Christianity's Ministry," *The Christian Ministry* 20:2 (March–April 1989).

8. Rudolf Otto, *The Idea of the Holy* (London: Oxford University Press, 1950).

9. Victor Turner, *The Ritual Process* (Ithaca: Cornell University Press, 1969), p. 2.

10. William James, *Varieties of Religious Experience* (New York: Collier Press, 1961); and *Faith and Morals* (New York: Meridian Printing Company, 1962). For an interpretation of James's vision of the moral life, see Don Browning's *Pluralism and Personality* (Lewisburg: Bucknell University Press, 1980), pp. 281ff. For a discussion of the probable influence of James's moral thought on W. E. B. Du Bois's concept of "double consciousness," see Robert Michael Franklin, *Liberating Visions: Human Fulfillment and Social Justice in African-American Thought* (Minnesota: Augsburg Fortress Press, 1990).

11. A famed black preacher, Dr. Charles G. Adams (aka the Harvard whooper), proclaimed from the pulpit that ecstatic religious experience ought to have measurable positive consequences for the individual's ethical and intellectual life. His sermon "Keeping the Child Alive" was delivered at Trinity United Church of Christ, Chicago, 1987.

12. Molefi Kete Asante, *The Afrocentric Idea* (Philadelphia: Temple University Press, 1987), p. 92.

13. Jawanza Kunjufu, *Countering the Conspiracy to Destroy Black Boys* (Chicago: African American Images, 1990), p. 48.

14. Lawrence W. Levine, *Black Culture and Black Consciousness* (Oxford: Oxford University Press, 1977), p. 32, quoting Mircea Eliade, *The Sacred and the Profane* (New York, 1961).

15. Henry H. Mitchell, "Toward a Theology of Black Preaching," in *African American Religious Studies: An Interdisciplinary Anthology*, ed. Gayraud Wilmore (Durham: Duke University Press, 1989), p. 369. Also see Henry H. Mitchell, *Black Preaching* (San Francisco: Harper and Row, 1970); and Ella Pearson Mitchell, ed., *Those Preachin' Women: Sermons by Black Women Preachers* (Valley Forge: Judson Press, 1985).

16. Asante, *The Afrocentric Idea*, pp. 91–93.

17. Ibid.

18. Martin Luther King, Jr., "Address at Mass Meeting," December 5, 1955, audiotape in the archives of the Martin Luther King, Jr., Center for Nonviolent Social Change, Atlanta, Georgia.

19. For a comprehensive and historical examination of the culture, I recommend C. Eric Lincoln and Lawrence Mamiya's superlative study, *The Black Church in the African American Experience* (Durham: Duke University Press, 1990).

20. Williams, *Community in a Black Pentecostal Church*, p. 51.

21. I hope that this model may urge pastors from other communities to examine, and perhaps strengthen, the ways in which social concerns are voiced in their own sermons. The model is inspired by Eugene L. Lowry's analysis of narrative preaching in *The Homiletical Plot* (Atlanta: John Knox Press, 1980).

22. Martin Luther King, Jr., *Strength to Love* (Cleveland: Collins Publishers, 1963), p. 115.

23. Ibid., p. 126.

24. Ibid., p. 76.

25. Carolyn Ann Knight, "The Survival of the Unfit," in Mitchell, *Those Preachin' Women*, p. 27.

26. Hortense Spillers, "Martin Luther King and the Style of the Black Sermon," in C. Eric Lincoln, ed., *The Black Experience in Religion* (Garden City: Anchor Books, 1974), p. 77.

27. King, *Strength to Love*, p. 109.

28. Ibid., p. 114.

29. Martin Luther King, Jr., "I Have a Dream," in James M. Washington, ed., *A Testament of Hope: The Essential Writings of Martin Luther King, Jr.* (San Francisco: Harper and Row, 1986), pp. 219, 220.

30. King, "Our God Is Marching On," in *Testament of Hope*, p. 229.

31. Caesar A. W. Clark, "Christ, the Center of History," in Walter B. Hoard, ed., *Outstanding Black Sermons*, vol. 2 (Valley Forge: Judson Press, 1979), p. 30.

32. James MacGregor Burns, *Leadership* (New York: Harper and Row, 1978), pp. 18, 36.

33. Ibid., pp. 19, 20.

34. Lincoln and Mamiya, *The Black Church*, p. 263.

35. Ibid., p. 221.

36. Peter J. Paris, *Black Leaders in Conflict* (New York: Pilgrim Press, 1978), pp. 21–27.

37. Lincoln and Mamiya, *The Black Church*, p. 289.

AFTERWORD

Keeping the Conversation Going

IN ONE SENSE the particular conversation which began at the University of Chicago in 1987 has ended. The seminar has adjourned, and the conversation partners have moved on to other projects and concerns. Yet in another sense the conversation continues. By means of the two volumes it produced and the dissertations it supported, the Congregational History Project invites others to join both this conversation and the much larger one that has been going on for much of the twentieth century. Moreover, the invitation is to join it as full-fledged partners who, "carried along" by the subject matter, advance the inquiry while participating in it. We believe there are many promising leads in this recent work which can stimulate conversations in seminary and university class rooms, in denominational headquarters, and in congregations themselves. We are also aware that several important new congregational studies projects are already advancing the field in their own ways.

The religious character of congregational life, the distinctive ways that congregations relate public and private life, the shifting American leadership ecology which manifests itself within congregations, the roles played by congregations in creating and transcending local cultures are topics that have received only initial attention in this project. Much more needs to be learned. Moreover, the ways that congregations serve as tradition bearers and creators and their capacity to serve as communities of moral and practical theological discourse also demand attention.

To the extent that the Congregational History Project fulfilled its purposes it has called attention to the congregation as a multidimensional reality which changes over time. Understanding these institutions requires many perspectives—in conversation. Through historical and ethnographic investigations of individual congregations and through larger thematic and interpretive studies of them, we can begin to approach a full appreciation of what is really going on within America's major institutional form of lived religion. As a result of these studies, our conventional wisdom about religion in America will need to make room for new perceptions of the full public reach and significance of congregations. Such studies will require an interdisciplinary openness, enticing scholars into new collaborative relationships in which they can both employ and transcend their distinctive disciplinary insights in the interest of a larger conversation.

This kind of conversation about congregations in America, we believe, has much to offer to the study of religion, to theological education, and to the congregations themselves. As scholars like Robert Wuthnow have argued, the end of the twentieth century seems to be a time of religious restructuring, a moment of distinctive transition. Old lines between sacred and secular seem to be blurring; the configuration of institutions that located religion "here" and other sectors of life "there" is shifting. Denominations are losing their traditional places on the American religious landscape; seminaries and universities are searching for new educational roles to play. Congregations are in the middle of this process of restructuring and reconfiguring. Studying them can teach many both within and beyond them a great deal about what is passing away and what is coming to pass in America's ongoing lively experiment with religion.

CONTRIBUTORS

DOROTHY C. BASS is currently the Director of the Valparaiso Project on the Education and Formation of People in Faith and Adjunct Professor of Theology at Valparaiso University. She is on leave of absence from Chicago Theological Seminary where she has served on the faculty since 1982. She has published numerous articles and reviews on church-related higher education, women and religion, mainstream Protestantism, and other issues in American religion.

DON S. BROWNING, the Alexander Campbell Professor of Religion and Psychological Studies at the Divinity School of the University of Chicago, currently directs a major research project there on Religion, Culture, and the Family. His most recent book is *A Fundamental Practical Theology*, published in 1991. His numerous books and articles deal with the intersections of psychology, psychiatry, theology, ethics, and religious education.

JAY P. DOLAN is Professor of History at the University of Notre Dame, where he also served until 1993 as Director of the Cushwa Center for the Study of American Catholicism. The recipient of many awards and honors, his work focuses on American Catholicism, particularly the immigrant experience. Written with three others, his latest book is *Transforming Parish Ministry: The Changing Roles of Catholic Clergy, Laity, and Women Religious in the United States, 1930–1980* (1989).

ROBERT MICHAEL FRANKLIN is Associate Professor of Ethics and Society and Director of the Black Church Studies Program at Candler School of Theology at Emory University. His book *Liberating Visions: Human Fulfillment and Social Justice in African-American Thought* was published in 1990. His numerous articles, book chapters, and reviews focus on the role of the African-American church in contemporary American culture.

LANGDON GILKEY, well known for his books on Christian theology, the history of theology, and the modern conflict of religion and science, is Professor Emeritus at the University of Chicago Divinity School. His recent publications include *Through the Tempest*, edited by Jeff B. Pool

(1991) and *Nature, Reality, and the Sacred: The Nexus of Science and Religion* (1993). He lives in Charlottesville, Virginia.

E. BROOKS HOLIFIELD is the Charles Howard Candler Professor of American Church History at Emory University, where he has taught since 1970. The topics of his several books and numerous articles range from Puritan sacramental theology to the history of pastoral care in America to antebellum theology. He is currently working on a history of theology in America.

JAMES W. LEWIS is Executive Director of the Louisville Institute for the Study of Protestantism and American Culture. He is the author of *The Protestant Experience in Gary, Indiana, 1906–1975: At Home in the City* (1992).

MARTIN E. MARTY is the Fairfax M. Cone Distinguished Service Professor of the History of Modern Christianity at the University of Chicago. He is also Senior Editor of the weekly *The Christian Century* and co-editor of *Church History*. He is the author of forty books, including *Modern American Religion*, vol. 1, *The Irony of It All 1893–1919* (1986), and vol. 2, *The Noise of Conflict, 1919–1941* (1991).

R. STEPHEN WARNER is Professor of Sociology at the University of Illinois at Chicago. He is the author of *New Wine in Old Wineskins: Evangelicals and Liberals in a Small-Town Church* (1988). His numerous articles and reviews deal with a broad range of issues in the sociology of religion in America. He is currently working on *Communities of Faith: An Essay on Religion in the United States Today*.

JAMES P. WIND is a program director in the Religion Division of the Lilly Endowment in Indianapolis, Indiana. In addition to numerous articles and reviews, he has published *The Bible and the University: The Messianic Vision of William Rainey Harper* (1987) and *Places of Worship: Exploring Their History* (1990). With Carl S. Dudley and Jackson W. Carroll, he edited *Carriers of Faith: Lessons from Congregational Studies* (1991).

INDEX

Ecumenism, 75, 146–47
Education, religious, 34–35, 65, 178, 263–64
Edwards, Jonathan, 159, 251
Ethics, 121, 129
Evil, forms of, 123. *See also* Sin

Fellowship, 67, 69–70
First Church, New Haven. *See* Center Church
"Floating," among Catholic parishes, 77–80
Flynt, Wayne, 73, 176
Fourth Presbyterian Church, 177, 184
Franklin, Robert, 16
Fundamentalism, 111. *See also* Protestantism

Gadamer, Hans-Georg, 193–94, 196
Gandhi, Mohandas Karamchand, 276
Gender, 32, 37, 40
Gilkey, Langdon, 6, 12–13, 62
Gladden, Washington, 3, 237
Goldman, Karla, 73
Groups, special-purpose, 147–48

Hinduism, 57
Hispanic Protestant congregations, 57–58
Holifield, E. Brooks, 10–11
Holy, the, 117, 121, 132 n.21
Hopewell, James, 7, 65, 202, 204

Identity formation, in congregations, 181
Immigrants, 57, 69–70, 241–42
Individualism, 104–5
Institutional church, 42–43, 45, 237, 240
Islam. *See* Muslims

Judaism, 40–41, 83

K. K. Bene Israel, 175, 176, 187, 241
Kaplan, Mordecai, 41
King, Martin Luther, Jr., 159, 266, 268–74, 279, 281

Korean ethnic congregations, 57, 70. *See also* Presbyterians

Lac La Biche Muslim community, 184, 187
Laity, role of, 258. *See also* Leadership, lay
Language, 33, 162
Leadership, 16, 29, 251, 267–68, 276; and African-Americans, 37–38; and class, 251, 252; congregational, 15–16, 250–53; styles of, 237, 245–46, 277–80
—, clerical, 159, 227–30, 234–35, 237–40; authority of, 31, 238–39, 240–41, 243–45, 248; professionalization of, 237–38, 252
—, lay, 45–46, 226–27, 230–31, 235–36, 242–44; authority of, 31, 77, 249, 251
—, women and, 37, 46, 77, 234, 239–41, 249–52, 280–81
Lifestyle, holiness and, 120–22

MacIntyre, Alasdair, 14, 171–74, 209
Mamiya, Lawrence, 177, 185, 258, 277
Mann, Hilda, 210, 213, 215
Marty, Martin E., 6, 7, 13–14, 56, 62, 64
May, Cheryll, 82
May, Dean, 82
Mediating structure, 140–43, 145
Meeting, the congregation as a, 150–52
Mega-churches, 43
Membership, 24–27, 28, 37, 43. *See also* Gender
Metropolitan Community Church, 72
Mission, 65–66
Mt. Hebron Baptist Church, 37, 175–76, 184, 186, 232–33
Muncie, Indiana ("Middletown"), 154, 237
Music, 262–63
Muslims, 57, 80–81